In the child's best interests?

In the child's best interests?

DIVORCE COURT WELFARE AND THE
SEARCH FOR A SETTLEMENT

Christopher Clulow
and
Christopher Vincent

In collaboration with
Barbara Dearnley

TAVISTOCK PUBLICATIONS
SWEET AND MAXWELL
London and New York

First published in 1987 by
Tavistock Publications Ltd
in association with Sweet and Maxwell Ltd
11 New Fetter Lane, London EC4P 4EE

© 1987 The Tavistock Institute of Medical Psychology

Typeset by MC Typeset Ltd., Chatham, Kent
Printed at the University Press, Cambridge

British Library Cataloguing in Publication Data
Clulow, Christopher F.
    In the child's best interests? : divorce court welfare and the
    search for a settlement.
    1. Children of divorced parents—Legal status, laws, etc.—
    England   2. Domestic relations courts—England
    I. Title   II. Vincent, Christopher
    III. Dearnley, Barbara
    362.7'95   KD772

    ISBN 0-422-61260-X
    ISBN 0-422-61270-7 Pbk

CONTENTS

ACKNOWLEDGEMENTS

Of the many people who have participated in and advised upon the work described in this book I wish to acknowledge the special contribution made by Christopher Vincent and Barbara Dearnley, my co-researchers. Although I must bear sole responsibility for the form and style in which this book has been written, Christopher Vincent undertook nearly all the statistical work and, along with Barbara Dearnley, prepared early drafts of some working papers from which the chapters finally emerged.

As a team we are indebted to the Probation Committee, chief officers and staff of the probation service where the research took place. They encouraged the work to go ahead and provided some financial support. Both the project and this book benefited greatly from their valuable contributions both in terms of the time they put aside and the guidance and experience they placed at our disposal. We have chosen not to identify the area in order to give additional anonymity to the clients. Our loss is that we are unable to name those from whom we learned so much. It goes without saying that we also owe a debt of gratitude to the clients of the Divorce Unit who gave us a memorable, and sometimes uncomfortable, education.

The project would not have been possible without the generous financial support of the Joseph Rowntree Memorial Trust and the Baring Foundation. The Institute of Marital Studies, which receives its major grant from the Home Office, also contributed towards the cost. Our colleagues shouldered some of the additional burdens that the project created for the Institute, and still had time to read early drafts of this book. To them our thanks. My thanks also to Linda Besharat and Margaret Spooner who converted sometimes illegible handwriting into processed text at a time when they were being introduced to the mysteries of microtechnology and teaching me the secrets of their new-found knowledge.

Of those outside the IMS I would like to acknowledge the help and criticisms offered by Austin Heady, Lisa Parkinson, and Margaret Robinson. Margaret Walker and her staff at the Tavistock Joint Library were as helpful as always.

I am grateful to Faber and Faber and Harcourt Brace Jovanovich Inc. for permission to reprint an extract from *The Cocktail Party* by T.S. Eliot (copyright 1950 by T.S. Eliot; renewed 1978 by Esme Valerie Eliot), and to William Heinemann Ltd for permission to use excerpts from *Waterland* by Graham Swift and *Casanova's Chinese Restaurant* by Anthony Powell.

It has become customary for authors to acknowledge the help and forbearance of spouses and partners. Researching and writing about family issues intrude upon family life in many ways. In expressing my gratitude to Pamela I am not simply observing a formality but registering my heartfelt appreciation to her for bearing with my preoccupation and frustrations during the fieldwork and writing-up stages of the project.

Christopher Clulow
February 1987

1

NO-MAN'S LAND

'We have all read what happened between the opposing armies, and how it came unexpected, undesigned, and yet willed with all the unconscious force of their natures. Not once or twice but again and again we hear of this sudden change upon the night of Christmas Eve, how there was singing upon one side answered by the other, and how the men rose and advanced to meet each other as if they had been released from a spell. Every one who tells of it speaks also of his own wonder as if he had seen a miracle; and some say that the darkness became strange and beautiful with lights as well as music, as if the armies had been gathered together there not for war but for the Christmas Feast.'

A. Clutton-Brock
Christmas 1914 (in *The Times*)

War is not too strong a metaphor to apply to the experiences of some who divorce. They fight for what they believe to be right, to protect their territory and security, and against forces that sometimes seem to threaten life itself. And there are social pressures to treat partners as adversaries once marriage ends. Divorcing men and women snipe at each other from their trenches partly through fear, mistrust, and sense of injury, and partly because those who define the 'rules of engagement' are understood to encourage such behaviour.

Clutton-Brock's account of an event which took place early on in the First World War, before bitterness set in, and when the chains of military command could be overridden by a higher imperative, invites an analogy with divorce. If the 'rules of engagement' were changed, might the experience be a less combative one than it frequently is at present? Both from within and from outside the judicial system the affirmative reply to this question is becoming louder.

The reasons for this follow recognition that there is a 'no-man's land' in divorce containing unintended hazards and unexpected opportunities. In a culture wedded to the ideal of life-long monogamy there are few social indications of how to behave, and to whom to turn, when marriage comes to an end. The resulting sense of disorientation constitutes a no-man's land in the sense that men and women are vulnerable to self-doubt, feelings of purposelessness, illness, hardship, isolation, and censure. These are just some of the commonly encountered consequences of leaving the security, if discomfort, of the marital 'trench'. There are few foxholes in the social landscape of divorce, and it is small wonder that many scurry for the cover of a new marriage, even when the shelter it provides is statistically less secure than that of a first marriage.

There is also concern that the cost of divorce may be unacceptably high for children. For them, divorce frequently results in the loss of one or other parent, usually their father. Although the family is unlikely to be a no-man's land after divorce in the literal sense (friends, uncles, grandfathers, and stepfathers all providing a male presence) the rupture of ties between children and parents who do not live at home is cause for disquiet. It is perhaps apt that Clutton-Brock's account observes an event which took place at Christmas, a festival which celebrates a child, assigns a position of privilege to a mother, but distances the natural father from the central drama.

But the image of no-man's land can also be a hopeful one. It is the ground between opposing factions which, if they have the courage to occupy it, allows for a different relationship between those who have formerly been in opposition. The recent growth in this country of conciliation services which exist solely to create the space for divorcing couples to meet and negotiate, is a tangible expression of that hope. The hope can be overstated, as if, indeed, 'everyone who tells of it speaks . . . as if he had seen a miracle'. And no-man's land is hazardous: goodwill missions often ended abruptly in the detonation of a hidden mine, or a shot fired by a comrade in arms who had mistaken his target in the confusion of war. The hope is founded on dissatisfaction with how things are and a vision of how they might be.

War is an extreme example of the axiom that behaviour receives its meaning from the context in which it occurs. War can convert a suicidal gesture into an act of heroism, a loving act into a statement of disloyalty. We must take account of the context of divorce in order to understand the behaviour of those who, having once chosen to throw in their lot together, now opt to go their separate ways. While divorce is initiated by personal acts and decisions, what follows is not always in the control of the partners concerned. There will frequently be no agreement between partners over the decision to end a marriage. Even when there is, divorce involves the judicial system as the executor of private *and* public interests. In extreme circumstances this can have alarming consequences, especially where children are involved. As one mother said: 'I went to court for a divorce and ended up with my children in care.' Divorce is not simply a private transaction, but a legal and social act, which removes the veil cloaking the values and assumptions of the community as a whole. The interaction of those inside and outside the family during the process of divorce may generate behaviour which neither side would condone in ordinary circumstances.

This book is about the meshing of private complaint and public response. It examines what happens to parents and professionals when divorce brings them together. More specifically, it examines the work of a group of divorce court welfare officers as they investigated the circumstances of divorcing parents. These investigations were undertaken at the behest of a judge or registrar when there was disagreement or disquiet about arrangements being proposed for children who were caught up in their parents' divorce. Divorce court welfare officers operate in the no-man's land between the interests of parents and children, between the conflicting parents themselves, and, ultimately, between the interests of the State and the individual. On the face of it their 'rules of engagement' appear to be in contradiction. By training they are equipped to offer personal help, by aspiration many endeavour to secure privately ordered agreements, by statute they are charged to investigate. They stand, therefore, both to help and encourage parents to accept responsibility for themselves and their children, and to prepare the ground for courts to override and appropriate that responsibility. The purpose of this book is to explore how far that contradiction is apparent or real.

Our method was to join and report upon the action at the front line. But we were combatants as well as observers. We worked with welfare officers, as welfare officers, to experience and describe what we both witnessed and were a part of. The research stance of participant observer is another kind of no-man's land. The opportunities afforded to the observer who occupies the middle ground between research and practice are offset by certain risks. By sharing and becoming involved in the work of welfare officers we had access to subjective data which might have gone undetected by an observer further removed. But our objectivity and sense of perspective may have suffered at times because of our direct involvement. This dilemma will be familiar to researchers and practitioners who work in the field of human relationships, and it is one which has particular relevance to divorce court enquiry work.

The origins and scope of the venture

Since 1948, the Institute of Marital Studies (formerly known as the Family Discussion Bureau) has operated as a centre of advanced therapeutic practice. Through its training and research activities with other agencies it has furthered understanding of relationships between couples, and made a contribution towards developing services to marriage and the family.

Situated in the Tavistock Centre, London, the staff of the Institute (which will subsequently be referred to as the IMS) have been greatly influenced by psychoanalytic thinking in formulating ideas about marriage and family relationships. The psychodynamic assumptions that inform practice at the IMS were evident in its first publication (Pincus 1960), as is the affinity between this book and the closely worked theoretical writings of Dicks (1967) which applied object relations theory to marital interaction. These assumptions have been developed to take account of the changing social and professional climate of the past 20 years. The IMS has continued to attend to the personal and psychological aspects of couple relationships, drawing primarily upon psychodynamic thinking to make sense of conflict within these relationships. In summary, this has involved grappling not only with what happens to people in the course of their lives, but what events mean for them in the specific contact of their past experience. This requires the juxtaposition of the past with the present, and considering together the realities of both inner and outer worlds and their interrelationships with each other. This knowledge has been applied to the complex problem of helping the wide range of practitioners who come into contact with distressed marriages to respond effectively and appropriately to the often ambivalent appeals for help which are made to them.

The three members of staff who were to become involved in the project were (and still are) marital therapists at the IMS. In the late 1970s and early 1980s we, like many others, became interested in the nascent conciliation movement in this country which, starting in Bristol, rapidly looked set to establish a new service for parents who were in the process of ending their marriages. This service offered the attractive proposition of reducing the destructive and costly effects which, fairly or not, had come to be associated with divorce litigation. No doubt, too, the enthusiasm engendered by conciliation was linked with a value system which favoured private ordering, and resisted procedures which intruded upon and undermined the freedoms and responsibilities of individuals in families. These values we shared, both personally and in our professional lives as therapists.

Along with our enthusiasm for the concept of conciliation was some scepticism about its implementation in practice. As therapists, we knew that reason was often the first casualty in battles between the sexes. Even in situations where separation was not seriously being entertained (and so where there was less at stake, in tangible terms, than during a divorce), partners were capable of behaving towards each other as if their very survival was threatened. Our experience of therapy was that dependable changes were usually achieved slowly and with considerable effort. A changing regard for others implied a changing regard for self, and such a shift in personal identity was not to be made lightly. We were critical of the courts when they operated in ways which failed to take account of the emotional purposes behind reasoned submissions, and when they encouraged and aggravated conflict between partners. Equally, we were sceptical about claims made by conciliators that rational, brief, and focused negotiations could achieve workable settlements at a time when passions were inflamed. We believed that effective agreements over the practical consequences of divorce depended upon laying broken marriages to rest in emotional as well as contractual terms, and feared that conciliation might underrate the powerful effects of the emotional realities of divorce.

Clearly, we were not to be easily satisfied. The only way we were going to find answers to some of our questions was to step off the sidelines and become directly involved in the work.

Learning of our interest, the Chief Probation Officer of the probation service which acted as host to the project (hereafter called HPS) raised the possibility of the IMS researching the work of an out-of-court conciliation service which she was helping to set up. The suggestion was warmly received, and a member of the IMS staff joined the steering group of the embryo service to offer her experience to that venture and to learn what might be involved for us in ours. However, it took very much longer than originally anticipated for the conciliation service to be funded, housed, staffed, and serviced. Even when it was operational a substantial amount of time elapsed before the service became well enough known to attract referrals. During the period in which the research was being negotiated there were real questions about whether the service we had been invited to research would become operational at all.

It was during this period of uncertainty that the Chief Probation Officer, along with a senior officer who specialized in divorce court welfare work, proposed that their newly formed Divorce Unit be included in the research. The HPS had recently decided to establish a specialist unit in the probation service to handle all divorce court enquiries in that area, and they were anxious to learn from it and to ensure its success. For the Chief Officer, research would provide the kind of monitoring of a new venture which was likely to produce information relevant to the debate then taking place about how – even whether – the probation service as a whole should continue to discharge its civil work responsibilities. For the senior officer, research promised an opportunity to firm up thinking about practice issues in a new area of work, and added to the enthusiasm and excitement already generated by a new enterprise. Both Chief and senior hoped to learn about the organizational implications of having a specialist unit. In particular, they hoped to discover how the stress associated with divorce court work might best be managed.

Uncertainty about the future viability of the conciliation service, combined with advice given to the IMS not to research both services (on the grounds that the project would become unwieldy and would generate rivalry), led to a decision to restrict the research to the operations of the Divorce Unit. It was decided to examine, as the focal point of the research, how feasible it was for welfare officers to assist parents to reach agreements acceptable to themselves and to the courts in the course of conducting welfare enquiries.

Having decided what we wanted to do, it remained for us to decide how best to do it. We were guided by three sets of considerations. In the first place, we were all practitioners who had a preference for dirtying our own hands, so to speak, as well as observing how others dirtied theirs. In line with previous IMS projects we wished to be participants as well as observers. This preference was supported by our hosts in the Divorce Unit. Second, a distinguished adviser urged upon us the view that the first base in social science research was accurate description, and that to that end we should aim to produce good case descriptions. We wanted our observations to be as detailed, and made from as close quarters, as we could manage. Third, a provincial welfare officer whom we consulted in the course of setting up the project urged us to 'tell it like it is' – to convey some of the guts of enquiry work – including the subjective realities of the job. These considerations implied that we should utilize several methods in our research approach.

To meet our overall objective we knew that we needed to describe the population seen by the Divorce Unit, to describe the Unit itself, and to give an account of the interaction between the two. We decided to build a profile of Divorce Unit clients by completing a questionnaire for each of the welfare enquiries undertaken by staff in the unit over a period of 12 months (the original period proposed was two years, but the work of compiling the information for one year was as much as we could manage in the time available and was, in any case, sufficient for our purpose). This profile was supplemented by questionnaires completed for 30 enquiries. These were enquiries undertaken by members of the IMS research staff, who worked as welfare officers in the Unit over a period of two and a half years. The questionnaires (see Appendix II) supplied the information for the three population samples referred to in this book. They are the *one-year sample* (consisting of the 110 enquiries undertaken in the 12-month period, but excluding core sample enquiries handled at that time), the *core sample* (consisting of 30 enquiries in which IMS staff were involved over a two-and-a-half year period) and the *Divorce Unit sample* (which is the sum of the one-year and core sample cases: 140 enquiries).

For the fieldwork life of the project the three members of the IMS research team participated in the weekly meetings of the Divorce Unit. On the whole, these alternated between case discussion and business meetings. Each meeting was recorded, and a note was made of the discussion. For case discussion meetings notes were kept on a standard form for the purpose of comparability (see Appendix II). These meetings were supplemented by the deliberations of a steering group consisting of Divorce Unit staff, IMS project staff, the Assistant Chief Officer with responsibility for the Unit, and the Chief Officer. This group convened infrequently (about every six months) and its purpose changed as the research went on. In the early stages, it helped to ensure that research procedures were running smoothly and to ease the tensions that the research presence inevitably introduced into a working unit. Later, it considered issues highlighted by the research. Finally, it was the body that commented upon, amended, and improved the drafts which have resulted in this book. The picture we portray of the Divorce Unit has been drawn from the various meetings we attended, and from our own impressions of what it was like to work as welfare officers for the one day a week on which we were attached to the Unit.

The main body of our material comes from work with the core sample of enquiries, most of which we and our welfare officer colleagues undertook together. The enquiry relationship was the meeting point between parents, children, and welfare officers, where different sets of expectations interacted with each other, generating different experiences. We paid particular attention to first meetings (tape-recording some) because they were occasions when important position statements were made by welfare officers and parents. When an enquiry was completed, a case profile was written up (see Appendix II) which summarized the work undertaken, attempted to conceptualize the experience, and evaluated, from the welfare officer's perspective, whether or not the enquiry had facilitated an agreement.

We were also anxious to obtain an independent view of how parents experienced the enquiry process. To this end attempts were made by an IMS researcher who had not been involved in preparing the report to trace and interview core sample parents eight months after an enquiry had been completed. In 16 of the 30 cases (53 per cent) we were successful in contacting both parents. In a further 11 cases (37 per cent) one parent was interviewed, leaving only 3 cases (10 per cent) where the views of neither parent were obtained.

The methods we employed will be described in more detail later in the book and in connection with the material they produced. Suffice it here to say that we hoped to obtain a profile of a Unit specializing in divorce court welfare work, a picture of the kind of clients for whom it catered, and first-hand accounts of what it was like to investigate, and to be investigated about child welfare issues. From these different vantage points we formed a view, not altogether encouraging, about the feasibility of helping parents to settle their differences in the course of preparing reports for the courts.

Many criticisms can be levelled at the kind of approach we adopted. In discussions with staff at the Home Office, and at senior levels of the probation service, doubts were expressed about how far it would be possible to generalize from a limited and atypical experience. We agree that caution must be exercised in drawing too many conclusions from this essentially small-scale research enterprise, although it allowed certain insights that might not have been possible had the scale of the project been larger. The question of typicality is more difficult. There is no doubt that our direct involvement in enquiry work – as people who were not welfare officers – will have had an effect upon the results, as will the fact that we operated from a specialist organizational base and usually worked in pairs with a member of staff from the Divorce Unit. However, civil work in the probation service is organized in many different ways at the present time, and we know there is substantial diversity in the approaches adopted by individual welfare officers. It would not have been possible to select a typical welfare unit, nor to find officers who could be said to carry out their duties in a way which was representative of the service as a whole. We therefore had few qualms about opting to work with a Unit which, in the estimation of the Home Office Inspectorate, was very competent, rather than pursuing what might have turned out to be an illusory quest for a typical base.

Although different practitioners have different approaches to the task of preparing court reports, so there can be no single typical mode of practice, it is fair to ask about the characteristic features of our reporting-cum-settlement-seeking methods. Because of the nature of the enquiry task and our attributes as practitioners we (the IMS and Divorce Unit teams) combined our skills as marital therapists, family therapists, investigators, and negotiators to form a hybrid approach that drew most heavily upon systems and psychodynamic theories for conceptual understanding. Structurally, we aimed to convene first meetings at which both parents and their children were present. Usually (in all but seven of the core sample cases) a member of the Divorce Unit and IMS team worked together on an enquiry, and they encouraged first meetings to take place on Divorce Unit premises and not at the home of either parent. Procedurally, initial meetings were convened with the express purpose of clarifying the nature of the disputes and exploring ways in which parents might be encouraged to settle their differences. However, there was no rigid adherence to any one technique or method of procedure. Professional judgement was used in deciding upon the kinds of meetings to set up and the course they followed. The families we saw had a powerful influence upon the structures and procedures that were possible and, of course, upon the enquiry relationship itself. We were not free agents acting upon passive subjects. We attempted to deploy the skills and experience we had towards furthering settlements between parents, but they had to be settlements acceptable to us as officers of the courts. We were influenced by our belief that children should remain involved with both parents after divorce wherever possible. Our approach and methods will become apparent from the case illustrations that appear later in the book.

The hybrid approach we adopted during the research is, no doubt, different from the approach that our Divorce Unit colleagues might have used had we not been working with them. Our presence at the Unit had unsettling effects upon a recently formed group of welfare officers. We discuss later in the book the impact of this, and the difficulties experienced on both sides in maintaining an appropriate boundary of involvement. Was our primary loyalty to practice or to research? This question, which exercised us and our Divorce Unit colleagues, might easily have been rephrased by parents and directed towards welfare officers in these terms: are you here to help us or to report on us? Neither question can be answered in either/or terms, yet maintaining an effective balance between the two positions is no easy matter. A practical stylistic consequence for this book has been the uneasy tension between the use of 'we' and 'they' when writing about welfare officers.

The research relationship reflected something of what was happening in the enquiry itself. Parents were subject to investigations initiated by the courts. They frequently under-stood the investigation to be concerned with assessing both their competence as parents and the justness of their cause. Reports were received by parents either as vindicating or criticizing their position. They were sensitive documents, especially when parents were expending considerable physical and emotional energy just to keep going, or to maintain a newly and tentatively acquired equilibrium. When much was at stake, and no agreement had been possible, reports were read as being either for or against them, supporting or undermining them.

In relation to our colleagues at the Divorce Unit we were like co-parents *and* welfare officers. We worked alongside them preparing reports for the courts, sometimes agreeing and sometimes differing about what was in the best interests of 'our' children. Yet we were also researching the work of the Unit during a period in which it was establishing itself and undergoing a transition. The staff had interests to protect, and much was at stake for them if the report (this book) presented their work in an unfavourable light. Moreover, it was as if one of the parents (the IMS) was being allowed to prepare the welfare enquiry (the research report), with the attendant danger that the point of view which ultimately emerged would be skewed or distorted in some way. Another danger was that our outside perspective as researchers would mean that enquiry work would be perceived and experienced by us differently as compared with seasoned welfare officers because we were not in the position of having the day-to-day responsibilities of the job.

No doubt distortions will have occurred in our account of the project. We became aware that the process of writing was one means of extricating ourselves from our experiences. No matter how hard we have tried to safeguard against distortions by reviewing our evidence and discussing our descriptions and considerations with our welfare officer colleagues, some will remain. Indeed, the sometimes painful process of working through the drafts of this book with the Divorce Unit may, in itself, have introduced a different set of distortions. No doubt, too, our relative unfamiliarity with enquiry work will mean that our investigative experience had a different impact upon us than it would have had upon an experienced practitioner in the field. Whether that is an advantage or a disadvantage remains to be seen. Certainly it is true that as participants, as well as observers, we were researching ourselves along with the other subjects of our research. If criticisms these are, we believe they can equally well be made of the practice of investigating families for the courts. When couples divorce, when enquiries are undertaken for the courts, and when research programmes are carried out, many discrepant realities come together. Providing the discrepancies represent genuinely experienced differences, the issue is not to select the one true story but to expose each account to the others in a way which ensures a hearing, so furthering the process of understanding.

This book is one account of the work of divorce court welfare officers, and of how feasible it is for them to help parents settle their differences while reporting to the courts upon their abilities and circumstances. We believe it will resonate with the experiences of many social workers, conciliators, lawyers, and judges, as well as with welfare officers themselves. We hope it will make a useful contribution to practice and policy discussions taking place inside and outside the probation service at the present time.

Those who are least likely to read this book are the parents and children who have been, or are yet to be, the subjects of court enquiries. They stand to gain most from a review of welfare practice and procedures. Through their consumer reports, the parents who were part of our research have added a perspective which was vital to our thinking, and which complemented our practitioner views.

When we contacted parents for follow-up interviews we made it clear that we wanted to see them for research purposes, not to reopen a court enquiry. They were told that the purpose of the interview was to obtain a consumer view of the enquiry experience which would be used to improve services. Most parents responded positively to this and wanted their views to be made known. The situation was rather different when information was gathered in the course of a court enquiry and the researcher was also the welfare officer. When parents were asked to consent to their first interview being tape-recorded, and to assist in the completion of the questionnaire, a brief general statement was made to the effect that the work of the Unit was being examined in order to evaluate the service it provided. We did not ask for their consent to be included in a research sample because considerable time would then have had to be devoted to explaining the purpose of the research. This would have changed the character of the first interview and skewed the enquiry experience as a whole. We were also unclear at that stage as to whether or how we would want to use the material. More important, a vulnerable, untrusting, and exposed population might have given consent, or withheld it, less through choice than through fear that to refuse would adversely affect the outcome of their enquiry. Either way, their decision might have had little connection with what we would actually have been asking of them.

As it turned out, we used only four detailed case descriptions from the core sample. We wondered whether we ought to trace these parents, obtain their consent, and discuss our written drafts with them. We decided against doing this. Our concern to do everything right by them might have produced unwelcome results. Reminders of past conflicts could have unsettling effects, even upsetting hard-won arrangements by resurrecting feelings which many parents would prefer to leave behind. Case descriptions could constitute a threat to those still feeling vulnerable, and provide a vehicle for others who wished to resurrect old conflicts. We were writing about times and contexts from which parents were likely to be well removed by the time the accounts were completed. Moreover, these accounts were intended to represent our perceptions of the enquiry experience; the clients' views were to be presented through the results of the follow-up interviews. There, our research purpose had been explicit.

We decided that the IMS and HPS should be jointly responsible for ensuring that the case illustrations were written in a way which would protect the anonymity of the people concerned. This responsibility was exercised through the steering group, and we are confident that it has been discharged conscientiously.

Charting the territory

Welfare enquiries intrude upon the privacy of family life, but that intrusion is rarely unsolicited. While the law requires that a judge or registrar should be satisfied about arrangements proposed for children before making final a divorce, it is usually the failure of parents to agree that leads them to turn to the courts for a decision. Many of these cases require the wisdom of Solomon to do justice to the conflicting needs of parents and children.

King Solomon's wisdom rested upon his soundness of judgment in difficult situations. A well known example of this was his handling of two women who claimed the same baby, when he ordered the baby to be divided in half so that each woman might have a part of the child. The real mother relinquished her claim, begging that the child be allowed to live, whereupon King Solomon judged her to be the true mother and ordered the baby to be returned to her.

Those who adjudicate upon family matters in the courts today often find themselves in similarly difficult situations, although their decisions tend to be less dramatic than those of their biblical predecessor. They are often assisted by welfare officers who explore the circumstances of parents and the nature of their disputes. This book is about divorce court welfare officers, the families they see, and the ways in which they assist the courts to arrive at decisions which will be *In the child's best interests*.

The next chapter considers *Solomon's lot*. Called upon to divine what is likely to be best for children according to the state of existing knowledge, beliefs, attitudes, and values, judges and registrars work on the intersections of public and private lives.

To assist them in their deliberations, the Solomons of the courts frequently use welfare officers to investigate the circumstances of those who appear before them, and to make appropriate recommendations. Divorce court welfare officers are probation officers (once referred to as servants of the court), and Chapter 3 describes the role played by *Solomon's servants*. It also describes the Divorce Unit in which the research project was carried out, and its clients.

Chapter 4 describes *The nature of the disputes* in the core sample of 30 enquiries. These disputes are organized into four groups, three of which refer to situations in which we considered unresolved attachments to a former partner or spouse to have been a crucial part of the context in which child custody and access applications were pursued. In this chapter we also introduce four courier cases: the Sheens, the Kings, the Hood/Hams, and the Robins. Each case serves to illustrate one of the four divorce groups. All four appear again later in the book, forming a thread of continuity between the chapters.

The next four chapters examine the enquiry experience from the perspectives of parents and welfare officers. In Chapter 5 a summary of their different expectations of the enquiry suggest they were frequently *At cross purposes*. Chapter 6 describes the four courier enquiries in detail and the different ways in which parents, children, and welfare officers were to be found *Playing the system*. More generally, Chapter 7 assembles a collection of consumer views of what it was like to be *Under the microscope* of a court-ordered investigation. Chapter 8 considers the same experience from the investigator's perspective, an experience likened by one welfare officer to being *On a roller coaster*.

Facts and fictions is the title we have chosen for the concluding chapter, which summarizes the main findings of the project and discusses the implications they raise for practice and policy. We suggest that procedures, while catering adequately for some members of some families, expose other needs which are not currently being met. We consider some ways forward which might improve on present practices. Having said this, we are very clear that the lot shared between Solomon, his supplicants, and those who serve him is not a happy or straightforward one. It is with Solomon's lot that we begin.

2

SOLOMON'S LOT

'And there came of all people to hear the wisdom of
Solomon . . .'

I Kings 4 (34)

The past sixteen years have seen an unprecedented increase in the
number of marriages ending in divorce. Within a decade of 1971,
when the Divorce Reform Act became law, the number of
decrees made absolute had doubled. They totalled 162,000 in
1983. In that same year the number of persons divorcing per
thousand of the married population was 12.2, a divorce rate six
times higher than that of twenty years before and one which had
outstripped other West European countries in its rate of growth
(Leete 1979). Since 1983 the increase in divorce has levelled off,
apart from a temporary surge following the implementation of
the Matrimonial and Family Proceedings Act in 1984 which
allowed petitions to be presented one year after marriage (instead
of three) and had the effect of advancing petitions which would
otherwise have appeared in the statistics of subsequent years.
Now it is predicted that one in three marriages in England and
Wales will end in divorce before the thirtieth anniversary of the
wedding, and one in five children under 16 will have parents who
have divorced (Haskey 1982, 1983). In 1984, 149,000 children in
England and Wales were in that position (68 per cent of whom
were under 11 years old and 30 per cent under 5). Today, as then,
around six out of every ten divorcing couples have children under
the age of 16.

Concern about the stability of marriage and family life has
stimulated fresh interest in the debate about whether marriage is
predominantly a public or a private institution. The intersections
between public and private spheres of life have been studied with

renewed vigour (Donzelot 1980, Morgan 1985). The concern about divorce reflects anxiety not only about the possible risks for individuals, but also about much recent social change. Established views about what it means to be male and female no longer find general acceptance. Conventional images of family life are confounded by the diversity of household living arrangements. Deeply held convictions about the sanctity of marriage are shaken by the statistics of marriage breakdown. Caught between the pull of the old and the push of the new, collective and individual responses to change may in certain respects be very similar. Those who reassert traditional values will find themselves in conflict with the advocates of change, but each will rely upon the other to provide a safeguard against the extremes of atrophy and disorientation. Conflicts produce symptoms. Certain issues gain prominence and provide a focus for more general anxieties, while others appear to be neglected. Those receiving attention can be expected to contain within them an amalgam of related concerns. Divorce has been constructed as a prominent social issue, a symptom of conflicts which have activated, and been activated by a shifting personal, social, and economic landscape. It is with this in mind that the boundary between the private and public dimensions of marriage and divorce needs to be understood.

Justifications for State involvement in the private sphere of family life are usually expressed in terms of the need to protect children from harmful influence and experience. Society has an obligation to protect its weaker members. Children stand in particular need of this protection, even against their parents, to whom they are especially vulnerable. The rudiments of social justice require that they be protected from anything that may harm or impair their future healthy development. In so far as divorce is a hazardous experience, it is proper for the State to ensure that the interests of children exposed to its effects are adequately safeguarded.

However, when the State intervenes in family life it effectively undermines the authority of parents and encourages an abdication of their responsibilities. Such an outcome is self-defeating, because the State relies upon the family to socialize its members. Even where action is taken to rescue children from manifestly unsatisfactory conditions, it is by no means certain that alternative arrangements will be an improvement on the existing state of affairs. The hazards attached to intervening in the private domain of relationships between parents and children are analagous with the iatrogenic effects induced by some forms of medical treatment.

The public argument for overriding parental responsibility is justified in terms of the interests of the community as defined by the knowledge and beliefs of the day. Today we have evidence for believing that family experiences influence whether children will grow up to become social assets or liabilities – whether they will contribute to the economic, social, and spiritual well-being of the community or constitute a drain on public resources. The well-being of the community is defined in terms of a shared system of beliefs and values. In times of change these may need revising or modifying. It is not difficult to see that, at an individual level, concern to protect a child from the stresses of his or her parents' divorce will reverberate with concerns about the value system of society as a whole. It is the lot of divorce court judges and registrars, the latter-day Solomons of judicial practice, to operate on this boundary between public and private issues. This chapter will review some of the arguments that have received attention in recent years at both levels of the debate, since they are relevant to deciding whether public intervention in divorce is justified at all.

The effects of divorce on children

It is sometimes thought that however unhappy parents are in their marriage it is always better for them to stay together 'for the sake of the children' than to inflict upon them the damaging consequences of divorce. In examining this belief researchers have found it helpful to see divorce as a process rather than an event, and to distinguish between its short- and long-term consequences. There is some consensus that divorce affects children adversely in the short term (and differentially, according to age and sex), but that these ill-effects do not necessarily persist. Short-term disturbances in children are associated with the temporary inaccessibility of parents and the impairment of their capacity to parent. Long-term effects are associated with those burdens from which children have found no relief since the time of their parents' divorce, and the socially and materially prejudicial circumstances to which divorce can give rise.

The child's burden

One of the early challenges to the belief that for the sake of the children it was best to preserve an unhappy marriage rather than to end it was advanced by Rutter (1971, 1975), who studied the differential impact upon children of the loss of a parent through death and divorce. His findings suggested it was not the *disruption* of the bond with a parent that was of greatest significance but the *distortion* of family relationships. From an examination of the backgrounds of juvenile delinquents he claimed that some intact families were capable of wreaking as much havoc in the lives of their children as some broken families. An American review of the effects of divorce on children arrived at similar conclusions (Anthony 1974). The temptation was to conclude that separation might be a better solution to marital discord than sticking out an unhappy marriage.

However, those who came into contact with children of divorced parents, either at the time of the divorce, or perhaps years later, were familiar with the impact a parent's departure could have upon a child's self-esteem and confidence in the stability of the world around him. The fear of separation in the intact home was replaced by an experience of actual separation from one or other parent which could result in long-term insecurity in relationships (Richards 1981, 1984). A review of the effects of separation and divorce on child development (Richards and Dyson 1982) estimated that between 20 per cent and 50 per cent of children of divorce showed degrees of upset which required outside help at some time. How far these figures referred to abnormal behaviour is open to question. A child's distress or poor performance at school – even delinquency – might be considered a normal reaction to (and protest about) being caught up in a stressful situation not of his or her making. Such behaviour was as likely to be found in an unhappy intact home as in a broken home. It remained true that children who came from broken homes were worse off than children from happy, intact homes. But was this disadvantage a permanent one?

As the tangle of divorce has been unpicked it has become evident that divorce is a multi-faceted process, spanning years rather than months. It affects children variously according to their age and sex, where they are in the divorce process, and how that process is managed. An American study (Hetherington *et al.*

1982) found that during the first year of their parents' divorce children functioned even less well than contemporaries who came from intact, discordant families. The boys were aggressive, difficult to handle, lacking in self-control, attention-seeking, and easily distracted. The girls showed similar symptoms but were better behaved than the boys (mothers had custody of the children in all cases). By the end of the second year, however, the position of the children of divorce and those from intact families had been reversed, and between two and six years after separation the children had, by and large, made a satisfactory adaptation to their new circumstances.

Wallerstein's and Kelly's (1980) study of 60 families attending a divorce counselling service produced similar findings. In their longitudinal study, which spanned six years, they identified three stages in the divorce process: the initial period of the first year after separation when responses were acute; the transition period, lasting between two and three years, in which adaptations were made; and the five-year mark, by which time family members had adapted to their changed circumstances. Divorce was viewed as an extended process in which children showed little diminution in their attachment to both parents. In the acute phase they distinguished between the fear, regression, macabre fantasies, and bewilderment of pre-school children, the sadness and yearning of the 6 to 8-year-olds, the anger, loyalty, and heightened sense of right and wrong in the 9 to 12-year-olds, and the anguish of the adolescents – who surprised the researchers by making frantic appeals to them to restore their parents' marriages. In the long run, neither age nor sex were the crucial factors in determining the outcome to divorce, although a subsequent follow-up indicated that children who were youngest at the time of the marriage break-up fared better than those who were older and had to live with troubled memories of family strife (Wallerstein 1984). The single most important variable associated with good outcome was that the children should have a continued and positive relationship with both parents after divorce, an outcome that depended upon the quality of the relationship between the parents themselves. Wallerstein and Kelly concluded that the central hazard posed by divorce for the well-being of children and adolescents was diminished and disrupted parenting.

Subsequently, Wallerstein (1985) noted the persisting ill-effects upon children overburdened by supporting their parents.

She argued that they were poorly served by interventions based on the prevailing paradigm of divorce as a time-limited crisis. Johnston and colleagues (1985) associated prolonged post-divorce distress in children with the extent and duration of disagreement between parents, with the degree to which children were involved in their parents' disputes, and with the extent of role reversal between the two generations.

Studies in this country which have taken the views of children into account are sparse, but they tend to confirm the American finding that it is not divorce *per se* which is the crucial factor for children, but how divorce is managed. In a project designed to test the reactions of children to divorce Lund (1984) interviewed (through play) 30 children aged between 6 and 9 years, two years after their parents had separated. She also interviewed their custodial parents and teachers. Three categories of post-divorce experience emerged from her study: children who had had no contact with the non-custodial parent for over a year; children who had access but whose parents were in conflict with each other; and children whose parents worked harmoniously together. In this last group, fathers were usually highly involved with their children. In terms of self-esteem, behaviour, emotional problems, and performance at school children did progressively better as one moved from the first to the last category. The outcome for the last group, the children of harmonious parents, was summarized in these terms: 'both teachers and mothers reported that these children had the fewest emotional symptoms and highest self-esteem of the three groups. They actually had fewer symptoms than is average for children of this age group' (p. 199).

Walczak and Burns (1984) interviewed 100 children, young people, and adults who had experience of their parents' divorce. The recurring themes emerging from these retrospective accounts were that children wanted to know what was happening when their parents separated (although not the detail of what had gone wrong), wished for assurance that divorce was not going to cost them one of their parents, and did not want to be placed in a position where they had to take sides. Poor communication in the family, a problematic relationship with the custodial parent, and dissatisfaction with custody and access arrangements were associated with a negative outcome to divorce. In their sample of respondents 26 per cent fell into this negative outcome category, one which included a high number of adults who may have reflected the effects of a period in which attitudes to divorce were less tolerant than today.

Mitchell's (1985) account of her interviews with 116 adolescents and their custodial parents, which were conducted five years after separation, provides a moving record of the initial loneliness and bewilderment that result from the inaccessibility of one parent following separation (and sometimes, in emotional terms, both). The remarriage of one or other parent constituted a second crisis for some of the children in her sample because it dispelled the last vestiges of hope (however unsubstantiated) that their parents might eventually come back together again – often the precondition children believed necessary for recovering two parents. They emphasized again and again their need to be kept informed about what was happening. Mitchell stressed the importance of good communication between separating parents to avoid an outcome in which a divorce is effected between a parent and (usually) his children, as well as between spouses. She argued that doctors, solicitors, teachers, and social workers were important attendants upon the process of marriage breakdown who therefore had a primary mental health care role to play in facilitating the reconstruction of family life after divorce. The case for educating professionals about the known effects of divorce on children and their parents is well made by Mitchell, and by other writers (for example, McLoughlin and Whitfield 1985).

The weight of research opinion favouring the struggle to keep children in touch with both their parents, despite the short-term stresses of so doing, has not gone unchallenged. Goldstein, Freud, and Solnit (1973, 1980) argue that when marriage ends, a child's greatest needs are for continuity and a low level of conflict in their relationships. They argue that the 'psychological parent' – in effect, the custodial parent – should have the right to decide whether and how much access a child should have to an absent parent. Their premise is that contact with the non-custodial parent is likely to be damaging if conflict between the parents remains high. The sooner a stable post-divorce family is established, the sooner children will find an end to uncertainty and distress. The role of the courts is then to establish who the 'psychological parent' is, and whether parents are able to agree over questions of access. A judgment is then made on the basis of the 'least detrimental alternative' open to the court, this being considered a more realistic basis for intervention than the 'best interests' principle, given the inability of courts to supervise interpersonal relationships or to make long-term predictions. These views have been challenged on theoretical and empirical grounds (Richards 1986). They have also been attacked for being unfair, and for increasing the likelihood of custody battles in Court (Mnookin 1979).

What seems to be clear is that the interests of parents and children do not usually coincide when a marriage breaks down. We have yet to read a study which concludes that children prefer their parents to go their separate ways than to stay together – even when the domestic atmosphere is tense (although, to be fair, this view has been represented by some of the respondents in some of the studies). What is required of parents is information about what is going on, so that children, in managing their own uncertainty, do not have to act like the detective investigators described by McGredie and Horrox (1985) who search for clues and explanations. Sadly, the toll of divorce on parents may be too great to allow them to hear and respond to that need, particularly when parents themselves may know that their children do not wish them to pursue the course of action upon which they are set.

What children prefer may not accord with what is in their best interests. But what these are, in terms of long-term outcomes of divorce, is hard to know with any certainty. As yet there is insufficient evidence to make hard and fast predictions, if ever this will be possible. The diversity of family forms, and the varieties of response to divorce and remarriage are not adequately catered for by research into predominantly white, middle-income families (Hetherington and Camara 1984). The work undertaken so far suggests that divorce is best understood as a process rather than an event, and that the post-divorce relationship between parents is significant when considering how children will adapt. Good communication about what is going on, plus the ready accessibility of the non-residential parent, is likely to be of considerable value in assisting children to come to terms with the reality of their changed predicament and in keeping both parents alive for them. These conditions help to relieve children of the burden of uncertainty, the burden of caring for themselves and their parents, and the burden of having to take sides.

The parent's burden

While the wishes of children and parents may conflict during divorce, the welfare of children is inextricably bound up with the welfare of parents. The interests of all family members are relevant to the burdens carried by each, and to that extent the distinctions drawn between the burdens of children and those of parents are arbitrary. Nevertheless, burdens carried by parents during divorce are so crucial to the well-being of children that they deserve separate attention.

For both divorcing and intact families the capacity to care for children is a resource and not a fixed attribute. As with other resources it can be depleted or supplemented. Some parents, by dint of inclination or experience, may be more predisposed to the job than others, but most parents acknowledge the wear and tear which, even in ordinary circumstances, is part and parcel of the job. Most vulnerable are parents with pre-school children, isolated at home with few friends and inaccessible partners, and lacking the financial and social buttressing afforded by employment and material security. Poverty, ill-health, and emotional upset can be as much a part of the ordinary experience of parenthood as of parenthood after divorce.

The absent father is also not a creation of divorce. The traditional distribution of roles in marriage has usually meant that the man has devoted the greater part of his time and energy to providing an income for his family (often trailing his dependents around the country – even the world – in pursuit of higher remuneration and status) while the woman has remained home and child centred. Changes of school and community have led to social isolation for many women, impairing their ability to parent their children, and sometimes compelling them to return to paid employment to relieve their own misery as well as to supplement the household income. The organization of social life around the workplace has compounded the risk of children being sacrificed on the altar of the greater economic good, certainly as far as men are concerned. The demands of work are at their greatest during the child-rearing years. The consequence, at least until recently, was that parenting and mothering were usually synonymous. The degree to which fathers could be involved with their children was circumscribed. A man exceeding the commonly accepted boundaries of parental involvement was as much a threat to sexual identity as the woman who took a career.

This division of labour is less rigidly adhered to today than in the past. Paid employment for mothers (albeit usually part-time) is the rule rather than the exception, and in some parts of the country, and for some families, this is nothing new. Chronic unemployment among men, however, is new for the post-war father. Yet the old patterns persist. Family poverty caused by the man of the house losing his job often goes unrelieved because women refrain from paid work for fear of compounding the injury inflicted by unemployment to their husbands' self-esteem. The chances are that if the man is out of work, so too will be the woman (Halsey 1985). As with divorce (and the connection may not be accidental) unemployment increases the lower down the social scale you go (Haskey 1984; Rimmer and Popay 1982).

Demarcation lines are drawn by both sexes. Jackson's (1984) vivid account of the reactions of first-time fathers to the birth of their children chronicles how their longings to be involved were tacitly discouraged by the closed shop of maternal interests. Their own uncertainty about whether they had a claim to press made it hard for them to counter such discouragement. Most of these men did not wish to be a father as they remembered their own fathers – benevolent but remote authority figures – yet they were ambivalent about involving themselves more actively. Those unfortunate enough to be out of work found it more difficult than the others to become actively involved as fathers because they felt dispossessed of their traditional roles.

Marital breakdown magnifies some of the ordinary conditions of family life and exacerbates their effects. In the short term it almost always results in impaired parenting. To begin with, there are usually serious social and economic consequences. This is especially true for women, who are the chief custodians of children. The financial and housing problems of single parent households were made startlingly evident in the Finer Report (1974): a third of mothers bringing up children on their own relied upon supplementary benefit as their main source of income. Among the one in five children who today come from families with an income below the poverty line, and the one in eight whose parents claim supplementary benefit (originally designed as a protection against the extremes of poverty), a high proportion will come from broken homes (Pugh and De'Ath 1984). Even the relatively well-off face a drop in their standard of living. Divorce results in downward social mobility, especially for women who choose not to remarry (Maclean and Eekelaar 1984). Most studies of divorcing families have highlighted the adverse financial consequences of divorce, and have charted how the return of women to work through financial necessity has left them exhausted and less available for their children than they would have wished. Material pressures add to the burdens of responsibility and day-to-day care which can so easily tip an unsupported parent into despair.

Separation and divorce have been shown to have adverse effects upon mental and physical health, work performance, and social confidence. This has been evident in symptoms ranging from alcohol abuse to attempted (and sometimes successful) suicide. Divorce has been described as 'a major health hazard', which isolates individuals and, in conjunction with constitutional predispositions, makes them more vulnerable to illness and death than other comparable adults (Dominian 1984). Degrees of disturbance are hard to predict, and at least one study has reported less shock and disturbance among divorcing couples than is commonly supposed (Mitchell 1981). The critical period of stress immediately precedes and surrounds the actual physical separation, and for many women divorce may come as a relief from this earlier stressful time (Chester 1971).

Research indicates that the first year after separation is likely to be the most unsettled. Close to the time of separation, when children are confused about what is happening and need the support and reassurance of their parents, parents are likely to be at their most preoccupied, often seeking reassurance and support in their own right. In that sense, their capacity to act as parents is impaired. Progress from an extended decision-making stage through a relatively brief negotiating stage to a new and consolidated position (the three phases of the divorce process most commonly cited) is rarely accomplished smoothly. Yet the indications are that between two and four years after separation parents have usually adapted satisfactorily to divorce, and this is generally reflected in an overall improvement in their health (Spanier and Thompson 1984). Parents and children tend to become reconciled to the inevitable, and while children may never quite come round to seeing the divorce as having been the right decision for the family, parents usually say they do eventually arrive at this conclusion.

There is, however, some evidence, that men find it more difficult than women to come to terms with divorce. A study of divorced men (Ambrose et al. 1983) found that years after their divorce, many were still angry about the way their marriages had ended, even when they had custody of the children. While there are methodological issues which may have weighted the findings (the sample was recruited by advertising and this method might be expected to attract those who had an axe to grind), their responses support intimations from our own work that divorce is a greater injury for men than for women, and one from which recovery can be slow.

There have been three main approaches to understanding the experience of divorce and the nature of the preoccupations which reduce the accessibility of parents to their children. The first identifies types of divorcing couples and families, emphasizing patterns of communication and behaviour that predate the marital rupture and which are, in some degree, 'givens' in the post-separation equation. The second considers social readjustments following separation. The third pays attention to the process of emotional adaptation following the ending of marriage. The three approaches are not mutually exclusive. Social and psychological processes of adaptation are affected by constitutional endowments. Behaviour associated with a stage of adaptation, caught at a moment in time, might be placed in a category of divorce experience.

Divorcing 'types'

In many divorcing couples, one partner will not want the marriage to end. An absence of consensus about the merits of a relationship distinguishes the decision to divorce from the decision to marry. Whether or not each partner expresses something for the other, attempts to classify the experience of divorcing families have referred to the degree of mutuality or ambivalence surrounding the decision to divorce, the frequency and openness of communication between partners, and the level and intensity of conflict.

A small study of fourteen couples (Kressel *et al.* 1980) has become an important reference point in the construction of a divorcing typology. Drawing upon systemic concepts the authors posit four 'types' of divorcing couples. Those exhibiting high levels of conflict, communication, and ambivalence about the decision to divorce (bitterly agreeing to and then changing their minds about divorce, and unable to implement a final decision) were termed *enmeshed* couples. Psychologically they were the least prepared to let go of their marriage. At the opposite extreme were *autistic* couples who, although ambivalent about the decision to divorce, avoided each other physically and emotionally. The *direct conflict* group displayed high levels of conflict and communication, but were distinguished from the enmeshed group by a moderating degree of ambivalence about the marriage ending and a capacity to work through the implications. Finally, there was the *disengaged* group, about whom the authors wrote: 'of all our couples these were the ones in which the flame of intimacy had come to burn least brightly – and so, too, the heat of conflict' (p. 112).

Whereas the last two categories made a good adaptation to divorce and were amenable to help, the enmeshed and autistic groups, plagued by high levels of anxiety and ambivalence about ending their marriages, were handicapped and inaccessible to mediation efforts. They appear in Wallerstein's and Kelly's study (1980) as *embittered-chaotic* parents. For them the disjunction between legal and emotional processes of dissolution, noted by Hagestad and Smyer (1982) among others, was at its greatest. They also appear as *non-communicating* (autistic) and *open conflict* (enmeshed or direct conflict) couples in Parkinson's (1983) classification, in contrast with *semi-detached* couples who are freer from ambivalence about marriage ending and can co-operate with each other over post-marital arrangements.

Little (1982) drew attention to the similarity between patterns of interaction before and after separation, a view challenged by other researchers in so far as it bears upon patterns of parenting (Maidment 1983). In her six categories of marital types she specified *fragile bond*, *fractured*, and *stalemate* families as bearing the hallmark of avoidance in the way conflict was managed. Among those who co-operated well after separation were the *perfect model* marriages, often very young marriages in which conflict was suppressed in the interests of protecting postmarital arrangements. Enmeshed or embittered families were to be found in her category of *unformed* families, where parents were emotionally (if not physically) young, and often more committed to their parents than to their spouse. In this group, separation constituted the loss of a family environment and personal viability as much as the loss of a partner. Open conflicts, and attempts to coerce and control, featured in the *dolls' house* marriages, where separation had followed a significant disturbance in the balance of power between the partners.

Little's typology extends to the roles children played in these different patterns of interaction. They acted to stabilize their parents' relationship, to care for them, compete with them, obstruct them, and sometimes to serve as hostages in post-separation battles. She comments that these roles were not the creation of divorce but were usually firmly rooted in family history.

Classifications of this kind are inevitably incomplete and offer a static, freeze-frame view of divorce. They run the risk of distorting reality by obscuring individual differences within general categories. At best they can signal features which are readily recognized by others. Indeed, ease of recognition is one yardstick by which the adequacy of a category can be gauged. A useful category is one from which fairly accurate predictions can be made with regard to the subjects in it. The value of Kressel's work lies not only in managing the complexities of idiosyncratic behaviour but also in identifying those groups where parents might (and might not) be expected to reach agreement with outside help.

In understanding the difficulties of adapting to divorce account needs to be taken both of conscious requirements (relating to role, status, and resources) and unconscious factors (the deep-seated psychological reasons for refusing to part with a redundant past). Together these determine the extent to which change and reorganization is possible. Both these tasks are facilitated by regarding divorce as a dynamic process rather than as an event.

Divorce as a status passage

Weiss (1975) likened separation to being despatched to a foreign country where one is confronted by new customs and new practices, and constantly thrown off balance by the strangeness of other people's reactions. But as he observes, for the separated there are no customs sheds to warn that the setting will be new, nor a foreign language to signal the possibility that others may behave oddly. Instead, the same people and the same places contrive to exist in a changed world.

The feelings of social disorientation depicted so vividly in this metaphor also featured in the accounts of many of the 63 separated and divorced men and women interviewed by Hart (1976). Her understanding of divorce as a status passage highlighted the lack of role supports available during the transition from spouse to divorcee. In part, the absence of supports was seen as a legacy of the view of divorce as social deviance (the study took place in the late 1960s), and it also reflected a more general uncertainty about how to behave towards those beyond marriage. 'Divorce is a process of endless becoming', she wrote, 'hopefully becoming something else' (p. 221). The 'something else' was usually a husband or wife in a new marriage. Burgoyne and Clark (1984) picked up the same pressures in a study of step-families undertaken in the late 1970s. Their respondents wished, above all else, to reconstitute a normal family life. The model for 'normal' was that of a first marriage.

Central to both studies is the understanding that new role identities require positive affirmation from others if they are to be taken on successfully. Whereas marriage is a highly structured status passage, with institutionalized rites and social supports, divorce is a highly unstructured change for which there is little preparation, minimal support, and no sense of going anywhere except into another marriage. With the collapse of social identity comes a sense of anomie, personal disorganization, and alienation from others. Increased illness, mental breakdown, social withdrawal, and suicide attempts can all be understood in the context of a collapse of social validation and meaning.

For both parties divorce will bring multiple losses, the impact of which may be more keenly felt by men than by women. In line with traditionally defined gender differences (the instrumental male and the expressive female) wives tend to be more at ease than their husbands with disclosing their feelings; when something goes wrong in a marriage it is commonly the woman who will signal for help (Brannen and Collard 1982). Commonly, too, it is the woman who creates and maintains a social network for both partners in a marriage. Men often express feelings primarily with and through their spouses. A wife's departure may not only close down the social network they had previously shared as a couple but also remove from the husband a listening ear. By the time the marriage breaks, of course, it is likely that each partner will have grown deaf to the other, so Chiriboga et al.'s (1979) argument that divorce constitutes a double loss for men (by removing a channel for expressing feelings as well as a sympathetic ear) may apply well before the stage of physical separation.

The differential impact of divorce also depends upon who initiates the break. This is seldom easy to establish. In 1984 72.7 per cent of petitioners were women (a figure which indicates the de jure instigators of divorce). The requirement of law which divides partners into petitioners and respondents is a very inaccurate guide to who has initiated what. Even if divorce is the outcome of mutual agreement, one partner must be seen to initiate proceedings. Similar complexities attach to the de facto ending of marriage. For example, one partner may be propelled into acting on behalf of his or her spouse in a manner which makes it difficult to be clear about who really initiated the break.

Nevertheless, separation comes as a shock to many partners, inducing disbelief that the crisis is anything more than a temporary aberration in their spouse, and reinforcing denial about problems in the marriage which may have a long history. Denial is a common means of managing anxiety, but over-reliance upon it not only affords little protection against unavoidable change, it may actually precipitate what it is intended to prevent. When separation is unwanted, unexpected, and believed to be unwarranted, the impact can be devastating. The 'goodbye' note left by the departing wife for the returning husband, and the affidavit dropping through the letterbox following a spouse's unexplained absence from home can trigger a chain of reactions which escalate the problems that families have to face after separation.

With separation, as with other major life events, it helps to be able to predict and rehearse what is to come. This reduces the sense of unfamiliarity, helplessness, and disorientation of the unprepared traveller described by Weiss. A predictable and planned conclusion to marriage is likely to ease the process of adapting to divorce. When partners have little control over and knowledge about the unfamiliar situations in which they find themselves, and are left to react only to a sense of having been stripped of assets, identity, and meaning in life, the results for themselves and for others can be very destructive. In so far as judicial procedures in divorce constitute a *rite de passage* (an institutionalized ritual assisting people to relinquish some roles and responsibilities in order to take on others) it is important that the social and psychological implications of procedural reform should be given adequate attention. It is no accident that the debate between those who wish to preserve marriage and those who wish to facilitate divorce should focus upon the judicial system at the present time. Judicial behaviour helps to shape the experience of divorce for those involved.

Divorce as bereavement

In a study of health reports on 50 American servicemen carried out in the 1960s, divorce ranked second to the death of a spouse in a scale of stressful life events (Rahe *et al.* 1967). Allowing for the fact that the study is twenty years old, and was confined to male subjects, it still contains a sobering message. Divorce can have an impact upon individuals comparable to that of bereavement. Some of the same features apply to both situations. As in bereavement, a process of mourning may be required in divorce before the threads of life can be picked up again in a way which is appropriate to the changes which have taken place.

Bereavement studies (Parkes 1972; Marris 1974) have described a definable progression from denial to realization in healthy reactions to loss. The shock and disbelief following news of a bereavement can result in a sense of numbness lasting anything from a few hours to a week. Such a reaction is much less noticeable when a death has been anticipated and there have been opportunities to entertain the idea of being a widow or widower. There follows a period of restlessness, yearning, insomnia, and general sense of ailing, symptoms which signal acute anxiety and may prompt a search for the lost person. Applied to divorce, these reactions explain many last desperate bids for reconciliation in the weeks and months following a separation. A woman in our study who had been left by her husband some nine months previously, and who said she did not regret the marriage ending, nevertheless described catching herself waiting for the sound of his key in the door at the time he used to return home from work. Those who offer comfort or condolence in either situation can expect a hostile response in return for behaviour which is rightly taken as confirming the loss as permanent. They may also become the target for anger which a death or departure can precipitate by evoking a sense of having been abandoned.

This period of mourning can last for months, even years. After more than two years of living apart from his wife, a husband bitterly attacked his welfare officer for wanting to discuss the custody of his child because, he said, it presupposed the marriage had ended. This he refused to accept. Feelings of anger and guilt may prompt self-destructive behaviour, as if the self has become identified with the departed spouse towards whom there is a wish that they be directed. Social isolation may be actively maintained out of a sense of personal injury. A lifetime's savings can be squandered prosecuting legal actions which have no chance of success. Recovering that part of the self previously contained by and related to in the absent partner is an integral part of the mourning process. Children who identify with their lost parent may inhibit that process by becoming proxy for the absent partner, unwittingly satisfying the remaining parent's need for comfort or for someone to fight. A physical resemblance, or a mannerism, may be sufficient to qualify for the role. In the end comes a period, sometimes protracted, of depression, disorganization, and even despair, before the phase of recovery and reorganization following the unalterable facts of change.

Observations made by Bowlby (1980) about the behaviour of children separated from their parents have relevance to the divorce process. He noticed that anger could have several positive functions. It could be deployed to restore a lost parent and so alleviate the suffering caused by separation. It could be a means of protest and of coercing others, enlisting their help and thereby reducing the sense of helplessness engendered by parting. It could also be the means of making a break from others in order to establish a separate, viable identity. In the last of these circumstances it is easy to see how an emotional need to disengage may conflict with attempts to counsel or conciliate. One man in therapy at the Institute of Marital Studies put the dilemma clearly. He wanted his marriage to survive but recognized his partner's determination to leave. 'I have to hate her to go', he said as he declined joint interviews in favour of separate sessions, 'I can be more civilized later on' (Clulow et al. 1986).

When the wish to protest or coerce is so overwhelming that it alienates those it is intended to win back, anger becomes dysfunctional and self-defeating. Fostered over time, anger may be directed less towards making a break than towards keeping a marriage alive, prolonging negative attachments to avoid separation. The man who contrives to watch his former spouse, or who haunts the places she frequents, is doing just that. Much psychological illness is an expression of pathological mourning. Accident-proneness – even suicide – may result from an unconscious identification with someone who has died. For the divorcee it may indicate that hostile or murderous feelings are being directed inwards towards the self rather than outwards towards others. It may constitute a plea for help – perhaps one designed to coerce a partner into returning. A compulsive need to care for others, or an assertive self-reliance, may camouflage an intense desire to be cared for. A sense of time being stopped at the point of separation may be reflected in the way lifestyles are organized. In all these instances what can be appropriate and healthy as a phase of mourning is inappropriate and unhealthy when it becomes a permanent resting place. The hallmark of pathological mourning is the undiminished belief that irreversible loss is reversible.

It is here that the realities for those who lose a partner through death, and those who lose a partner through divorce, become substantially different. For the separated and divorced there is no body; on the contrary, there is someone with whom a relationship will often persist. Weiss (1975) comments on the intense ambivalence of post-divorce relationships between former spouses. In the search for relief from confusion and uncertainty, former partners may fight each other or go to bed with each other. Irrespective of whether their feelings are hateful or loving they sustain an engagement with each other. The precondition for psychological divorce (a process that for some will never be completed) is a recognition of ambivalent feelings towards the former spouse. This allows for the recovery of good as well as bad feelings, encouraging awareness that time spent in the marriage was not totally wasted.

In giving expression to feelings stirred up by the loss of a spouse, the personal and social milieu of divorce affects the nature of catharsis, further differentiating the separated from the bereaved. Ambivalent reactions are handled differently. In the sorrow of bereavement a spouse is often idealized; self-reproach and quick-temperedness towards others may be the only channels through which anger finds an outlet. There is a finality about death which allows no reply to the anguish of the bereaved from the person who really matters. In divorce, the situation is reversed. Not only is there no *body*, but there is commonly an adversary who can be depended upon to reply. In these circumstances the former spouse is often denigrated, and good feelings are suppressed or channelled towards the children of the marriage.

Social pressures may reinforce these one-sided reactions. In divorce, to want a fight, to express rage, or to become a calculating tactician will be understood, if not approved of. In bereavement such behaviour would be considered bizarre or improper. The Obergs (1978) list reactions to separation tacitly encouraged by court procedures: slander, mistrust, distortion of the truth, poor relations between children and parents, self-justification, guarded behaviour, sleuthing, and blinkered self-awareness, to name but a few. Whereas people are discouraged from making far-reaching decisions immediately after a bereavement, a good lawyer will advise his divorce clients to act quickly, knowing that initial post-separation arrangements have a momentum of their own which substantially affect the final outcome. Court procedures are not designed to help people understand their part in conflict or to assist in the work of mourning. Except for children, who often have no choice, there are few who will listen to the adults and also ensure:

> 'that what will seem to the partners like demented outpourings will not be so regarded by the listener, who is not going to take anything down in evidence against them; that they are not going to be written off as untrustworthy potential murderers, unsuitable to care for their children because they have been able to express some of their own infantile rage which is an intrinsic part of grief.'   (Lyons 1981: 3)

The preoccupations of burdened parents provide children with opportunities for growing up and taking responsibility; they also create conditions in which they have to carry the burdens of adults in addition to their own. Through witnessing the death of their parents' marriages they may become involved in giving the past a proper burial, or perpetuating ghosts that refuse to be laid to rest. The opportunities for children to divide and rule between warring parents are endless, and provide them with some satisfaction. Torn by conflicting loyalties they may displace the parent who has left, and manage their own grief by caring for the parent who remains. A precocious step towards adulthood may be taken as compensation for a curtailed childhood. They may become arbiters of parental esteem, encouraging or discouraging the tentative claims of their parents by their behaviour. Garber (1984) commented on the failure of many non-custodial parents to sustain their involvement as parents in the face of their children's anger and disappointment. For the parent who remains, children may provide an outlet for frustrated anger or a source of emotional support. What children cannot rely upon, at least in the short term, is that either of their parents will be as alive to their needs as their situations warrant.

The current state of knowledge suggests that three main factors mitigate the effects of divorce on children: a continuing relationship with both parents, the quality of parenting from the residential parent, and the quality of what is created to take the place of the past marriage. Each of these factors raises questions about how far the social milieu of divorce encourages the conditions for making a good adaptation. It is to these questions that we now turn.

Divorce and social values

The postwar years have witnessed significant challenges to established views about marriage and parenting practices. These have affected the balance between the interests of the 'family' (using this as an umbrella word to cover the diversity of household living arrangements currently in operation) and the interests of the State. The divorce courts have provided a forum in which conflicts of interest have become evident not only between litigating partners, but also between the family and the State.

Changing attitudes to marriage, divorce, and parenting practices

Two changes have combined to affect the responses of courts to divorce petitions and child custody disputes. Since the Second World War (an event which resulted in the break-up of many marriages and paved the way for the removal of some of the economic obstacles to ending marriage through the 1949 Legal Aid and Advice Act) divorce has become an increasingly practicable and acceptable way of resolving marital conflict. In consequence, the concept of matrimonial guilt (which governed the divorce laws until 1971) has been in decline. The second change, perhaps not unrelated to the first, has been in connection with parenting practices.

Marriage and divorce

One reason for the recent change in attitudes towards separation and divorce has been a readiness to accept marriage breakdown as a social phenomenon rather than as a reflection of personal defect. Among the threads common to rising divorce rates in West European countries, Chester (1984) identified the changed situation of women as having been especially important. Released from unwanted childbearing by effective contraception and abortion, and experiencing social and economic freedom as a result of paid employment, women are today in a position to exercise choice about whether or not to stay married. For men, too, choice has been extended through rising affluence and social mobility.

For some, marriage has become a suspect institution. More than a hundred years ago Marxists were critical of the role of marriage in patriarchal, capitalist economic systems organized around the production and distribution of inheritable wealth. The sexual double standards of Victorian England were partly the product of a system which allowed no ambiguity about the paternity of sons and heirs. A century further on, the feminist critique of marriage is centred on the sexual discrimination that has been one product of this patriarchal system. Marriage has been portrayed as a social institution whose effect (if not purpose) is to perpetuate the relative disadvantage of women as compared with men. Following Bernard's (1972) distinction between 'his' and 'her' experience of marriage there have been a number of studies suggesting that marriage is physically and emotionally more damaging to women than men. Ideologies are capable of generating evidence to support their positions (and methodological objections have been raised about some of the marriage and health studies). There is no doubt, however, that the feminist critique of marriage has had a sobering effect upon those who may not previously have called into question the rightness of monogamous marriage. In this connection, it would be interesting to explore further the indications that men are more vulnerable than women after marriage breakdown, yet less likely to remarry in haste.

The self-defeating aspects of a monogamous ideology are no new discovery. Alvarez (1982) referred to an ancient Hebrew authority as a source for the view that nothing was more useful to marriage than the right to divorce, since it was likely to keep both partners agreeable to each other and to maintain peace in the family. The burden of choice can weigh as heavily as the burden of constraint. Today, much is expected of marriage as a personal relationship. Anticipating a long life unencumbered by material worries and heavy childrearing responsibilities, individuals may look to marriage to provide meaning and personal fulfilment throughout their lives. This can be especially true of those couples isolated from kin, fragmented by the demands of work, and dwarfed by the technology and institutionalized structures characteristic of life today. Marriage and the family may then be regarded as a retreat from the pressures of life rather than a springboard into society (Berger and Kellner 1977). But it is also true that marriage still represents the final transition to adulthood for many young couples, especially when restricted employment opportunities act to defer this step and restrict other routes to personal autonomy (Mansfield 1985). Marriage also remains a means of escaping from parental influence as, indeed, does parenthood. Despite these qualifications the functionalist sociologist's view of marriage as serving the wider interests of society has lost ground in recent years to the growth psychologist's view of marriage as a means to personal development, and this has given rise to a new set of tensions.

Askham (1984) pointed out the contradictory requirements of marriage when it is expected to provide partners with security *and* the means for personal development. Development requires that partners have outside reference points, opportunities for change and few publicly imposed definitions of role and status. Security demands the opposite. She asked whether the growing emphasis upon self-fulfilment in marriage had contributed to rising divorce rates and falling first marriage rates. The expectation that marriage should, in some objectified sense, be assessed in terms of its capacity to satisfy emotional and developmental needs carries with it the risk that marriage is regarded as a commodity and not as a relationship. The inevitable consequence of this view is that when one marriage is felt to have outlived its usefulness it is disposed of in preference for a newer (and possibly better packaged) model (Smail 1985). Monica Furlong sees real difficulties for those attached to a romantically idealized image of marriage:

'It may be the inability of some couples to endure the many minor deaths of a good marriage which finally brings about divorce; so fearful are they of anger, of loneliness, of separateness that they cannot manage the casualness that a true relationship demands. If *every* row feels like a life and death struggle, if living with someone evokes the huge emotions – terror, jealousy, envy, possessiveness, death-dealing rage – which normally we associate with grand opera or Shakespearean tragedy – then the situation may not be a liveable one.'
(Furlong 1981: 25)

In short, the shift in values and attitudes that has accompanied social and technological change has resulted in higher expectations for a relationship which is less supported today than in years gone by. The social meaning of divorce has changed in consequence.

Parenting practices

The declining influence of the matrimonial offence as an operational concept has, in certain respects, been aided by advances made in the field of child psychology. A central figure in this field has been John Bowlby, whose early work on the effects of maternal deprivation underpinned and strengthened the assumption that children were better off with mothers than fathers, and that the less disruption to the relationship between a child and his primary caretaker the better. The importance of fathers for children was overshadowed by the central position accorded to mothers, especially in the early years of life.

In the 1960s and 1970s, when patterns of family diversity were more openly recognized, the primacy of mothers was called into question (Rutter 1981) and the concept of attachment revised (Bowlby 1969, 1975, 1980). In the process, many firmly held views about child development have been unsettled. The boundary between science and doctrine has again been called into question. For example, the process of bonding, once thought to depend so heavily upon the skin-to-skin contact between a mother and her baby in the early hours and days of life, has been declared unproven (Sluckin *et al.* 1983). How otherwise, it is argued, can one explain the bonds that develop between children and their adoptive or foster parents? Bonding, it has been suggested, was a socially constructed concept intended to buttress the view that a woman's place was at home with her children. The consequence of this belief was that when things went wrong at home it was the mother who was to blame. The role fathers played for children, even from an early age, was a relatively neglected area of study, although there was research evidence to support its importance (Pilling and Kellmer Pringle 1978).

The current consensus among child psychologists is that the quality of interaction between parents and children is more important than physical care; a child's need for stimulation is to be accorded more importance than the need for proximity. The biological mother might not be the primary object of attachment and, most importantly, the infant might be attached to more than one person. The assumption that changes in parental care are necessarily damaging is questionable. Children can be resilient in the face of stressful circumstances providing the stress is not persistent and support is to hand.

These findings have crucial implications for judicial practice in relation to the children of divorce, implications which are only now beginning to filter through to the legal system. A mother who takes a substantial fall in income following divorce, sells up the family home which she can no longer afford to run, and moves with her children to a new house in a strange area, exposes herself and her children to considerable stress arising from the discontinuity in all their lives. If she takes a job to supplement the household income the overload of responsibility may result in her becoming emotionally inaccessible to her children despite the physical care she gives to them. For a judge to adjudicate in a custody dispute on the basis of a mother having had continuous day-to-day care of children in the past is no guarantee that she was then, or will be in the future, emotionally available for them. The assumptions that have guided so many child custody decisions in the past are now being looked at anew. The task of helping to establish a place for fathers in post-divorce families may require the special attention of judges and registrars.

The ability of courts to respond to social science findings depends upon the extent to which the judiciary, as a social institution, is shackled by the society of which it is a part. Shortly after the Divorce Reform Act became law, Mortlock (1972) took his legal colleagues to task for being prone to the dead ideas of the past, urging them to become more socially aware. Yet in certain respects the judiciary is designated by society to be a conservative influence, and this has its value in times of change and uncertainty.

Private freedoms and public costs

Since the second half of the last century, legislation facilitating divorce has been accompanied by measures designed to protect the welfare of children. As the State has relaxed the prohibition on divorce (formerly enforced by the Church) it has increased its direct interest in the child-rearing functions of families.

Historically, the socializing roles of State and family have been interdependent. In this country fathers were held to have sacred rights over their dependents and property, rights which were upheld by the Church and State and which dated back to Roman Law where *patria potestas* extended to the life and death of children. The family was the key instrument of social regulation, and the authority of the father over other family members was a local manifestation of the authority of the State. Stone quotes James I as saying in 1609, 'Kings are compared to fathers in families: for a King is truly *parens patriae*, the politic father of his people' (Stone 1977: 110). So long as a father controlled the behaviour of his kin, provided taxes, and co-operated with military conscription, the State allowed him and his dependents status, recognition, and protection. Those existing outside the family posed a threat to family interests in a system where property and influence was passed down the generations through marriage. They also threatened the security of the State, which depended on maintaining order and discouraging undue claims on the public purse (Donzelot 1980; Dingwall *et al.* 1983).

The echoes of this argument (in terms of the economic consequences of divorce for the State) are still to be heard today. It is argued that private freedoms involve public costs. In legal aid bills alone, the freedom to end marriage costs the taxpayer in excess of £40 million a year (£49.8 million was spent on legal aid in matrimonial causes in 1983). The Interdepartmental Review of Family and Domestic Jurisdiction published by the Lord Chancellor's Department in May 1986 estimated that expenditure on family business from the Legal Aid Fund totalled £114 million in 1984/85. More than four times that amount is spent on supplementary benefit each year, the principal means of support for many of the one and a half million children brought up in one-parent households today (Popay *et al.* 1982). While it is difficult to apportion the costs directly attributable to marital separation and divorce, it is safe to assume that the community bears a significant proportion of the financial burden associated with the process of restructuring in the post-marriage family. The 1982–83 General Household Survey indicated that only two-fifths of currently divorced women were receiving maintenance or alimony from their former spouses, and it is recognized that such payments often lapse over time. Many second marriages falter under the strain of financial legacies from the first, so repeating the cycle of economic dependence of the broken home upon the State (Maddox 1982). The repercussions affect the private sector of the economy too. The family is a consumer unit of prime importance, a fact well recognized by banks, building societies, and advertisers. Divorce reduces levels of disposable income and may destabilize existing economic interests. In that sense it can represent a threat to the security of the State.

How the costs of divorce compare with costs generated by tension in surviving marriages is a matter for speculation. One estimate of the direct and indirect costs of marital stress (including hours lost at work, expenditure on drugs, and the price of maintaining medical, psychiatric, and social services) amounted to one billion pounds annually (Dominian 1983). This compares with £1.5 million spent annually by the Government on marriage guidance services. Like the proverbial piece of string, the open-system nature of marriage (influencing and influenced by factors external to it) allows for elastic estimates of the costs of marital breakdown.

Divorce and the welfare of children

The evolution in this country of what has become known as *the welfare principle* can be traced in law from 1857. The transfer in that year of jurisdiction over divorce from the ecclesiastic to the secular courts created a need for guidelines in dealing with dependents of broken marriages which had not previously existed, divorce having hitherto been restricted to those very few who could afford to resort to private Act of Parliament. That is not to say that marriages did not frequently break down before then: desertion, wife sale, and diverse forms of family organization were common in Victorian times, as the novels of Charles Dickens and Thomas Hardy attest. What had changed was that the *de facto* reality of marriage breakdown received *de jure* recognition, although differentially as between men and women: the 1857 Matrimonial Causes Act required women to prove adultery plus one other offence to justify a divorce, whereas for men a wife's adultery would suffice.

In a painstaking synthesis of legislative change and social attitudes to divorce, Maidment (1984) describes how the welfare principle first came into being through the Courts of Equity as a means of protecting the property of children in a legal climate more concerned with enforcing patriarchal authority than with enhancing the practice of child care. Informally it was acknowledged that women brought up children, and this fitted the Victorian image of married femininity and wifely domesticity. Custody disputes would generally come to court only if property was at stake, a question of religious affiliation was raised, or the father had a particular axe to grind. Even then, disputes would not always be settled in favour of the father; the poet Shelley lost a claim to his child because he was a self-declared atheist.

Maidment argues that the history of the child welfare principle cannot be isolated from the Women's Movement of the late nineteenth and early twentieth centuries. In her view the 1886 and (more particularly) 1925 Guardianship of Infants Acts were, in part, designed to deflect the debate about women's rights from the public to the domestic arena by publicly conceding the importance of women to children. This can be seen as an attempt to reinforce the traditional gender divisions between the public (male) and private (female) spheres of life. In the public sphere the courts are the direct instruments of the State, and have acted as paternalistic *parens patriae* towards children whose welfare is considered to be at risk. In the field of child care legislation, there has been debate about how far the roles of parents – in the private sphere – have been usurped in consequence. An elusive yardstick, and one susceptible to the pressures of the day, the welfare principle has undoubtedly been the mantle under which behaviour which challenged established social beliefs and attitudes has been controlled and even punished. It is not so very long ago that a wife 'convicted' of the 'offence' of adultery would find that she lost her children to their father, irrespective of how good a mother she had been. Equating the welfare of children with the preservation of marriage through deterrent measures of this kind was not to stand the test of time. Maidment speculated that the practice of awarding custody to fathers and care and control to mothers (which began in the 1930s) represented an attempt both to preserve marriage and to recognize the facts of child-rearing practice. A distinction was drawn between the roles of parent and spouse which is being ever more firmly delineated.

In a relatively short space of time a minor revolution has taken place in the way the courts have interacted with divorcing families. There has been a transition between three models[1] of judicial behaviour. While they indicate a process of evolution in the assumptions which underlie practice, there is debate about how much evolution they indicate in practice itself.

Policing, paternalism, and participant justice

The first model of judicial behaviour can be described as the *policing* of divorce. In this model efforts were directed towards establishing whether or not an offence had been committed in the marriage. Private detectives were sometimes employed to this end and the court setting was particularly suited to enacting a public ritual which established guilt and innocence.

There was no half-way house. Any indication of spouses coming together to rig the evidence jeopardized the divorce. It is ironic that a stance which sought to protect the institution of marriage discouraged attempts at reconciliation through the bars against condonance, connivance, and collusion. As we have seen, the criteria for establishing the end of a marriage extended to decisions concerning the future care of children (as well as to property and financial matters).

This model characterized the operation of the judicial system in the years before the Divorce Reform Act was introduced in 1969. Some of its legacy remains. Adultery, cruelty, and intolerable behaviour are still grounds for deciding whether or not a marriage has irretrievably broken down. Although practices are changing, allegations submitted in affidavits to courts frequently add insult to the injury of separation. In consequence, the positions adopted by spouses over points of difference and disagreement can become polarized and rigid at a time when many far-reaching decisions are being made. Adversarial practices can then serve to enact and exacerbate a private dispute in public. In the process, individuals may be discredited as parents as well as spouses.

There is a strong movement within legal circles to combat the damaging effects of adversarial procedures. Special procedures introduced in 1973, and extended in 1977 to all undefended divorce suits, have simplified and speeded up the process of obtaining a divorce decree. The Code of Practice published in 1983 by the Solicitors Family Law Association commits its members to 'a conciliatory rather than a litigious approach' in conducting matrimonial business. The recommendations of the Booth Committee (1985) aim to shift the emphasis of courts away from the divorce suit to the consequences of marriage breakdown for the partners and their children. The proposed initial hearings will allow divorce decrees to be made early on, without affidavits, addressing the parties in other than the contentious terms of 'petitioner' and 'respondent', and aiming to promote and give effect to agreements.

The second model of judicial behaviour can be described as the system of *paternalism*. Its influence remains strong and is exercised primarily in the process of decision making in child-related issues. In this model, adversarial procedures are

supplemented by inquisitorial procedures. The probation service, through its divorce-court welfare officers, is implicated in
maintaining this system of behaviour, a system to which it is
fundamentally loyal but increasingly ambivalent. The court
welfare officer is the instrument of the inquisitorial system,
authorized by statute to investigate the circumstances of children
by gathering information, direct observation, and liaison with
official and unofficial figures relevant to the enquiry. His or her
report will assist the judge or registrar to adjudicate on custody
and access disputes.

The third model of behaviour, at present gaining ascendancy,
is that of *participant justice*. Here, a fundamental conceptual shift
is made from regarding the divorcing family as an object for
processing to a body which forms an integral part of the judicial
system. Murch (1980) describes the shift in these terms:

> 'all the actors in the drama of divorce proceedings may be
> perceived as forming a temporary social system. By including
> the family members themselves within the boundary of the
> system, instead of seeing them as external to it, it becomes
> possible to see them as having an important contribution to
> make to the decision-making process itself.'
>
> (Murch 1980: 226)

Within this model conciliation services have a crucial role,
whether operating in or out of court. Efforts are directed towards
empowering parents to exercise responsibilities which are properly theirs, rather than intervening to undermine or usurp those
responsibilities. This requires the courts to surrender control of
part of the divorce process which has traditionally been their
province. The Booth Report justified this surrender in these
terms:

> 'Our firm view is that conciliation requires that there should
> be a full and free exchange between the parties and that this is
> unlikely to occur if there is a possibility of matters disclosed in
> conciliation being referred to in subsequent proceedings. We
> would wish to see absolute privilege attaching to conciliation.'
>
> (4.60)

There is no hard and fast distinction between the three models
when applied in practice. Many courts wish to 'police' in a

'paternalistic' way, arrangements arrived at in a 'participant' model, since a declaration of satisfaction is still required regarding the arrangements for children. A judgment in the High Court in Manchester (Ewbank 1985) indicates that courts wish to retain key elements of the paternalistic, inquisitorial model in their dealings with divorce and child welfare arrangements.

The most unsatisfactory aspect of divorce settlements endorsed by law at the present time has been the likelihood that children will lose all touch with one of their parents. The reluctance of courts to assign custody to *both* parents often means that the resident parent becomes, in effect, the only parent. The fact that mothers are granted custody, care, and control of their children in between 85 per cent (Samuels 1982) and 90 per cent (Maidment 1984) of cases, effectively ousts fathers from any claim to real parental status and responsibility. True, there are indications that more joint custody orders are being made nowadays than before, but the picture remains substantially unchanged. Successive studies have shown that within two years of separation less than half of non-custodial parents have regular access to their children, and around one-third have no contact with them at all (Maidment 1976; Eekelaar *et al.* 1977; Eekelaar 1982; Fraser 1982; Gingerbread/Families need Fathers 1982; Burgoyne and Clark 1984; James and Wilson 1984b). This is the usual one-parent post-divorce family pattern.

The paternalistic, inquisitorial model of judicial behaviour has been held responsible for this state of affairs on two apparently contradictory grounds. The first is that the judicial system has an overbearing influence on how marriages end. It is said to coerce, demean, and even punish the individuals concerned while removing from them responsibilities which should properly be theirs. It sees judicial processes as exacerbating ill-feeling, generating disputes, and generally responding in a less than helpful and out-of-phase manner to the needs of those it is intended to serve. This argument smacks of the search for a scapegoat for the undesirable consequences of divorce, and plays down the responsibilities of parents in bringing their problems to courts for resolution. In rejecting the case for reforming adversarial procedures, the Booth Committee redressed the balance of responsibility by asserting that contention arises from the relationship between the parties rather than from the adversarial nature of the hearing.

The second argument is that the courts are redundant, they

only rubber-stamp arrangements already worked out and have no real power to enforce their rulings in the face of determined opposition by either party. What have become known as the Keele (Maidment 1976) and Oxford (Eekelaar *et al.* 1977) studies indicate that 94 per cent of divorcing parents agree arrangements for the care of their children after separation, rarely are these parental agreements disturbed by the courts, and there will almost always be a preference for preserving the residential status quo in the minority of cases where it is disputed. With so few contested custody cases, and so much approved private ordering, one might be tempted to ask what all the fuss is about. In connection with access, orders are less predictable and sometimes bear little resemblance to the requests or requirements of the parents concerned.

The two apparently contradictory criticisms of traditional judicial practices come together when account is taken of the context in which private bargaining takes place. Mnookin (1979, 1984) reviewed the impact of the legal system on the great majority who settle out of court but in the shadow of the law. Legal rules and precedents create bargaining endowments; solicitors may be tempted to advise fathers against contesting custody of their children on the basis that precedent indicates mothers to be more likely to win. There are transaction costs generated by litigation. The money, time, and energy at the disposal of each party will influence their willingness to embark upon a potentially costly claim. A wish to punish may be sufficient motive to warrant a costly and self-defeating battle. Risk-takers may have a bargaining advantage over those seeking security in that the prospect of the issue going to court will hold for them few terrors. Mnookin argued that the welfare principle favours the risk-taking parent, an unfortunate consequence, since a good parent is unlikely to gamble with a child's future. Exercising the wisdom of Solomon is then a particularly apposite description of the judge's role should matters come to court. About the Children's Appointment he has this to say:

'The review requirement may, ironically, send an inappropriate set of signals to parents at the time of divorce: it may suggest to them that because of the divorce they are no longer trusted to be adequate parents, and that the State will now assume on an on-going basis special responsibility for their children. Indeed, court review might conceivably induce more selfish behaviour on the part of parents who take the attitude that it is the court's job, not their own responsibility, to be concerned with the interests of their children. In fact, the State does not and cannot assume a broad role for child-rearing responsibility after divorce.'   (Mnookin 1979: 46)

While private ordering may be attractive in terms of preserving the autonomy of the individual and making the legal processing of divorce cheaper and more efficient, inequalities in bargaining endowments, and the implication of children in settlements, provide justification for imposing some limits.

For better or worse, the probation service finds itself at the sharp end of this conflict. Probation officers undertaking divorce-court welfare work assist the judiciary in carrying out its function. Although this work has developed logically from the historical involvement of magistrates with matrimonial disputes and the role of probation officers as servants of the court, there are those who draw sinister conclusions from the fact that an agency whose primary task is the supervision of offenders also has a prominent role in divorce settlements. It is for them confirmation that divorce is being treated as social deviance. However benign the conscious intent, the enquiries of judges and welfare officers may have the effect of undermining and even humiliating parents (Davis et al. 1983; Davis 1985). Although the manifest brief of the probation service is to safeguard the welfare of children in divorce proceedings, how is it to be sure that its officers are not unwittingly being employed under the child protection banner to act as agents of social control against a divorcing population? The next chapter will consider the place of the probation service in divorce proceedings, and describe the background to the project which forms the main body of this book.

Note

1 We are grateful to colleagues in the Probation Service for drawing our attention to these models, especially Mrs Bosie Swanton and Mr Andrew Taylor.

3

SOLOMON'S SERVANTS

'To think at all objectively about one's own marriage is impossible, while a balanced view of other people's marriage is almost equally hard to achieve with so much information available, so little to be believed.'

Anthony Powell
Casanova's Chinese Restaurant

Investigating for the courts

With the development of social science knowledge and the growth of professional expertise during the postwar years, divorce courts have increasingly come to rely upon an extra-judicial view when adjudicating on child custody and access disputes. For this help they have turned, in the main, to the probation service, with whom they have had a long association in the criminal field and who, in the 1950s and 1960s, had considerable experience of counselling troubled marriages.

Within a relatively short period of time the civil work emphasis in the probation service has changed from saving marriages to saving children. Following the report of the Denning Committee (1947) on procedures in matrimonial causes, probation officers were attached to the London Divorce Court as welfare officers to advise on the social and material circumstances of families in so far as these affected the welfare of children. In 1957 the scheme was extended to the High Court in the provinces and in 1959 the Divorce Court Welfare Service was formally established. The 1967 Matrimonial Causes Act required probation committees (the employing authority in the probation service) to assign a court welfare officer to every divorce county court. This, combined with the implementation of the Divorce Reform Act, has greatly increased the reporting function of the probation service in civil proceedings at the divorce court level. Wilkinson (1981) records that whereas only 880 reports were prepared in 1960 (when 24,000 decrees were made absolute) this figure had risen to 6,200 by 1970 (58,000 decrees absolute) and 14,500 in 1977 (129,000 decrees absolute). The number of enquiries completed for the county and high courts in 1982 had risen to 17,350 (Home Office 1983), and by 1985 the Booth Committee estimated that around 19,000 divorce court enquiry reports were being prepared each year. These reports provide a means of satisfying Section 41 of the 1973 Matrimonial Causes Act, which makes the granting of an absolute decree dependent on the court being satisfied that arrangements for the children are the best that can be devised in the circumstances.

Divorce court welfare officers have become key public figures in assisting the courts to arrive at settlements in contested (and sometimes uncontested) custody and access cases. As officers of the court they are expected, when directed, to assess arrangements proposed by parents for children. They observe relationships in the family and try to elicit the wishes and feelings of the children involved. They then report to the court with a view to assisting judges to decide with whom children should live, and whether or how much access they should have to the parent who is not responsible for their day-to-day care (Levy 1983). The statutory basis for this power is to be found in the Matrimonial Causes Rules of 1977, rule 95 (1). This states that a judge or registrar 'may at any time refer to a court welfare officer for investigation and report any matters arising . . . which concern the welfare of a child'. In 'exceptional circumstances' (Section 44 of the 1973 Matrimonial Causes Act) the involvement of the court welfare officer may extend beyond investigation to a supervisory role, an involvement which could last until the child reaches the age of 16. In both these interventions the guiding principle in law is that the welfare of children should be 'the first and paramount consideration', a principle formally established in 1925.

A number of criticisms have been levelled at the investigative role of the probation service in divorce proceedings. In the last chapter we referred to the stigmatizing effects which have been said to result from involving in the divorce process a service whose principal clientele is the criminal community. According to this argument, divorce court welfare officers are implicated in the process of constructing divorce as deviant social behaviour, and they operate, intentionally or not, as agents of social control.

This view has received tacit support from another argument which contrasts the expenditure of resources on preparing welfare reports with the results they produce. Officers may spend in excess of 10 hours on each enquiry, as frequently as not delaying hearings for up to six months or more (Eekelaar 1982). The Keele (1976) and Oxford (1977) studies referred to in the last chapter (see page 47) indicated that in custody disputes the welfare officer's report had little or no effect on existing child care arrangements. In the Oxford study, a real change in the status quo occurred in only two out of 652 cases studied. In one case this was against the recommendation of the welfare officer, and in the other no report had been called for.

The effects of welfare reports on access disputes is less clear. Orders for access have, in the past, been unpredictable, sometimes bearing little resemblance to the requests or requirements of the parents concerned. The effectiveness of access orders is called into question by the pattern of steady decline in the amount of contact between children and their non-custodial parents, a decline remarked upon by so many observers of the divorce landscape. When they are in agreement, the degree of reciprocal influence operating between court decisions and recommendations contained in welfare reports makes it difficult to know whether judges and registrars follow recommendations, or welfare officers recommend in anticipation of what they guess will be the court's decision. There is some evidence for the latter direction of flow (James and Wilson 1984a).

It may be, of course, that the time and effort expended by welfare officers in custody and access disputes is far from wasted, despite court outcomes remaining substantially unaltered (at least in custody cases). Coming to terms with what is unalterable can represent a significant change, one in which welfare officers may play an important part despite the outcome failing to register in the results of court adjudications. Moreover, outcries about divorcing parents being contaminated by exposure to the influence of a crime-oriented service may be evidence of a change in social attitudes rather than a commentary on the explicit or implicit purposes to which divorce court welfare officers are being deployed. When divorce was viewed as an offence, the involvement of the probation service was likely to excite less comment than today. Public acceptance of divorce has resulted in questions about how appropriate historically evolved processes and services are to a present-day phenomenon, and these questions cannot be restricted to the operations of the probation service.

A third criticism of welfare reports challenges the expertise of the officers who prepare them, and the scientific nature of court-initiated investigative procedures as a whole. Sutton (1981) argues that social workers have neither an empirical nor formal knowledge base to lay claim to professional status, and that the current state of social science knowledge does not allow for predictions on the basis of what is likely to be in a child's best interests or any other criteria. He argues that court-based social workers should regard themselves as good administrators, checking the unintended consequences of court interventions and mediating between courts and their users by balancing the supply of and demand for resources.

While the probation service would accept that it cannot lay claim to certainties which the state of social science does not yet allow, many court welfare officers, particularly those who specialize in this work, would argue that they keep abreast of developments in their field. They would also disavow any conscious intent to stigmatize the small proportion of the divorcing population with whom they come into contact. Moreover, many would not limit their contact with divorcing families to the completion of their investigative task. Their training and professional identity as social workers make it likely that they will regard themselves not only as reporters but as helpers, counsellors, therapists, and conciliators. They value their relationship with the courts and are committed to assisting them in protecting the welfare of children, but usually they recognize the conflicts to which this may give rise. Mediating the interests of individuals, families, and the courts is not a new role; it has been the bread-and-butter of their criminal work over the years.

In an important respect, then, welfare officers serve two masters: the courts (who are principally concerned with children) and families (where the well-being of the adults is considered to be as important and relevant as that of children). While there is evidence that welfare officers are experienced as helpful by divorcing parents, especially when their interventions take place early on in proceedings (Murch 1980; Fraser 1982), there is also evidence which goes the other way. Mistrust and suspicion attaches to their statutory role. Welfare officers are aware of this, and are anxious to overcome any unnecessary constraints stemming from their position.

Conciliating for the family

An important development that has affected the probation service in the last decade has been the arrival of conciliation services in many parts of the country. Located both in and out of court, these services to divorcing families are distanced from judicial procedures. Following the Finer Committee's (1974 para 4.288) distinction between reconciliation ('reuniting the spouses') and conciliation ('assisting the parties to deal with the consequences of the established breakdown of their marriage, whether resulting in a divorce or separation, by reaching agreements or giving consents or reducing the area of conflict'), conciliation services have emerged to help with the consequences of marriage breakdown. The probation service provided some of the momentum for the conciliation movement by pioneering in-court schemes and, in some cases, assisting enterprise in the voluntary sector. In 1977, the Avon Probation Service staffed the first in-court conciliation scheme in this country, while in 1978 the Bristol Courts Family Conciliation Service pioneered out-of-court conciliation by offering an alternative to litigation for settlement-seeking at any stage in the divorce process. Out-of-court schemes spread rapidly following this initiative and by March 1984, 24 were affiliated with the National Family Conciliation Council. In-court schemes spread more slowly but they are now widely available.

The central feature of conciliation is what lawyers call *party control*. Parkinson, who has a justifiable claim to being principal midwife to the out-of-court conciliation movement in this country, defines conciliation as:

> 'a structured process in which both parties to a dispute meet voluntarily with one or more impartial third parties (conciliators) who help them to explore possibilities of reaching agreement, without having the power to impose a settlement on them or the responsibility to advise either party individually.'   (Parkinson 1986: 52)

This process may or may not involve children directly. The protected and voluntary involvement of both parents, over a short period of time, in a focused and practical attempt to reach a resolution of disputed issues without recourse to an imposed settlement are the hallmarks of conciliation.

In some respects, then, the conciliation movement stands on the opposite bank to divorce court welfare services. In ideological terms, conciliation can serve as a flag around which those who wish to defend the family against the power of the State might rally. It is 'an organizational system which mediates between the private family system and the powerful system of State control, reinforcing the former against the threatened intrusion of the latter' (Parkinson 1985a: 245). Haynes (1981, 1984) is unequivocal about the stance of conciliation (or mediation, as it is known in the United States) being pro-family and anti-interventionist. For him, being pro-family means always aiming to maintain a family structure in which children have access to both parents after their marriage has ended.

The need for clarity in defining and differentiating conciliation from related activities such as divorce counselling and therapy (Parkinson 1985b) is understandable and necessary when a new service appears on the market. It must guard against either being ignored or appropriated by others. From the practitioner's standpoint, however, there must always be questions about whether people actually do what they say they do, and if they do, what effect their stringent practice has upon their clients. These are questions for the future. Undoubtedly conciliation has had its successes in this country and abroad (Parkinson 1982). It remains to be seen whether, as a technique, conciliation really is 'mightier than the sword', as probation officers have described it (Francis et al. 1983), or 'a shot in the arm', as one journalist has commented (Hills 1983). Those familiar with bereavement reactions will be familiar with euphoria as a means of coping with painful situations, or as an exaggerated response to glimmers of light in a dark world. In so far as conciliation favours an informal, non-combative and restrained approach to settling disputes, it commands widespread support. Conciliators share an attitude of mind which encourages party control and attempts to balance negotiations. But there are differences of view about conciliation as an operational concept, and it is early days to claim a breakthrough.

A lively debate has developed around the issue of whether conciliation is compatible with other activities, such as therapy and investigation. Is it a time-limited, focused negotiation with specific objectives, or a therapeutic process which enables parties to agree spontaneously? Does it only involve rational bargaining (requiring the conciliator to collate information, clarify the issues and propose solutions within a climate which strictly regulates the emotional temperature) or has it to touch upon the affective context in which that bargaining takes place (offering catharsis, and reframing or reinterpreting the nature of the dispute)?

In defining the issues for the probation service Davis (1982) posed a dilemma for divorce-court welfare officers. He argued that investigation, therapy, and conciliation had different objectives (child protection, self-realization, conflict resolution) and were based on different principles (child welfare, personal development, party control). He echoed Murch's (1980) fear that by bracketing such different activities together conciliation would be diminished and the control parents had over the outcome of their disputes would be undermined. He pointed out that negotiations conducted within the context of a welfare enquiry could not be privileged, and would therefore have a limiting effect upon what could be said or explored between the parties involved, a view which has been endorsed by the Booth Committee (1985).

The argument was taken up by probation officers (Shepherd *et al.* 1984) who argued that conciliation was compatible with investigation if reporting was confined to a neutral summary of the encounter. In their view conciliation was more than straightforward negotiation because of the emotional context in which conflict finds expression. As practised by these officers, conciliation was a therapeutic process (utilizing systems theory and family therapy skills) in which agreement was a product rather than an objective. Fearing that hard and fast divisions might result in difficult conciliation cases being abandoned to the traditional investigative approach, they argued that conciliation was always possible given sufficient time and skill, and a favourable setting. They argued, too, for the conciliator retaining a restricted reporting role, abhorring what they termed 'pseudo-professional judgments' in favour of assessing the emotional environment and dynamics of a family which might account for the persistence of the problem. If the Ewbank judgment (1985) is any guide, such reports may not be acceptable to courts unless clearly distinguished from conciliation services and demonstrably relevant to child welfare issues. Moreover, the indications are that judges want reports which contain recommendations (Dillon

1986). An alternative approach to therapeutic reporting is described by family therapists Bentovim and Gilmour (1981) who recommend that reporters make an explicit statement about their values (which in their case could be subsumed under the 'least detrimental alternative' principle) so that these can be taken into account when adjudication is made.

Pugsley and Wilkinson (1984), writing from their experience as court welfare officers, do not share the confidence of Shepherd and his colleagues about the universal potential of conciliation for resolving disputes. Even were this to be so, they argue, parental competence cannot always be assumed, and parents have a right to a court hearing and adjudication if they wish to settle matters in that way. They comment that assessing the dynamics of a family is as prone to value judgment as is orthodox reporting, and they are unapologetic about amalgamating the roles of conciliator and reporter, believing that in conciliation there is always enquiry, and in enquiry there is always an attempt to conciliate. They argue that the same person is capable of taking on both roles.

From his research experience Davis (1985) responded sharply to both probation lines of argument, accusing the service of attempting to appropriate conciliation. His interpretation of the reluctance to separate conciliation from other activities was that the commitment of probation officers to therapeutic or benign authority images had obscured from them the powerful effects they could have upon their clients, radically affecting the balance of power and undermining the principle of party control which is central to conciliation. He asserted that by merging therapeutic and child-saving principles with conciliation, the essence of conciliation was being sacrificed on the altar of professional self-interest.

It may be true that conciliation has evoked rivalry and competition among practitioners who are understandably anxious not to be excluded from what is perceived as a new and exciting field of work. It may also be true that professionals underrate their own power and the significance of what they do for their clients. But it is also likely to be true that there are real lessons to be learned from experience, not the least of which is that clients have a say in moulding the behaviour of practitioners, irrespective of how roles are formally defined.

Emphasizing the importance of context and attempting to hold together possible schisms, Roberts (1983) pointed out that *any* form of third party intervention transforms bilateral negotiations, and that those who mediate, and those who umpire, occupy positions along the same continuum between agreement and coercion. Bilateral negotiations should not be assumed to be free of coercion because no third party is involved. Even when there is a third party, different conciliators will hold different values and positions along the continuum which influence the kind of negotiations that take place.

He argued that the key variables to be considered in assessing the practice of conciliation are the *objectives* of the conciliator (whether primarily to offer supportive help or to assist joint decision making) and his or her *power* (the degree to which the relationship between disputants is regulated and control exercised over the outcome arrived at). Different strategies may be appropriate to different stages in the divorce process, but they may not be compatible when employed concurrently. A conciliatory approach to managing divorce proceedings can guide the behaviour of the parties themselves, of court conciliators, of court welfare officers preparing reports, and of judges who are faced with making decisions, but none will be free of the influence of context which vitally affects behaviour. It is necessary, therefore, to distinguish between the behaviour of different people in the divorce system on the basis of their primary objectives and the contexts in which they work.

The response of the probation service

The primary civil task of the probation service is to prepare reports for the courts. It occupies a powerful position in the divorce system. In responding to the challenges of the past ten years its members have had to ask themselves whether or not they should continue to serve the civil courts and, if so, how they should respond to the current conciliation debate.

In contrast to the argument that an offender-oriented service can only stigmatize those who come into contact with it is an alternative view which holds that the loss of civil work, and the contact with non-offenders it represents, would result in the probation service becoming an agency of correctional reform alone, which by its very nature would then further alienate from the mainstream of society those offenders with whom it continued to have dealings. This argument has been used to resist officers specializing in civil work, but it is one which has lost ground in recent years. There is no doubt that the probation service exists principally and increasingly for offenders, and that it will continue to do so. In 1984, the Home Office Statement of National Objectives and Priorities for the probation service placed civil work at the bottom of its list of priorities. While most probation areas have concurred in the low priority given to civil work there seems little immediate danger that this function will be surrendered to another agency. As yet, no appropriate alternative agency exists, and the service itself is unwilling to detach this part of its heritage from its activities.

In 1985, the civil work committee of the Association of Chief Officers of Probation anticipated that the probation service would continue to play a leading part in civil work in the next decade (Himmel 1985). This was to be performed both in the context of its statutory duties and also through promoting the development of an integrated system of in-court and out-of-court conciliation schemes. In noting the diversity of models which existed in the service at that time, three models were selected to illustrate the structures through which statutory duties were then being carried out: the specialist unit (covering either divorce court or all civil work), the semi-specialist unit (where officers had a specialist interest in civil work but were not necessarily sharing the same manager or offices), and, finally, specialist officers who acted as liaison officers to the divorce courts in accordance with probation rules. In addition, officers and probation areas involved themselves variously in out-of-court conciliation schemes, divorce experience courses, and other voluntary initiatives.

The probation service in which our project took place (HPS) selected the first of these models, and also supported an out-of-court conciliation scheme as its response to changes taking place nationally in the management of divorce. In 1980 an earlier decision to establish a specialist divorce court welfare team to carry out all the welfare enquiries in the area with its own offices, secretarial support, and full-time senior was fully implemented. The service also decided to provide professional, administrative, and practical support to a then embryonic local conciliation service. This action brought together people from the fields of social work teaching, marriage guidance, and the law, as well as from the probation service itself. Behind these initiatives lay a conviction that civil work required a separate and specialist place in the probation service.

Until the specialist team of divorce court welfare officers became operational, the preparation of welfare reports was organized and managed alongside criminal work, as it still is in many parts of the country today. In these circumstances, a probation officer, often of senior status, acts in a liaison capacity with the county or High Court for the area. Where necessary he or she represents the probation service in court and channels requests for welfare reports to probation officers inside and outside the probation area. Under this system, officers may or may not have had specialized experience of preparing welfare reports for the courts. They are less likely to have this experience today than in the past, when greater priority was accorded to matrimonial work. There is reason to believe that probation officers who work mainly with offenders are uneasy about the nature and demands of divorce work. Main grade officers have expressed concern about their lack of expertise in this area, and have thought that the requirements of civil work sit uncomfortably alongside work with clients referred from the criminal courts (Eekelaar 1982). More recently, a study covering slightly more than 10 per cent of all probation officers in England and Wales reported that 91 per cent of the respondents regarded the preparation of welfare enquiries as being more difficult than other report-writing duties, thus identifying a need for more training in this area of practice (James and Wilson 1983).

The limitations on the capabilities of non-specialist probation officers for divorce court welfare work were fully understood by the management of the HPS when the decision to establish a specialist team was taken. It was strongly believed that the shortcomings in training and morale evident under the old system could be made good by establishing a separate group of officers, working from a shared base, and led by a full-time senior. It was predicted that a more efficient and acceptable service would follow from this change, and that it would go a long way towards removing from divorcing couples the stigma of association with a service primarily geared to the needs of offenders. High priority was to be given to the recruitment and training of staff who, by inclination and past experience, would be interested and skilled in work with marital and family problems. To support this resolve it was decided that social work applicants who had no previous probation experience should be eligible for staff appointments. As recorded in an internal memorandum subsequently, this policy decision

'was the first tacit recognition of something essentially
different about the nature of divorce work, with the accom-
panying recognition that the different social work skills
required may be more readily acquired in the social work
context. It was also a recognition of the difficulty probation
officers have in the move sideways (from criminal into civil
work).'

A further important decision gave tenure to specialist divorce
court welfare posts, and so ended the convention of moving staff
in and out of civil work on a time-limited basis. The decision was
taken to preserve specialist skills following the investment that
was to be made in training and supervision. Both decisions had
the effect of weakening links between criminal and civil work in
the service. The boundary between these two spheres of activity
continued to exercise welfare officers during the period of the
research.

While the establishment of a specialist divorce court welfare
team anticipated the growing separation of civil and criminal
work in the probation service, the early support for setting up a
local out-of-court conciliation service reflected the keen interest
taken by the statutory organization in the potential of a new
voluntary body operating close to its traditional territory. There
were several strands to this interest. In the first place there was a
wish to encourage an exciting new area of conciliation practice
which, when introduced early on in disputes, had already
demonstrated its worth. As the elder sibling, there was a
willingness and enthusiasm to help a nascent service by training
volunteers to work as conciliators and giving administrative and
financial support to the enterprise. There was also an element of
self interest: the out-of-court conciliation movement as a whole
had an energy and momentum of its own that posed a challenge
to the established service. There were questions about whether
the lessons learned in the field of voluntary conciliation could be
applied in the divorce court welfare setting, or whether they
required a quite separate agency and structure. Should this turn
out to be so, there were fears that the voluntary movement,
having discovered a satisfying and satisfactory approach to
helping people overcome some of the difficulties arising from
family breakdown, might run off with the jam, leaving only the
less rewarding bread and butter work – the traditional investigative role – for the divorce court welfare officer.

With these new beginnings, the prospect of initiating research which might help to clarify the respective roles each service had to play excited much interest. A series of exploratory meetings between IMS and HPS staff took place in 1981 to consider the possibilities. Funding difficulties resulted in delays before the new conciliation service became operational, and at one stage there were doubts whether it would be viable at all. As a result, the focus of research interest shifted from studying the operations of the proposed conciliation service to the possibilities of a comparative study of the statutory and voluntary bodies. Advised against this, on the grounds of the scale of the operation and the rivalry which might develop, agreement was reached between the IMS and the HPS (and before the conciliation service became operational) to research the newly-formed specialist Divorce Unit.

The Divorce Unit

When the research began, in 1982, the Divorce Unit was responsible for all welfare enquiries in its Commission Area. The area had no natural geographical centre. The officers of the Divorce Unit were based at the westerly and more affluent end of the area, where 47 per cent of the population fell into social classes I and II at the 1981 census (OPCS 1983). The offices housing the staff were part of a modern magistrates' court building, situated close to the main shopping centre and within easy reach of bus, rail, and underground connections. Despite their central location, people who did not live locally or who were dependent on public transport, could find access difficult.

The approach to the Divorce Unit passed the magistrates' court building and ended at an entrance at the rear marked 'Probation Office'. Despite the absence of intent, visitors could be left in little doubt as they passed through the front door (and later shared the waiting area with clients of the probation team) that the Divorce Unit was part of the probation service.

In 1982 there were five welfare officers working in the Divorce Unit; all were women and most were well grounded in probation practice. Some had experience of social work outside the probation service and no member of staff had less than six years' post-qualifying experience. When the research began, the average length of professional social work experience of the staff was twelve years. The team covered a broad spectrum of therapeutic approach, utilizing psychodynamic insights, the concepts of systems theory, and the techniques of family therapy. While there were differences within the team in terms of experience and therapeutic stance, they shared a common desire to help parents referred by the courts to reach agreements over the care of their children, as well as to safeguard the interests of those children. In this, they were united by an aspiration to exceed their statutory brief.

The clients of the Divorce Unit

In order to look systematically at the clients seen at the Divorce Unit, a questionnaire was completed in respect of all cases handled by the service in the 12-month period from May 1983 to April 1984 (128 cases) and in a further 12 enquiries falling outside that period. The information was collected at the time of first contact between welfare officers and parents. In thinking about the design of the questionnaire, we were aware that previous research had suggested ways in which the clients of divorce court welfare officers might differ from other divorcing couples with children. We therefore asked questions which allowed us to compare our sample of cases with other samples. We also wanted to know how and why referrals were made to the Divorce Unit, and the structure and socioeconomic status of the families concerned, so that we might locate our sample in a wider context.

In placing our results alongside other research findings, three qualifications must be made. First, patterns of family life have changed significantly over the period in which the different samples have been obtained. A 10-year gap separates parents seen at the Divorce Unit from those seen by Murch (1980) in Bristol. During this period marriage rates have fallen for all age groups under 30, couples have opted to marry later and have delayed parenthood, second marriage rates have increased and, with them, the likelihood of divorce in remarriages (Mansfield 1985). Second, it is unwise to generalize from the experience of a few courts to judicial practice as a whole. In the Divorce Unit sample, over half of all referrals came from only two courts – 40 per cent from a local county court and 15 per cent from the High Court. Courts vary widely in the criteria used to decide when and with what frequency welfare reports should be called for (Eekelaar *et al.* 1977). As it happened, the local county court had a rate of referral for welfare reports similar to the national pattern. During the one-year survey period, the court asked for 102 reports, which was 9 per cent of all decrees nisi awarded in the court in 1983 (Lord Chancellor's Department 1984). In 1982, when probation officers in England and Wales prepared 17,350 reports for county courts and the High Court and there were 147,000 decrees absolute (Home Office 1983), the comparable rate was 11.8 per cent. Third, the accuracy of the questionnaire as a research instrument was not assessed during the run-in period. Earlier research has demonstrated that questionnaires completed by welfare officers are accurate in describing the circumstances of children, but less so when describing the circumstances of adults (Eekelaar 1982). These findings raise an interesting question about the accuracy of welfare investigations overall.

For the Divorce Unit to carry out an enquiry, a judge or registrar must have ordered a report and at least one of the children had to live in the probation area. In the first four years of operations of the Divorce Unit, an average of 125 couples were referred annually for reports. For the purpose of our project 140 questionnaires were completed in all. These comprise the *Divorce Unit sample*, which is made up of 128 cases referred in the period May 1983 to April 1984 and 12 cases which were part of the *core sample* of 30 enquiries. These additional cases were referred to the Unit in the 6 month period before the project started (a run-in period) and in the 12 months following the main survey.

A general overview of cases seen at the Divorce Unit is presented in Appendix I where the *one-year sample* (the 140 cases less the *core sample*) and the *core sample* itself are described. An account of work undertaken with the smaller group of 30 cases comprising the *core sample*, is described in detail in the main part of this book. These were the enquiries in which IMS staff participated directly. Cases were allocated to this group on an ad hoc basis. Usually we took on the next enquiry in line as part of the unit's general allocation procedure, but geographical convenience and the wish of both sets of staff to rotate working partnerships also affected whether or not an enquiry would enter the core sample. Statistical tables and sources for both the one-year and core samples can be found in Appendix I, along with a description of the two samples in terms of marital and divorce histories, family features, current disputes, and socioeconomic circumstances.

Four features stand out from the figures relating to the one-year and core sample cases. In the first place 'unreasonable behaviour' was cited as the ground for divorce very much more frequently in the one year (55 per cent) and core samples (74 per cent) of cases than for divorces nationally in 1982 (36 per cent). *Table 4*, Appendix I, gives the grounds for divorce for both samples. The Booth report (1985) observed that the bitterness and unhappiness of divorcing couples was frequently exacerbated and prolonged by the fault element in divorce, and that this was particularly true when the fact relied upon was behaviour. In contrast with the 24 per cent of divorces nationally in 1982 which rested on consent, using the two-year separation clause, only 4 per cent of the one-year sample and 7 per cent of the core sample chose to end marriage by that route. In summary, there were firm statistical indications that we saw a contentious divorcing population.

Second, the one-year and core samples (especially the latter) were socially disadvantaged groups of divorces relative to the probation area as a whole. In particular, the unemployment rate among men was very high (23 per cent for the one-year sample and 30 per cent in the core sample, as compared with 7 per cent in the area at that time). With little social and material cushioning against the impact of divorce one might expect these groups to protest and contest in order not to despair.

A propensity to fight is supported by a third observation: 31 per cent of the core sample and 34 per cent of the one-year sample of cases initiated divorce proceedings and/or child applications within six months of finally separating (see *Table 2*, Appendix I), as compared with 22 per cent in Murch's (1980) welfare sample and 7 per cent of his sample of couples who were not referred for reports. This would indicate that the parents we saw had instituted legal action more precipitately than other divorcing populations. Taken together, hasty litigation, social disadvantage, and a tendency to resort to the behaviour clause in divorce petitions suggest what we were later to endorse from first-hand experience, that our samples, and especially the core sample, contained a high proportion of embittered and embattled parents.

Finally, the decisions to marry and start a family coincided in around two-thirds of both the one year and core sample cases (*Table 9*, Appendix I). If marital and parental roles merge at the outset of marriage it is arguable that they will be difficult to disentangle when marriage comes to an end. We shall return to each of these points in later discussion.

The detail of the enquiry experience in the core sample of cases forms the substance of the chapters that follow. From our welfare role we hoped to discover how much scope there was for effecting settlements with families who had turned to the courts for a just decision. In our research role, we hoped to elicit from the families what it was like to be the subject of a divorce court enquiry. From both lines of enquiry, we hoped to make a contribution towards reviewing the role of the divorce court welfare officer in divorce proceedings. As a starting point, we wanted to know how the disputes between parents were understood by the welfare officers and by the families themselves.

4
THE NATURE OF THE DISPUTES

'All happy families are alike but an unhappy family is unhappy after its own fashion.'

Leo Tolstoy
Anna Karenina

Reilly: 'All cases are unique, and very similar to others.'

T S Eliot
The Cocktail Party

Managing the muddle

Tolstoy's oft-quoted observation is never more true than in periods of individual transition and social change. In such times, generalizations about the unhappy experience of divorce are especially likely to be flawed. Yet the discipline of teasing out common threads from the tangle of individual experiences to pursue Reilly's similarities, offers the best hope for advancing our understanding of what happens, individually and collectively, when marriage breaks down. The unhappy family experience of divorce seems sometimes only to be unified by contradictions and conflict. Many who resort to divorce courts to resolve their differences can be relied upon to perceive what is at issue between them in discrepant ways. The resolute prosecution of self interest seems set to ensure costly defeat or, at best, a pyrrhic victory. The pursuit of stability through an unbending defence of the past can accelerate change in a destabilizing manner. The olive branch offered in good faith will, as likely as not, be treated with extreme suspicion.

In this and the four chapters that follow we have attempted to assemble our endeavours, and the diverse responses with which they were met, when, with our divorce court welfare officer colleagues, we undertook 30 child welfare enquiries for the divorce courts. The material has been assembled under four headings. The first, the subject of this chapter, contains an examination of the disputes which brought these families to court. The remaining four look at the expectations, experiences, and levels of satisfaction of parents and welfare officers (ourselves included) which resulted from the 30 court-initiated enquiry encounters. The four areas overlap and interrelate at every turn. Satisfaction with the enquiry process was partly determined by the kind of expectations originally entertained by parents and practitioners. Impossible expectations constituted the nub of some disputes. The experience of an enquiry aggravated for some and ameliorated for others the problems with which courts had been asked to help. No one area could be defined in isolation from the other three. While they implied linear progress along a chronological sequence, there was every possibility of backward and forward movement. A dissatisfied parent – or welfare officer – could throw the whole procedure into reverse. The structure we have chosen in which to present our material is intended to convey something of the backwards and forwards movement which we came to associate with enquiry work.

The material itself is drawn from four main sources. Two are concerned with the views of parents, and two with those of the welfare officers. The voice of the parents (and some children) is heard through edited transcripts of tape-recorded first interviews (when parents – and occasionally families – met their welfare officers for the first time) and through follow-up interviews (conducted independently of the enquiry and carried out approximately eight months after completion of the report). The views of welfare officers are drawn from case profiles completed at the end of each enquiry which contained information of both a factual and inferential kind. They are also drawn from records of team meeting discussions kept during the fieldwork life of the project.

Each source presents a partial view of the enquiry experience. The case profiles and team meeting discussions posed fewest problems in eliciting the views of welfare officers because they were comprehensive and geared to that purpose. Moreover, when we were the welfare officers concerned, they registered our own views. In contrast, the first interview transcripts were available in only 17 of the 30 cases; some parents declined to be recorded, and the run-in cases preceded our decision to tape first interviews.

The material that was obtained in this way was secured during the course of a welfare enquiry and at a time when much was at stake. What parents said at this time will have been affected by these constraints. The follow-up interviews were carried out independently of the court enquiry, but often close in time to the hearing and adjudication (for reasons which are elaborated upon in Chapter 7). Feelings were usually still running high at this time. For many, the interview provided a means of registering protest or (less frequently) expressing gratitude and relief. Both parents responded to the follow-up invitations in 16 cases; a further 8 mothers and 3 fathers also agreed to take part, making a total response rate of 90 per cent for one or both parents.

In ordering the considerable quantity of material generated by the research we quickly became aware of how misleading it would be to present the experiences of clients and welfare officers in isolation from each other or, indeed, other key figures and events in their lives. To take the simplest example, a court decision favouring the application of one parent over another as a result of recommendations contained in a welfare report will affect the way in which an enquiry is remembered. This is likely to be especially true if parents were seen shortly after the court hearing and the decision was not in their favour. Divorcing parents, in common with the rest of humanity, are actively engaged in rewriting their own and other people's histories, and never more so than when circumstances are against them. In this, they are little different from the welfare officers they see, except that the latter are paid to do so on the basis that they have the children's interests to protect. The hope is that their relative objectivity will produce a less distorted account than that of the parents. Because of differences in perceptions, we have attempted to preserve a sense of context and coherence by presenting the experiences of clients and welfare officers in parallel as we and they moved through the enquiry process.

Past marriages and present conflicts

In the core sample of 30 cases, welfare reports were ordered in 17 custody applications (9 initiated by mothers and 8 by fathers), 8 access applications (7 of which were initiated by fathers), and 1 wardship application (initiated by an aunt). The remaining four enquiries resulted from a judge's need to be satisfied about arrangements proposed for children, even when there was no obvious disagreement between parents. Although it is tempting to see these enquiries as having been unsolicited by one or other parent (in contrast with parents who invited outside intervention by bringing their disputes to court) fathers had expressed unease in all but one of these cases when invited to do so in open court. In only one case (that of Mr and Mrs Robin, to be described later) was neither dissent nor dissatisfaction voiced in public by one or other parent.

Of 28 known divorce petitions in the core sample, 23 of the petitioners (81 per cent) were women, a figure which was higher than both the national average and the one-year sample of Divorce Unit cases. In contrast, the majority of applicants for custody and access rulings were men (58 per cent). Moreover, there were twice as many custody applications as there were applications for access alone, and despite their lack of success, men still formed 44 per cent of custody applicants. These figures invite speculation that applications initiated by men over child-care issues provided a means of protesting about, and even contesting, petitions for divorce initiated by women. This speculation is of interest in a context where only 1 per cent of divorce petitions are contested nationally.

The figures do not, of course, provide evidence to support speculation of this kind. It is misleading to imply that petitioners in relation to divorce proceedings, or applicants in relation to children, are the real initiators of action or instigators of change. To mobilize the machinery of law, disputes have to be processed and expressed in prescribed terms. Litigants must occupy one or other of the formal roles to which the courts have become accustomed over the years. These formal roles are poor guides to who is responsible for what in decisions affecting children and marriage. Of the two, applicants for custody and access may more accurately be described as initiators, although many applications will be reactive to other events. The concept of irretrievable breakdown as the only ground for divorce supports, at least in theory, a view of marital breakdown as something for which both partners carry responsibility. Accepting that it takes two to bring a marriage to its knees, and that one partner may be 'delegated' (consciously or not) to initiate the break, we were interested to find that the partners' own reconstructions of who was responsible for ending the marriage indicated that women initiated the divorce in 25 of the 28 cases (89 per cent), a higher proportion than that suggested by the number of petitions.

In the great majority of the core sample of cases it was our view that unresolved attachments to the past marriage formed a very significant part of the context in which child custody and access disputes took place. We estimated that for 25 of our sample (83 per cent) one or both parents had been unable to accept the ending of their marriage. Although some partners were explicit about their wish for a reconciliation, the shock of rejection and displacement more commonly resulted in vociferous and sometimes violent protest. A war of attrition could follow. Separation prompted the cut-off reactions of denial, the rapid substitution of another partner for the rejecting spouse and even seizing the initiative to divorce, so that the one who felt spurned was seen to leave rather than to be left.

We identified three groups of divorce which fitted the experience of these disputes: *nominal divorces, shot-gun divorces,* and *long-lease divorces.* These groups occupy different positions along a continuum, indicating degrees of persisting engagement with a former marriage. In that sense they represent the stage reached by parents in a process of divorce. However, the groups should not be taken to imply that parents will necessarily move from one stage to the next, nor that the partners of a former marriage are at the same stage in the process. Rather, they are a means of recognizing clusters of attributes characteristic of certain kinds of divorce. We believe there are broad implications for the kinds of service response best suited for each of these groups, which will be discussed in Chapters 6 and 9. We have selected 3 cases to illustrate the three groups, and added a fourth case to represent the five enquiries where we considered the attachment to a former marriage to have been of little relevance to the request for a welfare report. The 4 case illustrations are called the Sheens, the Kings, the Hood/Hams, and the Robins. They will act as couriers on this exploration of the experience of the enquiry process, providing a thread of continuity through its various stages. A full account of these 4 enquiries, and the issues they raise, is contained in Chapter 6.

Nominal divorces

The parents

The striking feature of the two couples in this group was their decision to continue living together despite having secured a decree nisi in the divorce courts. The parents remained ambivalently attached to each other, unable either to acknowledge their relationship as durable or to implement a decision to part. In both cases the man expressed the wish for the relationship to continue while the woman felt trapped, confused, and resentful that others had not enforced the break that she felt unable to make for herself. None of the adults came across as being in charge of their own destiny or that of their children. Seen together, the parents would cloud issues and obfuscate, as if to defer the date when clarity would make a final decision unavoidable. Seen separately, they would express frustration with their partner (and with courts and divorce court welfare officers) for failing to take the action required to break the deadlock. They resembled the *enmeshed* couples in Kressel's study (1980), although in one of the two cases high levels of direct conflict tended to be avoided.

The children

The children in these families expressed a wish for their parents to be reconciled, but were placed by them under some pressure to resolve the indecision by choosing with whom they would like to live. In both cases these teenagers appeared to function in a more adult way than their parents, behaving diplomatically and trying to resist the role of arbiter which they were under pressure to assume. There were also indications that they withdrew, sometimes physically removing themselves from home as much as possible, in order to escape the tensions generated by domestic uncertainty and indecision.

In both cases the stage of development reached by the children appeared to us to be relevant to the conflicts expressed by their parents. The struggle to achieve autonomy had an adolescent aspect. The search for sexual, physical, and emotional independence was pursued as if in defiance of a controlling or neglectful parent. The divorce petition can be understood as the tangible expression of a personal quest for autonomy. However, the separateness that divorce bestowed turned out to be an inadequate solution for the problems within the family. The interaction between the parents maintained their involvement whilst simultaneously keeping each other at bay. In many respects it would have been appropriate for these couples to have approached a counselling or therapeutic agency for help with their marriages. One partner had mooted the idea in both cases, but between them they were too ambivalent about the prospects to see it through. Of the 25 cases in which we considered an incomplete emotional divorce to have affected applications to the courts over children, those in the *nominal* group were least advanced in terms of having accepted that the marriage was over.

The Sheen family

The Sheens married young. Mrs Sheen was 18 and pregnant with her eldest child at the time; her husband was 21. After fourteen years Mrs Sheen left her husband and two teenage daughters to live with another man. Citing the unreasonable behaviour of her husband, she petitioned for divorce and was granted a decree nisi within three months of leaving home. Following eight months of living apart (in which time her physical and emotional health deteriorated, leaving her unemployed, penniless, and dependent on hostel accommodation) she applied to the court for custody of her daughters. A welfare report was ordered. Within two weeks of the application she returned to live with her daughters and their father in the matrimonial home.

The comments which follow were made in the context of a first meeting between Mr and Mrs Sheen and one of their two divorce court welfare officers (a man who was also an IMS researcher). The central preoccupation at that meeting was with the parents and not their children.

The problem (Mrs Sheen)

'To be honest, my feelings are very mixed . . . I don't think anyone really knows what's happening emotionally. I wouldn't say we are husband and wife . . . in most people's eyes it's probably a peculiar situation [she goes on to say that they share the same bedroom but not the same bed; she cooks and cleans, and he decorates]. But we still do things together and go to places together with the kids.

I was the one who started it all. I seem to be the one with the emotional problem, really . . . I felt as if I'd no personality or individuality of my own . . . I tried to explain to him that . . . when you have children you can vegetate unless you still retain your own personality. Unless you have outside interests you can become a very boring person if all you can talk about is babies and nappies. Every woman feels that – at least at the beginning. I just think it somehow enveloped me. It's only as I got older that I thought "Oh God, there must be more to life than this". I love children, but at the same time I can still feel rather hemmed in. This is what I tried to tell him. He used to play football every Sunday, and play darts, and go down the pub. He used to have nights out . . . I think we drifted. We just went our separate ways. To be honest, I can't stand football or darts or pubs.

My only outlet . . . was traipsing round the country with the two kids. I did that a long time on my own . . . I am very much into what they do, and wish it was me . . . I think, sometimes, I'm reliving what I wanted to do through them [she explains that her parents were very much against her doing what her daughters had achieved]. [The welfare officer asks if one of their problems was that they were undecided about whether to keep the marriage going or not.] I don't know how he feels on that point, but I don't think I could make a decision right now. But I think that things have gone this far, and deep down if I had wanted to retract or come back I probably would have done so a long time ago [she adds that she believes the girls are for their father and expresses some bitterness that he should have turned them against her; he should have explained that their mother wasn't very well and was trying to find out who she was].'

The problem (Mr Sheen)

'[In response to a question about the future of the marriage] This is the whole crux of the matter . . . No, I couldn't see what was wrong. We've got two fine daughters. We both work. We've money in the bank, a nice house, holidays every year – I thought "What the hell's wrong with this woman!" Like you say, I didn't understand – then. [The welfare officer asks whether he'd thought it was all her problem.] No. I couldn't see what the problem was. Life is as complicated as you make it. If you can go about doing your business without it being complicated that's the easiest way. That's the way I normally like to run my life.

I used to think "She's coping, that's nice". I didn't want fussing over every five or ten minutes of the day. Yet every woman needs some kind of love and attention at times, and perhaps that's why I haven't been the right person for her. It became automatic that she didn't want to come [to the pub] although it would have been much better to have her with me . . . she's very independent at the moment. She's very detached . . . it's almost laughable we're so detached now.

[In response to the possibility of other men coming into Mrs Sheen's life] Why should I, as the significant person in their life, tolerate them being in their mother's and another person's presence? The girls shouldn't have anything to do with anyone who isn't going to be significant in their life.

[At the follow-up interview more than a year later Mr Sheen summarized the issue] The divorce proceedings were nothing to do with me. My wife instigated it all, but she was unsure of what she was doing. I was sure of what I wanted – I did not want a split.'

The problem (the welfare view)   There was an overwhelming sense of stalemate in the Sheen's predicament. Ambiguous messages served to confuse the welfare officers and frustrated their attempts to clarify the central issue. With hindsight, they wondered whether the ambiguity served to avoid the conflict and feelings of guilt which might follow from one or other partner laying claim to what they wanted. They had the distinct feeling that words had failed adequately to communicate within the marriage, and so behaviour was being relied upon to succeed in their place. Separation and divorce could not, therefore, be taken at face value. They might be the metaphorical sledgehammer applied to crack the nutty problem of 'getting through' in the marriage. As the husband in the other *nominal* divorce case put it: 'Initially, I just wanted to give her a short, sharp shock; to say "If you're treating me like this, I'm treating you like this, and see how you like it." '

For the Sheens, as with the other couple, the aftermath of a temporary separation left them angry, and the anger found expression through intransigence. Mr Sheen was resentful about being caught up in a chain of events which he could convince himself that he neither initiated nor wanted. Mrs Sheen may have known more about what she wanted than she was prepared to say, but her dissatisfied presence ensured that their problem would not go away. Pressure was therefore applied (not necessarily with conscious intent) first on the teenagers, and then on the welfare officers, to assume the decision-making responsibility that the parents found so hard to accept at that time. It was the inappropriate burden of responsibility placed on the two girls which constituted the problem as far as the welfare officers were concerned.

Shot-gun divorces

The parents

The 21 cases in this group accounted for 70 per cent of the core sample. They included 17 men and 4 women who viewed the decision to divorce as one which had been taken unilaterally by their partners and against their wishes. As far as was consciously acknowledged, these were one-sided divorces. The sense of one partner having been coerced by the other into a situation he or she had no apparent wish to be a part of, led us to describe these cases as *shot-gun divorces*.

The shocked reaction of those who had been left resulted in behaviour which was significantly different for men and women. Men tended to react with anger, abuse, and sometimes physical violence, to what they regarded as a gross offence:

'I think the person who takes your wife away from you should be made to maintain the children. That would stop divorce. If a guy takes your – he's as good as a murderer. If a woman takes a man away she should be made to pay for the crime. I think adultery is a crime – full stop. It's a terrible crime. Nobody knows how my children will turn out in ten years' time. I think somebody should pay for it . . . I don't see why I – as the innocent party – should be made to pay . . . to walk out on children is terrible. They are criminals as far as I'm concerned.'

They were also more likely than women to seek out, engage, and even pursue their partners, or others who threatened their position:

'I'm a fairly tenacious sort of man. I've found out the name of my wife's boyfriend and I've had him CRO'd [checked his criminal record] because someone told me he wasn't very nice. So I had him CRO'd and he's been involved in drugs, burglary, petty theft, car theft – it's the drugs bit which worries me – very, very much. [He adds later] Imagine my humiliation seeing him changing the locks on *my* home to keep *me* out!'

Women who were left tended to want to make a clean break, and would try to eliminate existing channels of communication between themselves and their former spouses, sometimes using as a pretext the upset caused to a child:

'One day he brought the children home with the eldest screaming in the car. I asked him "What the hell's wrong with her?" – and he drove away. It took me four hours – the best part of the evening – to calm her down and find out what was wrong. [After a break in access] he wrote via his solicitor saying he wanted to resume access. I told my solicitor to tell him to go to hell. Children – they're not just things you pick up and drop. [Now] I don't need him for property, nor for money (I live on supplementary benefit), I don't need him to talk to. I don't need him for anything. I totally refuse to meet him and will have nothing to do with him. I don't like him, and I don't see why, because he's the father of my children, I should have to subject myself to being in his presence. Had he played fairly from the beginning, things would have been civilized – but he was totally uncivilized.'

Cut-off reactions of this kind were particularly noticeable where, as in most of these cases, women had initiated the separation. The rupture was often experienced as violent by both parties. In 5 instances women left home in order to effect a separation. In a further 8 cases they applied for ouster and/or non-molestation orders in order physically to remove their partners and, through the courts, to protect themselves from the repercussions they anticipated for having ended their marriages. The changing of door locks, listing telephone numbers ex-directory, and moving to undisclosed addresses were frequent occurrences, indicating a high level of anxiety about being pursued and intruded upon by former spouses. The fear of persecution combined with low levels of trust were capable of creating a monstrous environment in which the process of reality-testing through direct communication could become well-nigh impossible. It was as if there was no belief that former partners could survive direct contact with each other. 'As far as I'm concerned, you don't exist in my life', said one woman to her former husband. Another described her husband as 'a monster, a bloodsucker, a gigantic spider', and lived with a terrifying conviction that he was going to kill her. A third expressed her fears in terms of helplessness: 'It's too dangerous for me [to talk to him]. Any feelings I express he uses against me later [these included positive feelings] . . . he can become very violent very quickly. The only power I have is to keep ourselves so he can't invade our privacy and come into our house.'

In terms of the strong wish to avoid former partners, and the determination to reduce or eliminate all contact with them, these women were similar to the autistic families described by Kressel *et al.* (1980). However, 'autistic' behaviour (more properly described as cut-off behaviour in our view) was usually one-sided, and in that respect Kressel's category does not apply. What we witnessed was a self-reinforcing pattern in which tendencies to fight or take flight were accentuated by the behaviour of former spouses towards each other. Usually it was the rejected male who would be inclined to fight, whereas the rejecting female would (sometimes very aggressively) take flight. Positions could quickly become polarized, leaving little middle ground on which separated parents might meet to discuss the implications for themselves and their children of what had happened in the marriage.

Fundamental to this alienating pattern of interaction was a difference of view about the future of the marriage, and a conviction that action was the only possible way forward. On neither side had it been possible to arrive at a considered decision to part because there was no agreement about ending the marriage and no confidence that talking about this disagreement would produce anything other than a deteriorating state of affairs. The consequence was that all members of the family were precipitated into a situation which was unfamiliar and threatening to them, and with little or no forewarning. For some, separating succeeded where words had failed, but too late to make a difference:

'He never believed I would leave. It shook him. He then wanted the marriage, and by that time it really was too late. I felt free of him, relieved, stronger. He was sure I would return. He flew at me at court. I think what I did was right. Even my vicar says "You should have done it a long time ago." '

Others, too, read into their partners' reactions confirmation of the rightness of their decisions:

> 'He's still attached to us – still wants us and the marriage – though it's all over and done with for me. You could talk 'til you were blue in the face – he'll contest everything: the divorce, the custody, the lot. He's always done that. He's done it in both his marriages. The judge was mad with him. It makes no difference. No one can.'

Part of the fear of talking to the partner who had been left behind was that intentions would be misconstrued. Friendliness might be read as a willingness to reconsider:

> 'Quite honestly, if you spoke to him now he'd still have hope of coming back. Everybody's said the same. He still really believes there's going to be hope, although I tell him – believe you me, I don't give him any false hopes whatsoever – I tell him it's absolutely finished. The day I went to court and got my divorce, that was the end of it.'

We came to identify a pattern of marital history with shot-gun divorces which one of our welfare officer colleagues termed the *turned worm* syndrome. Fifteen of the 21 cases were similar in this respect. Typically, the wife had felt disadvantaged in comparison with her husband and neglected by him. In consequence, she withdrew from the marriage, increasing her commitment to the children in compensation. For years the couple may have continued living together in relative isolation. The wife would be well aware of her dissatisfaction but her husband would, as often as not, turn a blind eye to the situation and busy himself elsewhere. When an opportunity to leave presented itself, the wife would seize it. Her departure would be received with shock by the husband who would protest that it was totally unexpected and incomprehensible. Dispossessed, he would protest angrily, turning hastily to solicitors and the machinery of law to right an intensely felt sense of being wronged. However, the experience of litigation would frequently heighten feelings of frustration and powerlessness, leaving him embittered and defeated by what he would see as the weight of bias and discrimination in favour of women.

The *turned worm* syndrome is illustrated by the recollections of a couple after they had come through the experience of divorce and established themselves with other partners:

The woman

'I didn't leave until I was ready. I knew that when I was ready I would leave, and that was over a period of about five or six years. Even before our girl was born I knew our marriage wasn't going to last. In some ways I thought she would bring us closer together, but she didn't. It drifted us further apart . . . I used to say to him – oh, for four or five years – "John, if things don't improve there's no point in us carrying on." And I carried on and carried on, and I suppose eventually you stop and you do what you're going to do. It took me a week. I decided, and I asked my parents if I could go and stay there. They said yes. It took me a week to do it, and I left a note. There was no way I could tell John 'cos he'd cry and everything . . . He thought the breaking of the marriage was due to the adultery. It wasn't. The adultery was due to the breaking up of the marriage.'

The man

'After committing adultery with someone who was then a good friend, my ex-wife decided to leave, taking the children and, I might add, half of the house possessions – and while I was at work. When I arrived home at 6.50 p.m. that evening, I was confronted with a note requesting me not to try and contact her and the children. The following day I, of course, contacted my solicitor to start proceedings and to secure legal permission to locate and see my children . . . As the innocent party, and as both children clearly wanted to be with their dad, I felt disgusted that their feelings and mine seemed to be insignificant. It appeared, no matter what, that the children would be better off with their mother.'

The children, as well as being important in their own right, were very important levers in attempts to restore the marriage. Only when this husband was able to hear his wife say that were he to obtain custody she would come back to him, but only out of her love for the children, did he relinquish his custodial claim on both the marriage and the children.

The strength of feeling in the *shot-gun* divorces indicated little distance from the experience of a traumatic ending to marriage. Emotionally, these couples were further along a divorcing process than those in the *nominal* divorce category, but feelings were still raw, suggesting that welfare officers had first met them soon after the event of separation. In fact, this was true of less than half of the 21 cases in this category. Of those who had been separated for less than a year, 3 were still to part when the welfare report was ordered, 5 had been separated for less than six months, and 2 for more than six months. Of the remaining 11 cases, 6 had been apart for between one and two years and 5 for two years or more (these last 5 cases all resulted from reapplications to the courts). One third of the separated sets of parents were living with other partners.

The children

The uncertainty following a sudden rupture in the relationship between parents affected children as much as adults. Not only were they having to contend with unexpected changes in their environment, over which they had little control, but they also found themselves the focus of their parents' conflicting needs. All this was taking place when, on their own account, they were trying to come to terms with contradictory feelings and divided loyalties. It is not surprising, then, that children from two families were attending child guidance clinics for symptoms which were directly attributable to the breakdown of their parents' marriages; that children from two other families were in trouble with the police; that one child was expelled from school because of behaviour disturbance and the work performance of others affected adversely; or that social services departments were actively involved with children from four other families in this group. The impact of separation on children was graphically described by one father:

'The night she left I went to my neighbours. I couldn't stand it. Simon hid in the bushes in the front garden and heard my neighbour say that she [his mother] was deserting the children. He rushed up to his bedroom and barricaded himself in. He messed his trousers. He handcuffed himself to me for a week . . . he was incontinent for a year after my wife left.'

The reactions of other children may have been less visibly extreme, but were a matter of concern to their parents and to the welfare officers when they became involved.

Children played many different roles in the post-separation period. They were called upon to console the rejected spouse and to alleviate the leaver's sense of guilt. 'It leaves each of us with someone to have', explained one mother, justifying her decision to ask the eldest son of the family to live with his father. The children often assumed premature responsibility in the home, worried about money or accommodation, supported and comforted the parent with whom they were living, and generally carried a burden of distress which was sometimes in marked contrast to the vigorous warfare being conducted by their parents. Added responsibilities had their positive side: '[It] makes me feel important, almost being the man of the house . . . we do have to comfort mum . . . we get upset because she does . . . a good talk comforts mum best', remarked one 14-year-old.

In so far as they carried a disproportionate share of responsibility for their own and their parents' care, and were fought over by their parents, they fit precisely the description of the overburdened children described by Wallerstein (1985) in her Californian sample. It remained an open question whether the cost of this responsibility was that these children would need to go in search of a lost childhood in later life; the American study indicated that overloaded children might well suffer long-term adverse effects.

Broadly speaking, the children of the *shot-gun* divorces played two roles in their parents' disputes. They functioned as *arbiters* and as *allies*. *Arbiters* tended to be allowed too much influence and control by both parents, and were in a position to play off one against the other. More benignly, they would 'go between' their parents, providing a link that was otherwise unavailable to the adults. Their role gave them an unwelcome amount of power: messages lost or distorted in transit could add fuel to the fight between parents. We judged that these children (usually aged between six and twelve years) were motivated by a wish to reconcile their parents – if not in reality, at least inside themselves. Sometimes welfare officers provided them with an escape route from impossible dilemmas:

'My dad told me I had to go to court and I'd have to say which one I wanted to live with. Mummy said he was lying, and was probably trying to find out which one I wanted to live with. I didn't want to say to mummy that I wanted to live with daddy 'cos then mummy would get upset, nor say to daddy that I wanted to live with mummy 'cos then daddy'd get upset. So I just left it up to them [the welfare officers].'

Faced with divided loyalties, it is easy to understand how children might be tempted to say what they thought each parent wanted to hear, however contradictory or inflammatory their messages turned out to be.

Children who functioned primarily as *allies* were more concerned with buttressing one parent against threats posed by the other. They related to a perceived fragility in their parents and supported them against a hostile world outside. They would frequently act as parents to their own parents, sacrificing some of their own needs as children to maintain the security and stability of the household in which they were living. Occasionally they were able to relate to both parents in a supporting way, but more usually they prosecuted the interests of one parent against the other, sometimes with considerable vigour:

'I don't know why, but I just hate him. Ever since he came round and starts shouting and that, I've hated him. He was shouting at me 'cos I wouldn't go out with him, and then he was shouting at mum because he wanted mum to force me to go out with him, and that's the time he went to hit mum. And so I've just hated him. I just wish he'd stop and leave us alone . . . he should be paying us maintenance and he's not. And he's getting all these new clothes when he comes round, like suede jackets, and new shirts, and ties, and trousers and that. If he's meant to be paying us maintenance and he's getting all these new clothes, where's he getting the money from? . . . I think he wants to ignore us most of the time, because he doesn't buy us things like clothes, he doesn't give us any pocket money. But he's probably buying things for this other little boy, and giving him pocket money.'

It is not hard to detect this 11-year-old's disappointment with his father, and his attempt to deal with it by identifying with his mother. Later on in the interview he was to say: 'If he listens to the tape and on it, like, it's got "I hate my father", that would be one of my biggest reliefs I've ever had . . . then I would be satisfied.' Children who functioned as *allies* tended to be amongst the oldest in the shot-gun category of divorces, their ages ranging from 7 to 15 years.

In one third of the families, the children played a more passive role than that implied by the titles of *arbiters* or *allies*. They were often under 8 years old, and were commonly regarded by both parents as the repositories of all that was good in their lives. Phrases like 'my treasure', or 'my life', would convey their importance. These young children tended to evoke the strongest feelings in their parents and the welfare officers because of their vulnerability.

It was not possible, however, to draw hard and fast distinctions between children on the basis of ages or roles. Older children might be as special, or as overlooked, as younger ones, and comments like 'we needed to hide', or 'I go away until it all calms down' were common among teenagers. *Allies* and *arbiters* might be found among different children in the same household, and sometimes the same child would play both roles at different times. The point of central importance is that parents were seldom able to protect their children from their own preoccupations with surviving the break up, and, knowingly or not, recruited them into a drama which properly belonged to the adults. This occurred in the case of the King family, whom we have chosen to illustrate the *shot-gun* divorce group, as in other families in our sample.

The King family

Mr King was 25 when he married his wife. She was three years older than him and had recently divorced her previous husband. She brought a son from that marriage into the new family, and four months after the wedding she gave birth to Mr King's child – another boy. Six years later she ejected her husband from the matrimonial home and petitioned for divorce on the basis of his unreasonable behaviour in the marriage. She also obtained an injunction restraining him from returning to the house and molesting her. Mr King applied to the court for custody of the youngest boy, and when his application was heard three months later a welfare report was ordered on both the children.

The problem (the views of the Kings and their welfare officers) Mr and Mrs King were first seen together by two welfare officers, a man and a woman. In the course of that interview the nature of the

problem was redefined, and the perspectives of the two parties
and their welfare officers became apparent. Rather than present
separate statements about a changing problem, we have repro-
duced four sections of the initial interview in chronological
sequence. This more accurately portrays the emerging nature of
the problem than a brief statement from the partners concerned.
At first, the custody application prompted Mr King to question
his wife's competence as a mother, and Mrs King to portray her
husband as a violent father:

Mr WO	'We're curious about why we needed to become involved in your . . .'
Mrs King	'[interrupting] That's what I can't understand!'
Mr King	'I don't think she can look after them properly – that's the problem. Every time I pick my boy up on Saturday he's always hungry. My mother feeds him. You know, I don't think all of them are looked after properly.'
Mrs WO	'[Ascertains they have been together for six years and asks how they got on over the children in that time.]'
Mr King	'Quite reasonable.'
Mrs King	'Just about . . . if they weren't well fed, the school would have reported by now, and the doctor.'
Mrs WO	'I thought I heard your husband say that things were going reasonably well when you were together?'
Mrs King	'Up until we went for a divorce, yeah; until he started hitting my boy around.'
Mr King	'He bleedin' well needed it.'
Mrs King	'Not round the head he didn't.'

From this initial definition of the problem followed questions
that exposed the difficulties reconstituted families can encounter
when parenting children from different marriages. The allegations and counter allegations over parenting turned out to have
some of their roots in past history. The welfare officers picked up
how the children from the two marriages had been treated
differently when there was tension between the parents, and how
they had absorbed some of the impact of the anger in the
marriage. In other words, there was a history in the marriage of
confusing parenting and partnering issues:

Mrs King	'He suffered from the first marriage, my eldest.'
Mrs WO	'So you have protected the boy from your first marriage?'
Mrs King	'Yes, I have looked after him specially because of his problem.'
Mr WO	'It sounds as if Mrs King felt that if she controlled Jason [the youngest] Mr King would take it out on her other boy.'
Mrs King	'We tried to treat both the children the same.'
Mrs WO	'But were both the children treated alike?'
Mr King	'They weren't ill-treated, no. But I did smack them sometimes. It's obvious.'
Mrs King	'But you kicked Neil a few times.'
Mr King	'It's not him that wants the kicking, it's you that wants the kicking . . .'
Mrs WO	'[Confirms that Jason is now six and learns from Mrs King that she was already pregnant when they married.]'
Mr WO	'It would be helpful if you could say what went wrong in the marriage – what happened between you.'
Mrs King	'Well, he was out of work and drinking.'
Mr King	'But you were nagging all the time, that's why I went to the pub. You were nag, nag, nag.'
Mrs WO	'What did she want from you?'
Mr King	'Gawd knows!'
Mrs WO	'What was she nagging about?'
Mrs King	'I was left indoors to look after the children all the time.'
Mr King	'That's your job.'
Mrs WO	'Her nagging was trying to tell you something.'
Mr King	'I don't mind being nagged at but it was nag, nag, nag all the time.'
Mrs WO	'What did you do when she nagged?'
Mr King	'Sometimes I lost my temper.'
Mrs WO	'And who would you hit?'
Mr King	'Well, I hit the wall sometimes . . . then sometimes I hit him, sometimes.'

Later in the interview Mr King's preoccupation with the marriage became clearer as his anxiety about the children merged into his unease about there being another man in his wife's life.

Attempts to restrict discussion to child-care issues could not dam his feelings of jealousy and hurt at having been displaced:

Mr King   'I didn't mind her going out, but when she got back at one or two o'clock in the morning – and occasionally the following day – what am I to think? Wham!'

Mrs WO   'Now you've shifted the argument to each other. Earlier on you were talking about the difficulties of bringing up the children and the disagreements you had had.'

Mr King   'It all really started when my wife started staying out.'

Mrs WO   'Let's go back to the parenting issues. Who would look after the children if Mrs King went out?'

Mr King   'I would.'

Mrs King   'Not always. [She adds that she came back early one night to find he was out at the pub and the two boys were at home on their own.]'

Mr King   'I used to get a few beers in and a mate would sometimes come and stay.'

Mrs King   'Now Neil is 15 and old enough to babysit.'

Mr WO   'It sounds as if you both feel quite blamed at the moment, so when it comes to talking about how the children are being looked after . . .'

Mr King   'I just want them properly looked after.'

Mrs King   'They are being looked after.'

Mr King   'But there are other blokes around there . . . I know for a fact that she's got a bloke round there.'

Mr WO   'Why should she not?'

Mr King   'Well, I don't think she should. She's got two kids to look after.'

Finally, the question of custody becomes less contentious as real differences emerge over the ending of the marriage. The welfare officers understood this to be the central issue which lay behind Mr King's application for custody of Jason. Not only did his application provide a means of getting back *at* his wife, he still hoped that it might be a means of getting back *to* her:

Mr WO   'So I was wondering about the real problem that you're up against.'

Mrs King   'The main problem is who is going to fight for Jason.'

Mr WO   'As his parents, both of you need to fight *for* Jason,

	but what is happening is that you're fighting with each other.'
Mr King	'Yeah, we are.'
Mrs King	'In most cases the mother gets the child.'
Mr WO	'You're still on about the fight between you. You want to win by getting custody. Whoever gets custody "wins".'
Mrs King	'I've already got the house, I've already got three-bedroomed accommodation . . .'
Mr WO	'You're still on about winning. And the question you asked was: who's going to fight for Jason. The more you're at war with each other the harder it is for him and indeed for you both, I imagine.'
Mrs King	'When this thing's over I'll feel a lot happier.'
Mr King	'I'd like to have him. But if I know he's being brought up and looked after properly I don't mind Mrs King having him.'
Mrs WO	'Yes. I keep coming back to that. I think there is a lot of anxiety on both sides.'
Mrs King	'Another thing is you say that if I remarried again you wouldn't want me to have Jason, but you took on the other boy.'
Mrs WO	'Maybe he doesn't really want to let you go. It was you who chose to end the marriage [Mrs King agrees] so it's quite difficult for him to let you go.'
Mrs King	'He said once that if he couldn't have Jason I wouldn't have him.'
Mr King	'Yeah, but that was anger.'
Mrs WO	'I think, that Mr King has a few regrets about this marriage ending.'
(SILENCE)	
Mr WO	'That is a difficult problem that one, isn't it?'
Mrs King	'I've got no intention of getting back together again. It's finished and that's it.'
(SILENCE)	
Mrs WO	'Can you understand that it might take him a bit longer to come to terms with that than you . . . and that is what a lot of the fight is still about, really?'
Mrs King	'You see, I've accepted the end of the marriage but he hasn't.'
Mr King	'I don't think I have really. Not really. Really deep down, I haven't.'

Mr WO   'It's a very short time – it's very recent that all this has happened.'

Mr King   'Really deep down in my heart I'd still like to be there, really.'

Mrs King   'There's no way. The marriage has ended and that's it.'

Long-lease divorces

The parents

The third group of divorces consisted of two families where the parents had been apart for six and four years respectively when the enquiry was ordered. In only one of the cases had the marriage been ended in law, although both parents in each case were living with other partners. Further along the road to breaking the emotional threads of marriage than either the *nominal* or *shot-gun* couples, the men retained a distant affection for, interest in, and control over the affairs of their former spouses. There were indications that, despite protests called for by propriety, their spouses reciprocated this positive regard. The continuing attachment between the partners (both sets of whom were childhood sweethearts) was of a chronic but distant kind, suggesting that the idea of their belonging together lingered on despite the passage of time and circumstance. We have described these as *long-lease* divorces because of the sense of ownership and proprietorial regard which persisted among the men, and the tacit recognition and acceptance of this by the women.

While the men allowed their former partners considerable latitude in going their own way, they reacted sharply to any action which threatened to squeeze them out of the picture altogether. Court applications were triggered in one case by the remarriage of a spouse and the application by the new husband and wife to adopt the only child of the former marriage. In the other case, court proceedings followed a father 'snatching' his children from school and refusing to allow them home to their mother. She had formed an unwelcomely strong attachment to a man whom the father believed (with some justification) to be a detrimental influence on his children. In both cases, the courts were used by the men to try and restore a previously existing balance.

Overt conflict was fiercest between the present and past male partner (a situation not exclusive to the *long-lease* group), sometimes erupting in what might best be described as a stag fight. Publicly, the woman supported her present partner, but in private there were indications she might discreetly hold a torch for her former partner. It so happened that both sets of parents were familiar with the criminal community and had themselves been convicted by the courts. They inhabited a world where conning was a way of life; 'a beautiful conner' was used as a tribute and term of endearment by one man to describe his former wife. Courts and court procedures were there to be used, with due wariness, and there was frequently contempt for and anger with welfare officers who, in Mattinson's and Sinclair's (1979) terms, seemed bound to fall into one or other category of 'suckers' or 'bastards'. Both sets of parents had their own ways of securing what they wanted. The legal system constituted but one channel through which pressure might be brought to bear.

The children

By and large, children featured less prominently than adults in the *long-lease* disputes. When they did, they acted as *allies*, corroborating their parents' stories and abandoning any bids for the absent parent for fear of the storm that might be expected to break over their present household in consequence.

The Hood/Hams

Mr Hood was 24 when he married his wife, who was two years his junior. Two years later she gave birth to twins. After some separations, Mrs Hood petitioned for divorce on the grounds of her husband's unreasonable behaviour and was granted an absolute decree. Mr Hood was granted reasonable access to his sons. The marriage ended after six years, although the Hoods continued to have reason to meet.

Two-and-a-half years after the divorce, Mrs Hood married Mr Ham. One year later, Mr and Mrs Ham applied to adopt the twins who, by then, were approaching 8 years of age. Access was interrupted during this period (at least), and three months after the adoption application Mr Hood returned to court to enforce his sons' right to see him. A welfare report was ordered.

The problem (Mr Hood) The first meetings between Mr Hood, Mrs Ham and their welfare officer were not tape recorded. The

comments below come from the follow-up interviews which
invited recall of events occurring a year or so earlier. They had
lost none of their intensity with the lapse of time.

> 'She wants security. She gets upset. Maybe he is pressing her.
> Perhaps he is threatening to leave her so that she will do what
> he wants. So she might be stuck again. It's all gone wrong
> since she married. We got on perfectly before, we were like
> brother and sister. We ran a little business together . . . but
> [now] she's the bullet and he's the gun . . . she and I have been
> together since we were schoolchildren: it's him; he's the
> trouble-maker . . . The thing they are angry about is I would
> not agree to adoption, and that turns out to be right because I
> would have been cut off completely.
>
> I daren't go round because, as I explained to the welfare
> officer, I've got quite a violent temper and her new husband
> rubs me up the wrong way. And if it came to a row I'd
> probably have no chance of seeing my sons again. I've got the
> legal right of access – but he's got the legal right of his house.
> And that's another bone of contention never brought up: the
> house they've bought now is with the money I've given my
> wife. And he considers it's his house, but it's something I did
> for my sons, not for him.'

The problem (Mrs Ham) It was a distinctive feature of both
enquiry and follow-up interviews that Mr Ham acted as the
spokesman for his wife; she managed to be either elusive or
absent. Mr Ham spoke for his wife at the follow-up interview:

> 'We considered it was counter-productive to allow Mr Hood to
> have access. When the boys are 16 we will provide them with
> their father's address and they can please themselves. Until
> then we consider access is not beneficial. Mr Hood is a
> roughneck and not suitable. The welfare officer thought
> differently – I had two rows with him. How would you like
> your children to go to a stranger? . . . We wanted to adopt; Mr
> Hood would not agree.'

The problem (the welfare view) The discrepancy between Mr
Hood's and Mrs Ham's account of the contact kept up between
father and sons over the previous six years was so great as to make
it certain that one party was lying. The timing of Mr Hood's

application supported the view that however much contact he had kept with the twins he was not prepared to be cut out of the picture altogether. The proprietorial interest he took in his boys, his former wife, and the uses to which the financial provisions he had made were to be put, all of which were threatened by adoption proceedings, provided an adequate explanation for the court application. The application was pursued with determination because of the feelings of rancour existing between Mr Hood and Mr Ham. For Mrs Ham, remarriage required complete allegiance to her new husband. That appeared to be what he demanded of her, and he was the person to vent most anger towards Mr Hood during the enquiry. The application for renewed access, and the refusal of consent for adoption, posed threats to family stability which might have increased had she wavered in her support for Mr Ham's position.

In 25 out of the 30 core sample of cases we judged that strong feelings about the ending of marriage formed a very important part of the context in which child custody and access disputes took place. This is not to deny the real attachments between parents and children in many of these cases, but to offer an explanation for why parents found it extremely difficult to agree upon arrangements which might protect and foster those attachments. Five cases remained.

Other conundrums

These five remaining cases did not fit our hypothesis of child-related applications to the courts being linked with a persisting attachment to a former marriage. One application followed an argument between a father and his brother-in-law. His sister, who had day-to-day care of the child, applied for the child to be made a ward of court when the father threatened to escalate the family quarrel by withdrawing the child from her care. Another application, this time for custody, was made under the Guardianship of Minors Act following the break-up of a temporary relationship between two parents. In a third case, an access application followed a couple's request to adopt a child of the mother's previous marriage which had ended six years earlier (when the child in question was a baby). The timing of this application coincided with the breakdown of the father's second marriage in circumstances remarkably similar to those in which his first marriage had ended. A fourth application arose from a mother's frustration with the inconsistency of a father's contact with her son. The fifth case was that of Mr and Mrs Robin.

The Robin family

Mr and Mrs Robin married when he was 20 and she was 18. They had three children, two boys and a girl. After eight years of marriage they separated at Mrs Robin's instigation. She and her daughter went to live with a relative and the following year she moved into a flat with her daughter and a male friend. Mr Robin continued to live at the matrimonial home with their two sons. He petitioned for a divorce under the two-year clause, and proposed to continue the arrangements for the children, which had worked satisfactorily during the two years of separation. The judge was concerned about the care of the children being divided between the parents and ordered a welfare report.

The first (and only) interview with the Robin family was not tape-recorded. When Mr and Mrs Robin were interviewed separately at follow-up they were very much more open than they had been during the enquiry. The problem they described concerned their past marriage, and not the present arrangements they had made for their children, although some of the reasons given for why arrangements were as they were would have given the welfare officers pause for thought had they been known at the time of the enquiry. The marital problem had been resolved by divorce, although some residual effects were still apparent.

The problem (Mrs Robin)

'He was so dominating, so possessive. I could not have a life of my own. He played up if I went out. He used to ration my cigarettes and I had to ask him for the two he allowed me each day. He made all the decisions. He could be aggressive – he's much mellower now. [The interviewer remarks that he sounds like a strict father, not a husband.] Yes! That's just it. That was what he was like: a father. What he wanted was a daughter – and that's what I was to him. You see I was only 18, I didn't know my mind. I didn't know anything then. It's too young, 18. [The interviewer asks 'Why 18?'] My mum was an alcoholic. When she wasn't drinking she was the best mum you could have, but I remember dreading going home from school – it was awful when she was drinking. [Interviewer asks whether she had married young to escape.] I suppose you could say that. I suppose it was that.'

The problem (Mr Robin)

'You see, mine was an untypical case. My marriage was broken up by a woman . . . Even when she was here I did everything except the cooking – all the cleaning, shopping, washing, ironing. I was a fool to myself, but I drew the line at cooking. Then the boys came of age to go to school and she met this woman . . . I was silly. I used to take her round there. I looked after the kids while they went out together – until one day I rebelled, and drove off leaving her and the kids.

My wife was funny that way, she doesn't like boys. She never even took to ours, never wanted anything to do with them – right from nappies – even before the break-up. I think she might not have wanted any of the children, but I thought "Why should she get away with that? Why should I have it *all* again?" So we decided on the split, and they do say that girls should have a mother because of all things about growing up – periods and such like.

The judge had a bad day. He heard about us dividing the kids and said "We can't have this", and ordered an enquiry. I couldn't really understand his objections as the arrangements had been working well, but he's a funny man, that judge. So we saw the welfare and got it rubber-stamped.'

The problem (the welfare view) The welfare officers in this case, not being party to the information which emerged at follow-up, concluded that the problem belonged primarily to the courts and not to the parents. An atypical arrangement had alerted the judge to the possibility of there being risks for the children. These were not apparent to the welfare officers. For them, the enquiry felt like an unwarranted intrusion upon arrangements which had been working well enough for more than two years. This case, and the issues it raises, will be described in more detail along with the other courier cases in Chapter 6.

The fight for survival

Whether recently separated or not, we judged that all but four of the 30 sets of parents in our core sample were preoccupied with their own psychological survival. Their emotional equilibrium and social viability had been seriously disturbed. As one woman described the predicament of her former husband: 'He didn't want the divorce. This is why he was being what he was. He felt to himself that the house and children – everything – was being taken away from him. He said his whole life was being taken away from him.' His grim quip – 'I have a soft spot for my wife: about 20 cubic feet of quicksand' – confirmed her estimate of the impact divorce had had upon him.

The roles of spouse and parent act as life support systems to many people. They can also constitute a threat to personal autonomy. When the integrity of the individual is threatened, it is not surprising that the fight for survival is carried out in relationships with partners and children. Shock, denial, fear, anxiety, protest, intransigence, and rage are all understandable reactions to the threat and realization of being dispossessed. 'The argument wasn't rational', one mother observed, 'I felt I would lose my rights. I think my husband felt the same way.'

At the time we saw them, much was at stake for the parents we met. Not only were they fighting for material and emotional security, they were having to reconstruct their view of themselves and the world outside. In the process, one or other parent (and often both) showed a propensity for attributing to their former partners all that was bad, shameful, and blameworthy in their present circumstances. The degree to which allegations were made and reinforced suggested that many parents were strug-gling to keep at bay their own feelings of guilt and failure, and wishing to disown responsibility for what was happening between them. While the paranoid reaction of externalizing all that is experienced as bad is one means of protecting against the fear of personal disintegration, it is a psychological process which is incompatible with the kind of bridge-building necessary for the development of joint parenting after separation and divorce.

It is of little use decrying a necessity. The prevailing ambience of persecutory anxiety which often existed between parents was there because personal survival was felt to be at stake. When the actions of others are experienced as, in one man's phrase, 'a declaration of war', the world is divided into enemies and allies. The capacity to be concerned about others is necessarily limited by the amount of energy expended in sustaining the self. The condition may be described as one of *necessary narcissism*.

Involvement with others is restricted to activities which underpin and support the self. In the struggle to establish and maintain a sustainable view of events (and sustainment is more important than accuracy in this context) the activities most warmly embraced are those that absolve the self and vilify others.

It is at this time that court procedures can complement the psychological needs of parents. Litigation provides a formal channel through which vindication may be secured and blame established. There is a reciprocity between judicial procedures and the needs of some divorcing couples at certain stages in the divorce process. Much attention has been paid to the effect of adversarial procedures upon the behaviour of parents. Less weight has been given to the part played by parents who might need to invent an adversarial system if one did not already exist.

We have argued that an incomplete emotional divorce provided an important part of the emotional context in which child custody and access disputes took place in our core sample of cases. We have also suggested that one means of registering a protest about marriage ending, short of defending the divorce itself (a course taken by only 1 per cent of respondents nationally) is to dispute arrangements made for children. Many of our sample were unprepared for the ending of their marriages, and separation precipitated a crisis which threatened personal disintegration. Endowments of social disadvantage and past loss (to be considered in the next chapter) provided few buffers against the impact of marital breakdown, making change even more difficult to manage. In these circumstances protests were registered, and the need to vindicate and convict made the courts a natural forum for the prosecution of self interest. A favourable adjudication not only provided a solution to disagreements between parents over practical arrangements following divorce (at least, sometimes), it represented a public seal of approval and a form of absolution. While the law struggles to rid itself of the concept of matrimonial offence, this concept is very much alive in the minds of some divorcing couples if our sample of parents is any guide. This has implications for understanding the gap in expectations we discovered between parents and welfare officers about the nature and purpose of enquiries for the courts, and helps to make sense of dissatisfactions with the enquiry process frequently expressed on both sides.

5

AT CROSS PURPOSES

'Oft expectation fails and most oft there
Where most it promises, and oft it hits
Where hope is coldest and despair most fits.'

William Shakespeare
All's Well That Ends Well

The petitions and applications presented to divorce courts usually signify that parents are at cross purposes. In Chapter 4 we suggested that for a large proportion of parents, child custody and access disputes take place against a background of disagreement over a bid by one partner to sever all ties with the other. The consequence for those upon whom a welfare report is ordered is that they find themselves in the unfamiliar territory of a court investigation. In the enquiry relationship, the different purposes of parents interact with those of welfare officers. Each embarks upon the process of enquiry with more or less defined sets of expectations about what might come out of the experience.

Expectations are defined by a mixture of hope and experience, one usually triumphing to some degree over the other. They are an amalgam of received wisdom, lived experience, and fantasy. Frequently they become clear only when they have been fulfilled or disappointed. Sometimes they remain outside the reach of consciousness, motivating behaviour in a driven but sightless way. Occasionally they are over-defined and impermeable to experience. Parents and welfare officers often approached each other with incompatible sets of expectations about what the enquiry might portend.

Every time a judge or registrar orders a welfare report, parents and practitioners are bound to ask themselves why this has happened. The parents in the core sample of enquiries may not have been aware that they constituted a statistical minority (9 per cent of all couples granted a decree absolute at the local county court in 1983) but they were likely to feel they had been singled out for special and unwelcome attention. Even when the court had stated clearly why a report was being called for, all the parties involved (and these included children and welfare officers) were likely to draw their own conclusions. These conclusions affected the way they behaved, and so contributed towards defining the nature of the enquiry encounter itself. In this chapter we shall be looking at some of the hopes and fears surrounding the welfare enquiries in our core sample from the points of view of ourselves as welfare officers and the parents we saw.

The welfare officers' perspectives

Many parents in our sample were unclear as to why a welfare report had been ordered in their case and, while entertaining their own preconceptions, were often confused over what to expect from the enquiry itself. Because they were in a subordinate and vulnerable position, they often did not feel free to ask for clarification as vigorously as they might have wished, and they sometimes said they emerged from the enquiry as confused as they had been at the outset:

'Really, what I should have done was said "What do you want out of me? What is it all about? What is it for?" And I feel, now, they should tell people what it's for, really.'

'When they actually ordered the divorce welfare in I hadn't a clue what to expect. I didn't even know these people existed. I didn't know what they were aiming for. I still don't know what they're aiming for. I assume it's to get you back together again.'

How far this confusion reflects a failure to communicate effectively about the nature and purpose of welfare enquiries, and how far it is an expression of the general sense of disorientation, frustration, and ambivalence common to the experience of divorce, is a matter for conjecture. It does, however, draw attention to the welfare officer's understanding of his or her role and purpose, and to the possibility that confusion is generated by a mismatch between parents' and practitioners' expectations of the enquiry process. Studies of marriage guidance clients (Hunt 1985; Blampied and Timms 1985) have drawn attention to the expectation gap which sometimes exists between the providers and users of services, suggesting that the problem may not be an uncommon one.

In connection with the core sample of cases, our role as welfare officers and the expectations we had of the enquiries were affected by three factors. First there were our professional aspirations, including those of our welfare colleagues. Then there were the expectations generated by the research. Finally, there was the influence of statute and court.

The professional context

The welfare officers in the Divorce Unit and the IMS researchers had in common a background of being professionally trained social workers. Broadly speaking, the wish to be of some help to others was the main conscious reason for choosing social work. Of course, occupational choice is many-faceted, and the decisions we took were influenced by opportunity and circumstance, as well as by the kinds of unconscious factors described by Daniell (1985). Guilt and reparation, alienation and identification, all combine to make philanthropy a complex and sometimes suspect activity. Be that as it may, personal motivation and professional training inclined us to view our activities as offering a service to individuals, couples, and families.

Defining our clients in these terms immediately raises some of the differences between our two agencies. We marital therapists from the IMS defined our 'client' as the relationship between spouses or cohabiting partners. The marriage relationship was therefore of particular interest to us. In contrast, welfare officers were most concerned with the well-being of children, their function being to advise the courts on the kinds of post-divorce arrangements best suited to safeguarding their interests. Straightforward as this might seem, the impact of systems theory on the practice of family therapy has encouraged many welfare officers to define their clients in family-centred rather than child-centred terms (using the word 'family' in a generic sense to include people significant to the child by dint of kinship and household circumstance). The implications of systemic concepts can be confusing to those, including clients, who look no further than to the individual for an explanation of behaviour.

Strictly speaking, the welfare officer's client was the court. It could, at times, seem as if the statutory duty to furnish courts with reports was in direct conflict with the professional duty to provide a service for divorcing families. The relationship between welfare officer and client is an enforced one in which the court is an ever-present third party. This configuration is familiar to the probation service, which has traditionally operated as the honest broker between public and private interests. The professional struggle to exercise authority in a manner that reconciles individual and community interests is the hallmark of probation practice. Welfare officers were therefore inclined to view the courts as having an important but not exclusive claim upon their services.

The nature of the service offered to family members, again described in broad terms of ethos, was to enable those disabled by endowment and circumstance to recover and develop their resources in order to exercise the fullest possible control over their own lives. This philosophy of care has been described in operational terms by Sutherland (1979) as 'good parenting', a concept which is not to be confused with paternalism – or maternalism – but describes the kind of involvement with others which tries to promote the development of personal autonomy and not to encourage a regressive dependence or precocious independence. It is a philosophy which allows a place for control as well as care.

The Divorce Unit and the IMS had this philosophy in common. Applied to divorce court welfare work, we shared an interest in encouraging former partners to work together as parents in the belief that their children would benefit as a result. In this we started out by adhering to the value system of those who maintain that children need access to both parents after divorce. We also shared a desire to resist the transfer of parental responsibility from parents to others. These values provided an affinity between ourselves and the conciliation movement in this country. The enquiry relationship constituted one point of access to parents who, in dispute with each other, were in danger of ceding their parental responsibilities to the courts. Sitting uneasily with a desire to encourage parents to discharge their responsibilities was the knowledge that some would be unable to do this, and that children could be placed at risk if this reality was ignored. Welfare officers were not deaf to criticisms levelled at social workers in child abuse cases (see, for example, Blom-

Cooper 1985) which added to their anxiety and, by making them feel more responsible, could work against the principle of party control.

While in no sense offering a conciliation service, the enquiry process was envisaged by welfare officers in a way which incorporated some of the objectives and techniques of conciliation. Conciliation training was seen to be relevant to the job, as relevant as knowledge about child development, marital interaction, and family therapy. Tellingly, training in research methods (which might well be considered to have something to offer to investigators) was not considered to be relevant.

The research context

Developments in the field of conciliation are very much a part of the professional context for welfare officers. In Chapter 3 we described the debate which has been taking place about the kind of relationship there should be between the activities of investigation and conciliation. Our research focused on the feasibility of encouraging private ordering while reporting for the courts. This focus affected the aspirations and expectations with which we, and our Divorce Unit colleagues, approached the enquiry relationship.

In describing how the project came about, we referred in Chapter 1 to the hope and enthusiasm with which the Divorce Unit and the IMS launched the research enterprise. Morale in the Divorce Unit was high given its recent inception and following a very good report from the Home Office Inspectorate. As an officer was later to remark, 'the world was fresher then'. At one level, the staff of the Unit hoped that the project would justify the decision to set up a specialist unit, validate their work, and even provide a blueprint for civil work in the probation service as a whole. There was an optimism about the prospects of helping parents to reach agreement, and a desire for success in these terms. Equally, however, there was a realism about the stressful nature of the work and the limits upon what could be achieved. We, from the IMS, vividly recall the initiation of two of our number to the world of the Divorce Unit when we encountered the brick wall of a failed negotiation with a couple who had been referred by a solicitor for voluntary help. Experiencing total defeat at the hands of a woman who was convinced that her husband's wish to leave her was a symptom of mental disorder, we received the kind of cheery condolence which could only come from seasoned campaigners in the field. Hope therefore seemed only tenuously linked with experience.

On the IMS side, the research project we completed was less ambitious than the one we had originally proposed. The weight and volume of the material generated by the work led us to monitor one year's intake of clients to the Unit as opposed to the two years originally proposed, to limit the core sample to 30 rather than 36 enquiries, to restrict follow-up interviews to core sample parents, and to tailor certain other procedures. We had anticipated a very much more circumscribed project than the fluid, messy, and intrusive experience it turned out to be.

If we are honest, we also thought that by harnessing the resources of marital therapists to those of experienced welfare officers we would combine forces which might prove irresistible to warring parents. We had yet to meet our Waterloo! Undaunted by Saposnek's (1983) warning that effective mediation must utilize the skills of brief behavioural therapy, crisis intervention, and negotiation, and that conciliators need emotional sensitivity, firmness, understanding, and other attributes besides, we launched forth with expectations of ourselves which, in retrospect, seem just a trifle omnipotent.

Perhaps our grossest miscalculation was to expect to engage responsible adults at a time when parents were preoccupied with the hurt and frightened child within themselves. Operationally, this was attempted by inviting parents to attend a first appointment at the office in company with each other (such invitations were issued in 25, or 83 per cent, of the core sample cases). In 13 of these cases (43 per cent) parents were also asked to bring their children for a family interview. The reasons for this practice included the need to explore and define contentious issues, to appraise the interaction between family members, and to negotiate with the objective of securing an agreement. Separate appointments were offered when parents were known to have attended a previous conciliation appointment which had failed, when there was the prospect of violence, when parents had been separated for a long time, when they lived far apart, and when there was an important secret that one partner wished to keep from the other. Time and again the welfare officers would make it clear in these first joint interviews that as well as reporting to the court they wished to help parents come to their own decisions about issues concerning their children.

The court context

As welfare officers, we were well aware that the principal concern of the courts was to protect the interests of children. The welfare report was a vital instrument in this process, although what it contained and how it was conducted were matters that were assumed to rest with the welfare officers concerned.

The judiciary has recently been explicit about what it expects from welfare officers. The Booth Report (1985) and the President of the Family Division (Arnold 1985) have required conciliation services to be operated quite separately from welfare enquiries, so that privilege attaches to the former in a way which would be quite contrary to the purpose of the latter. This view does not prohibit welfare officers from attempting to help parents come to agreement in the course of reporting to the courts (thereby increasing the likelihood that court decisions will be acceptable and adhered to), only from attempting to conduct privileged negotiations in the context of a court enquiry. The irritation caused by reports which omit to make a recommendation following attempts to achieve agreement has been expressed by Lord Justice Dillon (1986). A certain ambiguity has crept in, however. In 1985, the liaison judge of the Family Division in Manchester directed welfare officers to confine themselves to reporting upon family circumstances and to exclude anything that had a bearing upon the content of conciliation. If this directive is interpreted as excluding from both the process of welfare enquiries and the content of welfare reports accounts of attempts to facilitate workable settlements between parents (who know from the outset that a report is to be prepared) this is indeed a confusing and retrograde step.

At the outset of an enquiry, the nature of concern about a child or children may not be clear. The specific reasons behind court orders for welfare reports were frequently as obscure to welfare officers (among whom we include ourselves in relation to the core sample of cases) as they were to parents. That is not to say the orders were considered unnecessary or that their general purpose was misunderstood. Rule 95 of the Matrimonial Causes Rules (1977) makes it clear that 'a judge or registrar may at any time refer to a court welfare officer for investigation and report any matter which concerns the welfare of the child'. However, in most cases welfare officers had to infer why a judge or registrar had called for a particular enquiry, and to assume that parents would not necessarily understand the reasons for this course of action.

The information we first received about an enquiry was contained in the court order for a report. A typed entry or deletion on a standard form indicated whether the report was wanted in connection with one or more of the three broad issues of custody, access, and satisfaction. Marginally more revealing was the statement of arrangements proposed by parents for their children. Sometimes, the divorce affidavits of the parties would be included amongst the court papers, providing a background of alleged behaviour and events indicating the emotional climate in which parents were seeking to decide upon their children's futures. Frequently, a welfare officer in attendance at court would note the particular circumstances that prompted the order. This information could be invaluable. In none of our cases, however, did a judge or registrar commit to paper his or her particular reasons for ordering a report. There was therefore no formal means of conveying what might have been said in open court to parents or welfare officers who were not present at the time. In terms of the needs of parents, welfare officers, and courts for an explicit understanding of why a report is necessary, this was, in our view, a serious omission.

It was not part of our remit to investigate why reports were ordered in some cases and not in others, nor to interview those making the orders about their expectations and experiences of the services performed by welfare officers. Evidence from other research suggests that welfare reports are likely to be ordered in contentious cases (Eekelaar et al. 1977; Maidment 1984; Murch 1980) but there is little evidence associating reports with cases in which fathers care for their children. Courts vary greatly in the frequency with which they resort to welfare reports and presumably, also, in their reasons for doing so. Eekelaar and colleagues (1977) found the range of variation to be between 3.1 per cent and 18.4 per cent of the cases heard by them. Family size, change of address (experienced or proposed), separation of children, and the presence of people in the household who were not related to children (other than cohabitees) have been linked with court orders for reports. So, too, have difficulties over access, custody disputes, split custody proposals, children in care, a mother in prison, and questions about the quality of care.

In the absence of detailed information about the reasons for instigating an enquiry, we and our welfare officer colleagues were left to draw our own conclusions. For welfare officers, these conclusions were based upon informal contacts with judges and registrars as well as formal communications. It was assumed, for example, that in addition to needing other sets of eyes and ears to collate material which would inform their decisions, judges wished to avoid the damaging effects of stage-managed fights in open court, and wanted to save court time wherever possible. These reasons might be sufficient grounds for ordering a welfare report even before taking account of the idiosyncracies of particular families which might give cause for concern. They encouraged welfare officers to infer that judges hoped enquiries would take the steam out of custody and access disputes by giving them opportunities to work with families in conflict, as well as by the sobering impact of the reports themselves. Reading the expectations of the courts in this way synchronized with their own expectations in so far as enquiries were regarded as opportunities to reduce, if not resolve, conflict in families afflicted by divorce.

The parent's perspectives

With or without a clear explanation of their purpose, parents tended to entertain two broad kinds of expectations about welfare enquiries. First, there was apprehension about having to submit to an uninvited and unwanted experience. The welfare report introduced an element of uncertainty about future arrangements. It added to existing uncertainty resulting from the disputes between parents. It postponed the date by which courts might be expected to have arrived at a decision. It also exposed children to the realities of their parents' divorce, an arena which, until then, they may have been protected from knowing too much about. Mothers who had day-to-day responsibility for the care of their children were usually the parents who had most difficulty in accepting the enquiry. They were predisposed to view welfare officers, if not as agents of former spouses come to unsettle a new and hard-won equilibrium, at least as potential critics of their abilities. The enquiry was therefore expected to add to, and not to diminish, an already heavy burden.

Parents who did not have *de facto* custody of their children (usually fathers) were less threatened by the prospect of an enquiry, at least to begin with. Although not immune to the fears of custodial parents, they tended to see themselves as having more to gain than to lose from a welfare report. In some cases they had specifically asked the court to investigate their partner's circumstances, or had readily acquiesced to this suggestion from their legal advisers. Orders for a welfare report were therefore frequently perceived by custodial parents as weighted in favour of their non-custodial adversary.

The second set of expectations concerned the wishes of parents (and some children) for welfare officers to meet particular needs. Such wishes were sometimes acknowledged, but more usually implicit. Sometimes they remained outside awareness, and were surmised by us from our involvement as welfare officers. While enquiries were capable of generating certain needs (for example, the need for information about procedures) they were more likely to focus attention upon existing needs than to create new ones. The nature of these needs, and the investigative context of the enquiry encounter, usually conspired to ensure that they would not be met.

Enquiries in a court context

We have drawn upon the comments of parents at follow-up to deduce and illustrate the expectations they had of the enquiry process. The limitations of this method are discussed in Chapter 7. It was sometimes unclear from their comments whether parents were talking about courts or welfare officers. This ambiguity needs to be kept in mind when interpreting what was said, but in so far as it affected how parents saw welfare officers it constitutes an important part of the phenomenon of the enquiry experience.

Without exception, one or both parents in our core sample of cases experienced the court order for a welfare report as an unwelcome imposition. In three cases parents colluded to minimize this intrusion upon their lives, but more usually one parent felt that the report was yet another manifestation of their former partner's persistent and unwelcome presence. For the custodial parent in particular, the welfare enquiry threatened to unsettle a new-found equilibrium and to undermine a sometimes tenuous sense of control over events, and it could come as a shock when it was unexpected:

'Quite honestly, I didn't know what to expect. I think it's the parents fighting for themselves, actually. You get a letter saying you've got to go to the welfare court and you really don't know what to expect . . . It absolutely terrifies you, quite honestly – well, it's not knowing how it's going to go. They're either for you or against you, and until you go in you don't know the answer to that.'

'I don't actually know to this day why I got a letter from the welfare. Apparently he went to court (it was a great shame, my solicitor bungled things a little bit: I got a letter from him stating that I didn't have to attend the court) . . . and the judge said "Is everything alright, and everything?" And he said "No" . . . Out of the blue I got a letter from the welfare: "Would I like to attend – with my husband and son – at the welfare office?" I went absolutely bananas! I don't know whether it was the secretary I 'phoned – I felt so sorry for that poor woman – but it was such a shock, and I thought "What the hell have I got this for after two years?"'

There was a noticeable difference between the shocked and indignant reactions of women to welfare reports, and those of men who expected welfare officers to investigate the situation and even maintain surveillance on a former spouse. Non-custodial parents often hoped that the enquiry would restore their sense of control. The following comments were both made by men in this position:

'My barrister was asking for a welfare report because I couldn't figure out why my daughter wouldn't come down. I thought they would find out mainly why she wouldn't come down to see me, and get our views on what we thought was a reasonable access.'

'I . . . think that visits by officers to the parents in homes should continue up to two years after any decisions on a random time and scale, to be sure that conditions and circumstances are as they should be.'

By and large, parents expected welfare officers to be neutral and unbiased. This did not lessen their fears of being undermined as parents or losing control of a delicately balanced situation:

'I knew they [both welfare officers were women] weren't going to side with either of us. I knew they were going to smooth things over to everyone's satisfaction without causing too much of a disruption; and I knew they were going to get my daughter to see her dad again. . . . You sometimes get the nasty feeling that because they are trying to be fair to both parties the person in the middle, which is my daughter, would be forced back into a situation I couldn't control. That was my fear at the time. Obviously my ex-husband's fears were the reverse – that they were going to tell him he could never see her again, and they were going to side with me. That's the first sort of thing you think when you walk into the building.'

Many parents approached the courts feeling that an offence had been committed, that someone should be placed on trial, that their case should be given a fair hearing, and that someone should act decisively to acquit, convict, and sentence. We know that at least nine parents in the core sample had criminal records, which might go some way to explaining the fusion of criminal and civil procedures. Even without prior contact with the criminal courts, parents, especially custodial parents, felt they had been placed on trial and assumed guilty until they proved themselves innocent:

'I felt threatened because I'd been the one to walk out and had to justify taking her back [not returning her daughter from an access visit] – and I knew there'd be a lot of muck-raking and that didn't particularly cheer me up.'

'when the judge actually ordered the welfare, and my husband was fighting so much, and said no way would he leave home and that he wanted the child . . . I didn't really know what this was about. In the end I felt as if I was the criminal. Because of what he'd actually said about me – trying to run me down in front of the court to make me look a bad mother (of which they had no evidence at all; I had been a very good mother and I know people who will stand by that) – only through what he had said they ordered the welfare unit in.'

Arising out of the sense of being on trial as parents and as people, two further expectations were associated with the welfare enquiry and the court context in which it originated. The first was that there would be an opportunity to present a 'case' and that this would be given a fair hearing. The second was a wish for prompt action. An adversarial court system which leads to resolution of conflict through adjudication is well matched to both these expectations. The wish for a 'fair hearing' often bordered upon the need for an effective ally or advocate, a point observed by Murch (1980) in his study of divorce court welfare clients. Without an alliance, some parents felt their case had not been adequately heard. In this respect, the more welfare officers strived to retain their neutrality, an objective which required an approach not dictated by either parent, the more frustrating they could become. When neither parent felt they had enlisted the support of their welfare officer, each could feel their case had not been properly heard. The following remarks come from a father and mother who were contesting the custody of their young daughter; the father was also considering defending the divorce:

'I thought both parties would go to him and be free to talk to him, and he would work something out on the basis of what he heard. The report he made, he ignored entirely what I'd said. He made his own decisions.'

'I expected him to concentrate on where we are now, and how well I am caring for Diana, and how well she was doing, how she'd come through it – but more on her. In fact, the whole of the first interview was only what had happened in the marriage, and I don't feel he believed me. Even now, I don't feel he believed me . . . I had welcomed him into our home and given him a cup of tea – he didn't want tea; it felt unfriendly.'

After being given the chance to make their case, parents often expressed the hope that courts and welfare officers would act authoritatively to end an injustice or break a deadlock. In this area, feelings could run high. It is easy to read into the frustration expressed towards authority figures who will not, or cannot act, projections of the feelings of helplessness and impotence experienced by parents as a result of their entangled circumstances. The two comments which follow come from a father and a mother:

'I didn't think the whole situation was necessary. It's just that she would say this, and that's it. She won't give way. And I think she should be made to give way – not demanding this and demanding that, and people sitting back and saying "OK, we'll have a welfare report". I don't think it should ever have come to that.'

'Could not somebody put an end to it? . . . what I would like is somebody to stop him running rings around the system. He made the law seem like utter rubbish. He made fools out of us all – judges, barristers, solicitors, and social workers.'

Enquiries in a personal context

The wish for public vindication in a court of law, which was shared by all the parents in our core sample once a court settlement was accepted as unavoidable, is closely related to the need for personal confirmation and support. However angry they might have been with each other, however dismissive of those around them, however protective of themselves and their children, all the parents in our sample were under stress and preoccupied with their own needs at the time we saw them. In the course of the enquiries they asked for information and advice about judicial procedures, legal terminology, state benefits, welfare rights, housing applications, and other immediate practical problems with which they were having to contend. Often they confided about more personal worries regarding themselves and their children, although the solution was often perceived as resting with the other parent, and welfare officers were expected to direct their attentions 'out there', rather than concerning themselves with matters closer to home. Occasionally parents would acknowledge their own difficulties and make a direct appeal for help with these.

Most commonly, however, there was ambivalence towards welfare officers. No matter how longed-for was the opportunity to talk about their own worries, parents were often deeply mistrustful of how such disclosures might be used. The end product of the enquiry was, after all, a report to the court, a report which would be seen by 'the opposition' and be influential in the decision-making process. In those cases where a follow-up interview was agreed it was therefore not uncommon to find the hope for personal help expressed alongside a sense of disappointment, and sometimes a sense of realism:

'I did sometimes wish somebody would have helped me more

with my boy. He was vulnerable. When I tried to discipline him he would run off and telephone his father. I couldn't discipline him at all. It was very difficult for me. [The interviewer asks what help she would have liked.] I don't know, really. For someone to tell his father – tell him that he was affecting the child.'

'The welfare concept is a bit misleading, if you ask me, because people go in there thinking you've got all the answers and that's the last thing you've got. You've got ideas, but it's they who've got to find the answers at the end of the day. It implies you're handing your problems over to someone else, which you're not, really. All you're doing is getting an independent assessment of what your problems are; the problems still remain.'

In addition to the stresses and strains of current circumstances, we gained the impression that enquiries were sometimes implicitly expected to put right former wrongs as well as present losses. These losses, sustained in the current reorganization of family life, were very apparent for adults and children alike. Children sometimes expressed the wish that their parents would come back together again, although it was unclear whether they expected welfare officers to be instrumental in this process. Our impression was that they regarded it as a forlorn hope and wished, most of all, to be relieved of the pressures associated with warring parents and their own feelings of loss. Displaced husbands often entertained private hopes that the marriage might be retrieved, but their anger was usually more in evidence than their distress. If they looked to welfare officers to restore their marriages at all, it was usually as agents who might be able to coerce former partners and effect a controlling influence upon them in a way that they felt unable to do.

The ending of a current marriage resurrected memories of earlier losses for some parents, compounding their difficulties in the present. We were surprised by the number of cases in which these past losses were disclosed. Specific events were described to us in 12 of the 30 enquiries. They were significant because they were disclosed as being relevant to the issues about which parents were in dispute. Other losses would almost certainly have been sustained by other parents but not disclosed, despite their relevance to current reactions and behaviour. The losses described concerned parents, children, and former partners. In one case, the tragic death of a child had frozen a family in silent recrimination for eight years before action was taken to end the marriage. In another, a father recalled his own father dying when he was the age of the daughter for whom he was contesting custody. In a third case, a man frantically (and unsuccessfully) opposed the efforts of his wife to oust him from the home which had been left to him by his parents upon their death a short time earlier, and with whom they had lived as an extended family.

Connections between present-day disputes and past losses were made by parents – especially men – who had lost contact with children from earlier marriages. In these circumstances, current disputes carried a double burden, making their resolution that much more difficult to achieve:

'Twenty years ago I was married previously, and there was a child. Everything was in my favour. I had just come out of the Navy and was finding my feet. . . . had I wanted, that child would be here today, but I just couldn't. My wife decided to look after her. The court passed adoption papers without me knowing, without me saying. That child was adopted by her second husband, and it's not going to happen again. I'm close to 50; that's why I'm being difficult.'

'I'd already lost one [daughter] and I wasn't intending to lose any more. That was my main concern.'

The investigative context, the attribution to the authorities of responsibility for failing to alleviate painful predicaments, and the burden of past losses, all served to make it impossible for some of the personal hopes and expectations of parents to be realized by welfare officers except through securing the kind of support that would result in a favourable recommendation, so reinforcing their standing as parents. When spouses separated, children became important not only in their own right, but also as a means of meeting their parents' needs for support and affirmation and compensating for earlier losses. In many cases it seemed to us as if a fiction of parenting had to be created, especially by men, in order to secure children who offered the best chance of mitigating acute feelings of need, grief, and distress. This fiction created its own set of expectations which were relatively ungrounded in experience and therefore doomed to disappointment.

The fiction of joint parenting

We have estimated that in 83 per cent of the core sample of cases an incomplete emotional divorce was a significant background factor in child custody and access disputes for one or both partners. The ease or difficulty with which a relationship is given up depends, among other considerations, upon its meaning for the individuals concerned. While it was not possible to explore with parents the complex question of meaning in their marriages in anything other than a superficial way, we did accumulate information which led us to speculate that the children in our sample retained a special personal significance for some parents when those marriages came to an end.

Our observations must remain hypothetical given the circumstances in which the information was obtained and the fact that our informants (the parents themselves) were often anxious to establish their own credentials as parents and to discredit those of former spouses. Despite these considerable qualifications, our impression was that the majority of marriages in our sample lacked the characteristics of peer relationships, and that there were more than usual manifestations of parent/child interactions between the partners. In at least three cases it was our view that the refusal of one partner to surrender an attachment to his or her own parents prevented an effective marital partnership from ever having been established. In several others, the drive to infantilize a partner or to treat them as a parent seemed to have been the dominant pattern of marital interaction. We wondered whether the 'child' which lives on to some degree in all parents might be more than usually prone to finding expression in the behaviour of these parents towards child-related issues during divorce. The needs of parents to be supported by their children might then override the needs of children to be supported by their parents. Our impressions, while subjective, derive from the chronological coincidence of marriage and parenthood, and one-sided patterns of parenting which operated during and after marriage.

One third of the marriages in the core sample (33 per cent) were preceded by the conception of a child. This includes the one unmarried couple in the sample, whose decision to live together was similarly precipitated by pregnancy. A further 7 couples (23.3 per cent of the additional 33 per cent of couples whose first child was born within two years of marriage) conceived a child within six months of marriage. Altogether, of the 29 cases in which the date of marriage or cohabitation was known, the decision to marry or live together coincided with the decision to start a family in 17 cases (56.3 per cent of the sample). If there is an overlap between partnering and parenting roles at the beginning of marriage, we wondered whether there might be particular difficulties separating the two roles when marriage ends.

There may be no special significance attached to these figures in an age where couples increasingly live together and defer marriage until a child is conceived. The legal contract of marriage is then an inextricable part of the decision to start a family. Yet two-thirds of the 9 marriages in which the bride was pregnant took place between 1968 and 1975, a period when cohabitation was a less established stage of courtship than it is today – especially among the very young.

Seven of the 10 pregnant brides were 22 years old or younger at their wedding, and 4 of these were teenagers. Three of the teenagers married men who were at least ten years their senior. We speculated that in some cases, the primary motivating force behind the decision to start a family was to establish a family and parents for the partners (perhaps as an alternative to the families from which they came), rather than to become parents themselves. By creating children, parents may hope to create the conditions in which they can be cared for, nurtured, protected, affirmed, and generally allowed to live unlived aspects of their own past lives. In hoping for this, parents in our sample would be no different in kind from other parents. Creating a family is the most intense way for adults to reconstruct and recreate their own childhood experiences; therein lie the pleasures and pains of parenthood. If a difference exists, it may be in the degree to which the needs of these parents to create families (and parents) for themselves predominated over other considerations. From the outset of marriage there may have been a greater than usual confusion between the need to create a child and to recreate the self, a confusion that may provide a basis for the special difficulties so often encountered at the time of divorce in distinguishing between parenting roles and personal needs.

The cautions attached to information supplied by parents during the course of welfare enquiries apply much more strongly to what they said about parenting practices in the later stages of marriage, or after separation. Accepting this limitation, it was our impression that in two-thirds of our core sample cases practical parenting responsibilities had been very unevenly divided between men and women during marriage, women usually carrying the greater (and sometimes exclusive) share of the day-to-day care. In a few cases men had played no part at all in their children's upbringing.

This estimate may again correspond with the division of parental responsibilities in families generally; the core sample might well reflect patterns of child-rearing practice in the community as a whole. However, if one accepts that fathers are likely to become more involved with their children as they get older (an assumption which is often made, although not necessarily grounded in fact), one might expect fathers in the core sample to have been more practically and emotionally involved with them than they were. Of the children in our sample 85.5 per cent were at school and 30.9 per cent were over 12 years old (these statistics overstate the ages of children at separation which occurred months, and in some cases years before our contact with parents). Some mothers felt intensely about having been left 'holding the baby' (a term that they sometimes also applied to husbands) and drew a direct link between the burden of feeling unsupported as parents and the breakdown of their marriages. The uninvolved men in our sample divided between those who accepted such descriptions as more or less true (defining their chief contribution to family life as having been through their breadwinning role) and those who contested such minimization of their involvement as parents. The sense of there having been a history of single parenting in the family, when it was agreed by partners, was attributed not only to the failure of men to assert themselves as fathers, but also to women who operated a closed shop at home. In the context of divorce, and in the context of the enquiry relationship, it was common for women to complain about the interest men were showing in their children in comparison with their past involvement as parents:

'Before all this cropped up he didn't care a sod about his children. . . . The only time you'd think he cared about the children was when his mother'd come, or his family, and this was to impress them. Any of his family would tell you the same. That was the thing with him, he'd have to impress people. I wondered if the welfare officers could see that – see that he didn't really care.'

The phenomenon of men showing an unprecedented degree of interest in children following separation (if phenomenon it is) might be accounted for in a number of ways. It would not be surprising for parents to experience a renewed surge of feeling for children during divorce, associated with a keen appreciation of what they might be in danger of losing in terms of family life, affection, parental esteem, and the marriage. Mixed feelings about the breakdown of the marriage might be managed by splitting, recognizing in the children all that had been good in the marriage, and in the former spouse all that had been bad. A child might be envied for retaining the love and affection of the spouse, and claimed as a means of restoring what had been lost from the marriage. Dispossessed, parents might feel an intensified need to cling to children to provide personal meaning, self-esteem and social position in their lives.

However compelling the reasons, joint involvement as parents after separation was difficult to achieve. Of the 20 cases in which mothers had sole *de facto* care and control of their children at the time reports were ordered (fathers looked after their children in 3 cases, while joint arrangements were operating at that time for the remaining 7) there had been no access in 9 cases. Access was irregular or infrequent in a further 4 cases, and in 1, where a father had *de facto* custody, it was made impossible for a mother to see her children. At a conservative estimate almost half of the cases in our sample had either introduced or perpetuated a serious disruption in the relationships between children and one of their parents after separation. It was ostensibly dissatisfaction with this state of affairs which resulted in applications to the courts and in the welfare enquiries themselves.

If our impression of there having been little joint parenting in the core sample of cases was borne out by fact, then the applications to courts to instigate and enforce joint parenting may have been based more upon wish than experience. At its extreme, the bid for joint parenting may have rested on the experience of single parenting practice. That is not to disqualify the intent as being impossible to fulfil, but it does suggest there is a gulf between what is expected to come out of applications to the courts and from welfare enquiries, and what can be sustained on the basis of past experience. Should the core sample of cases be little different from most other families in terms of parenting practice, one could argue that what is being attempted and encouraged at the time of divorce (where circumstances are, to say the least, unfavourable) has yet to be realized in the more favourable environment of unbroken marriage.

The courier enquiries

In the last chapter we identified four groups of cases in our core sample. Three described patterns of divorce in which a lingering attachment to the marriage formed a significant part of child custody and access disputes (the *nominal*, *shot-gun*, and *long-lease* divorces). The fourth loosely assembled together those cases in which such an attachment was not considered to be particularly significant to the disputes.

It would be misleading to suggest there were clear differences between the four groups of cases in terms of their expectations. Most couples anticipated an investigation rather than an offer of a service. Many were unclear about the role of the welfare officer when it extended beyond reporting. Some looked for an advocate, for an ally, and for decisive action. All wanted to be given a fair hearing and to be vindicated by the report and the court decision. Several wanted practical help and advice, and a few made ambivalent bids for a therapeutic or counselling response.

The two couples in the *nominal* group were amongst the most confused in their expectations, both as to what they wanted and how they understood the welfare officer's role. Mr and Mrs Sheen oscillated between anger over the intrusion of courts and welfare officers into their lives – 'it was very unfair, other people deciding about intimate things and about one's own property' – and an intense wish to be relieved of the responsibility for deciding what should be done. Mrs Sheen was the more outspoken of the two parents about her frustration, and also the more open about her confusion. At one level she wanted expert intervention, 'a sort of specialist jury, so that different things could be dealt with by different people'; at another she invited a therapeutic response:

'I really don't know what's going on inside me. [She refers to a conversation with a marriage guidance counsellor who said that she might need to go and see someone who could "Go within her, and find out what's inside her, and bring it out".] I don't seem to be able to explain to people what's deep down inside. It's not just a case of sitting here and saying "I want to he free, I want to go out into the big wide world". It's not just that. It's sort of mixed up feelings . . . perhaps I need a doctor to analyse and say "This is what's wrong with you".'

Mr and Mrs King, of the *shot-gun* category of divorces, reacted defensively to the order for a welfare report. Mrs King had come into contact with social workers and welfare officers during her previous divorce, an experience which had resulted in the child from that marriage being taken into the care of a local authority for a short period. She feared losing her child again. Accurately sensing her husband's wish to return to the family, she repeatedly stated that the marriage was at an end. Mr King's application for custody of the child of their own marriage was motivated by wishing to respond to his son's attachment to him, wanting to obstruct his wife's divorce, and hoping to regain his position in the family. He also thought that a successful custody application would provide a solution to the practical problems he faced – especially those of unemployment and having no home of his own. The welfare enquiry was therefore regarded as a possible means of obtaining reinstatement to a number of roles from which he had been displaced.

Mrs King was one of only four wives in our sample who were older than their husbands. She was Mr King's senior by three years, and, unlike him, had been married before. Sometimes she talked about Mr King as if he were the third of her children. Mr King's welfare officer sensed his loss to be connected with feelings about being ousted from home and family as well as from a marriage; he had returned to live with his own parents when the marriage broke down. In certain respects, then, Mr King wanted to be restored to a family.

Mr Hood and Mrs Ham (of the *long-lease* group of divorces) were out to discredit each other. In this, they looked to their welfare officer to uphold their own claims and to conduct a thorough investigation that would expose the weaknesses in the case of their opponent. The welfare officer was designated as a pawn in a process of strategic manoeuvrings which had a long antecedent history. Each side looked to him for unqualified support and would be content with nothing less. 'We provided the house', observed Mrs Ham, 'and the welfare officer should have supported that.' Mr Hood complained that the enquiry had not been rigorous enough: 'When I explained to the welfare officer he could easily have found out what a liar she was, but he didn't. He didn't follow anything up that would have made my case more solid by proving her to be a liar.' Both parents were familiar with the criminal courts, knew how to play the system, and were experienced in the kinds of leverage that might be applied to good effect.

Of the four courier cases, Mr Hood and Mrs Ham were the exception to the 'parental marriage' pattern. They had a long-established peer relationship, one which was competitive, mistrustful, but affectionate. They knew each other well, and could rely upon each other for mutual support in scapegoating the system.

From the fourth group, Mr and Mrs Robin regarded the order for a welfare report as intrusive and unnecessary, and put it down to the judge having had a bad day. They maintained a collusive agreement which was designed to deflect unwelcome attention from outsiders and to preserve the situation as it was. By doing this they avoided the uncovering of certain issues which might have complicated the arrangements already worked out between them for their children, and which could have delayed their divorce. The cost of this collusion for Mr Robin was that he had to forgo an opportunity to talk over his feelings about the marriage ending, and the chance to elicit the appreciation for his efforts he anticipated a more thorough enquiry might have produced. These were needs which the enquiry prevented him from disclosing, but which could be expressed in the neutral context of a research interview.

In the next chapter we look in detail at the experiences of these four sets of parents as they underwent the process of being investigated for a court report and were encouraged to reach agreement. We record how satisfied they were with the outcome and how far their expectations were met. In two cases, parents and welfare officers remained at cross purposes; in one some headway was made in reconciling these purposes; in one the outcome can be described in retrospect as a collusive agreement.

who had remained with their father during her absence. Despite having a decree nisi, the parents continued to live together throughout the enquiry period and were still doing so when contacted for a follow-up interview ten months later.

The enquiry: the welfare officers' story

The enquiry was undertaken by a man and a woman (from the IMS and Divorce Unit respectively). It spanned a period of five months from case allocation to filing of report with an active interviewing period of three months. There were six meetings with one or more members of the Sheen household, representing 10½ hours of interviewing time (but considerably more if occasions when both welfare officers conducted an interview is counted as double time). Reports were obtained from the schools attended by the two girls. The Sheens declined an invitation to come to the office to discuss their welfare report, although Mrs Sheen wanted to hear the recommendation by telephone. Two years after the report was filed their case had not come back to court. They were one of eight enquiries in the core sample where parents did not return to court for a decision.

The welfare officers decided to open the enquiry by seeing the family together; the girls were considered to be old enough to participate in discussions about their future. At this stage it was thought that Mr and Mrs Sheen were living at different addresses and letters were sent to them separately, inviting them to a family meeting at the Divorce Unit. On the day of the appointment the female officer was ill and the male officer, who by then had learned that the parents were living together, decided to drop the family interview in favour of seeing Mr and Mrs Sheen on their own to clarify whether or not their marriage was at an end. The girls were seen briefly to explain this change of plan, and the rest of the time was spent talking to the parents together. The interview focused upon the ambiguity about the status of their relationship introduced by their decision to live under the same roof.

The Sheens described a marriage in which they had become estranged from each other and had derived major satisfactions (some of them vicarious) from the achievements of their children. Mrs Sheen was confused about herself and what she wanted from the future, while Mr Sheen adopted the position of one who waits (resentfully) for another to sort themselves out. An appointment with a marriage guidance counsellor had been made but not kept. While there were clear indications that Mr Sheen wanted a reconciliation, his wife clung to the idea of divorce as if it represented some kind of lifeline for her.

The male welfare officer was not at all convinced by this and subsequent interviews that the marriage was over. In his mind this question needed resolving before going on to consider who should have custody of the children. However, the issue about children was very much alive for both parents. Mrs Sheen was anxious to resolve the question despite her confusion in other areas – perhaps because of it – and applied pressure on the welfare officer to take responsibility for deciding. Mr Sheen indicated that if she wanted her divorce the girls should be asked to decide with whom they wanted to live; he remained secure in the knowledge that they were more likely to choose him than their mother who had left them for the best part of a year. Anxious to avoid being precipitated into premature negotiations about custody, and equally anxious that the weight of responsibility for making a choice should not rest with the girls, the welfare officer arranged to visit Mr and Mrs Sheen at home to try and clarify the confusion that surrounded their relationship.

He discussed the interview with his colleague when she returned to work, and they decided upon a division of labour which would leave him free to continue to explore the ambiguities in the marriage with the Sheens while she saw the girls to assess the impact of the situation upon them. They agreed that at some future date, when the time seemed right, parents and children should be brought together for a family meeting.

In connection with both marital and parenting issues discussions took on a circular and locked nature. A see-saw pattern of interaction ensured that if one partner initiated movement in one direction it would be counterbalanced by movement in the opposite direction by the other. Confusion was introduced to issues which showed signs of becoming clear. The result was an impasse.

While this was frustrating to both welfare officers, it worried the man (familiar with the prevarications and uncertainties encountered in his mainline work as a marital therapist) less than the woman, who had spoken to the two girls. She reported that, unlike their parents, the girls seemed clear about what they wanted. They wished to know whether they were likely to have to move house; they did not know what the situation was between their parents but wanted to be told; whatever the outcome, they hoped both parents would be actively involved in their lives; they wanted their parents to take charge of the situation. By implication they looked to their father to effect these changes. Of their two parents he was thought to be the better financial manager and disciplinarian. The female welfare officer discerned their need for someone who could be clear about where they stood and could provide the boundaries which make for security. The elder girl (the spokeswoman) also thought that her younger sister and mother 'rubbed each other up the wrong way'. Aware that the prevailing climate was unsettling for the two girls she suggested to her colleague that a family meeting was called in which some pressure might be brought to bear on the parents to encourage them to relieve their daughters' burden of uncertainty.

A family meeting was convened with the express purpose of clarifying for the two girls what was happening between their parents, and to consider whether there were issues on which there might be agreement. Mr and Mrs Sheen responded by saying they thought the girls would fare best if the family continued to live under one roof, but Mrs Sheen made it clear that she intended to press on for her divorce decree to be made absolute. The girls agreed that they would prefer their parents to stay together, but indicated that if it came to the crunch they would feel more secure with their father. As there seemed to be agreement, the welfare officers proposed that a report was written supporting an arrangement which would uphold joint responsibility for the day-to-day care of the girls. They suggested a further meeting after three weeks, to allow the parents time to reconsider the proposal and to enable the welfare officers to enquire about the legal implications of what would be an unusual recommendation for joint care and control.[1] Despite the agreement, Mrs Sheen expressed dissatisfaction with the welfare officers for not injecting sufficient clarity into their discussion and for failing to supply practical information (the example she cited was about her rights as a DHSS benefit claimant). She also pressed them to decide what should be done on their behalf. In contrast, Mr Sheen registered his appreciation that efforts had been made to help them exercise their own responsibility over future arrangements for the girls.

Three weeks later the Sheens had changed their minds. They thought that living together was an unreal option and believed they should sell the house and divide the proceeds. Mr Sheen added that he had mixed feelings about being left to bring up the girls single-handed. His wife had obtained a job and seemed more composed and confident than before. Both parents said they thought the enquiry had gone on for long enough and the welfare officers should decide. Irritated by the Sheens' prevarication and determination to offload responsibility, the welfare officers explored whether Mr Sheen's statement represented a real change of heart. Satisfied that it was more a criticism directed at his wife than a change of heart (now that he had landed on a snake?), the welfare officers agreed that the time had come to write the report. They said they would be recommending an order for joint custody, with care and control going to Mr Sheen but providing the girls with reasonable access to their mother.

At the time the report was filed the welfare officers thought there had been modest gains as a result of their efforts. The male officer felt rather more hopeful than his female colleague, who had reservations about how much either parent really wished to be involved with their children. Nevertheless, the girls had been given an opportunity to state their feelings and their views, and channels of communication had been opened between all the family members. They thought that, on balance, the Sheens would separate, although they were by no means convinced that this would happen nor that it would resolve the problem to which divorce was supposed to provide an answer. In their assessment profile they concluded:

> 'A positive outcome will be either that they have customized the joint living/parenting relationship, without the friction evident in the enquiry period, or that one or other parent has left and accepted the change – evidenced by a continuing and appropriate involvement with the girls. No change would mean that they continued living together, stuck in the same doubts and frustrations as during the time we saw them.'

The enquiry: the parents' story

The woman researcher, who interviewed Mr and Mrs Sheen after the enquiry, failed to secure a personal meeting despite two months of trying. She had to settle for a separate telephone conversation with each parent. Mr Sheen at first blocked access to the lady who was still legally his wife, saying that she was in a precarious emotional state and an interview would be experienced by her as intrusive. When she finally spoke to both parents the impression was that they were as deadlocked as ever, and that the criteria for no change spelt out in the profile was exactly the situation that had pertained earlier. She concluded the couple were back at square one.

Overall, Mr Sheen had found the enquiry experience helpful, although contact with the court system had exacerbated the trauma of divorce for him:

> 'My wife did not envisage how much distress it was going to cause us all. We never discuss it now. It was very unfair other people deciding about intimate things and about your own property – very uncomfortable. [He went on to say] I would have liked earlier voluntary help.'

He valued the welfare meetings for the opportunity they provided to talk about the marriage, although this process had become more taxing as the enquiry went on. Home visits which 'eased the stress' were preferred to office appointments. He saw in the male officer an ally who was prepared to listen to his story and who encouraged the couple to take responsibility for their predicament:

> 'He gave us a breathing space between solicitors. He was a breath of fresh air and such a relief after all those solicitor types. He sat and listened and did not want money. He was relaxed, easy, no pressure. He made it clear that the decision lay with us alone.'

However, he had also wanted a halt to be called to long drawn-out proceedings:

> 'We were disheartened and exhausted and needed the court to decide . . . it's like my father said to me "Time is the greatest healer" but the pain has not disappeared overnight. It can't ever be the same, but it's made me think a lot more now. I am quite happy about the outcome; it's best for the children still to have us, and not to split.'

It is interesting that although he said he had needed the court to decide, the court never did decide. Once the report was completed the legal process was left in abeyance.

At the fourth attempt, the researcher made contact with Mrs Sheen. On the telephone she sounded anxious and still preoccupied with preserving herself against potentially overwhelming outside forces. Her experience of the enquiry had been one of unwarranted intrusion which had threatened to take over her children as well as herself:

'It was too painful . . . the entire welfare process was unhelpful. It contributed more to the friction between me and my husband than anything else . . . home visits were an invasion of privacy . . . they tried to impress their views on you too much. In trying to get my views out I felt overwhelmed by them . . . Like I said, I'm trying to forget the whole painful business, so I have not asked them [the children] and I hope they are forgetting like me. I can tell you that they [the welfare officers] put things in their minds that weren't there before. It was grotesque.'

As frustrating and threatening as the intrusion was her experience of there being no-one to bump up against who could help her to define herself and where she stood: 'They listened, you could see them digesting but they didn't react to me . . . their passivity was off-putting . . . they were too introverted; their extreme passivity was very disturbing. It was unbearable.'

Comment

The Sheen's marriage can be said to have been experienced as a prison by Mrs Sheen and a fortress by her husband. This was one way of looking at it when the enquiry was in progress. At follow-up the metaphor changed: for Mrs Sheen the marriage can be said to have served the function of an asylum, a soft-padded cell, which provided a kind of restrictive security against the lunatic world threatening to invade and engulf her. Either way Mrs Sheen was designated, or designated herself, as the prisoner or the patient. She was the one who longed to break free, and who was confused and unable to know her own mind.

To write about the Sheens in such terms is to write in the language of therapists. Images convey experience. As marital therapists we hypothesized that the struggle for identity experienced so painfully by Mrs Sheen was one in which her husband also shared. For this reason they generated in their marriage a

pattern of interaction resembling an adolescent daughter rebell-
ing against a controlling father. But the roles could have been
reversed, and nearly were when Mrs Sheen became stronger.

At one level, both parents wanted someone to take responsibility for their predicament. They avoided coming into the limelight
to fight their own corner, and they preserved a twilight existence
halfway between marriage and divorce. Part of the reason for this
may lie in their not really knowing what they wanted, and feeling
it was restricting to be too clearly defined by others yet unsafe not
to be defined by them at all: Mrs Sheen was as frightened of
passivity as she was of intrusion.

Divorce can be said to have thrown into relief the needs of a
fragile psychological system (in the marriage and in each parent)
which was by-passed by a legal system concerned to process
divorces and promote certainty for children. The welfare enquiry
came within hailing distance of the adolescent conflicts of the
parents, but was bound to relate more to the needs of the real
adolescents than to those of their parents. The girls made it clear
they wanted to be told what was happening between their
parents. Their parents were less clear about what they wanted.
Welfare officers offered something which was both longed-for
and feared: freedom from responsibility. That freedom risked the
removal of structures which had defined the Sheens throughout
most of their marriage: their role as parents. While they might
wish to jettison the burden of parenthood, by doing so they
risked jettisoning an important part of themselves in the process.
Perhaps it is not surprising that the welfare report was not acted
upon. A court decision was not to provide the solution for the
Sheens.

In circumstances like these we would argue that a therapeutic
service was required to help make sense of the dilemmas and
confusion presented by parents. Neither marriage guidance nor
the Divorce Unit was quite right for the Sheens. Marriage
guidance was seen as a process for saving the marriage, whereas
court welfare suggested too final a break for them at a time when
they were in two minds. It is possible that the ready and early
availability of information about the implications – practical,
procedural and emotional – of instigating divorce action would
have helped them to anticipate the effects of their actions.
Divorce counselling may have been a more acceptable form of
help than either marriage counselling or litigation. The decision
to seek counselling about divorce is voluntarily entered into and

easily reversed. There is less pressure on time than in a Divorce Unit, which has to furnish courts with reports and has different sets of priorities. In short, Mr and Mrs Sheen drew attention to a possible deficiency in the range of services to those considering divorce. Whether or not they would have been able to use a divorce counselling service had it been available is another matter, although a very important one. The point to be taken here is the general one that divorcing parents may need therapeutic or counselling help for which the welfare setting cannot cater.

Musical Chairs: the King enquiry

The distinctive feature of musical chairs is that there is always one chair less than the number of players taking part. When the music stops, somebody is bound to be left out. The music stopped for Mr King when his wife ejected him from their home and took out a court injunction to prevent him from returning. Mr King suspected, correctly as it turned out, that his place had been taken by another man.

The enquiry was initiated by Mr King applying for custody of the only child of this, his wife's second marriage. He had been encouraged to apply by hearing his six-year-old son suggest he would like to live with him. Because he had alleged that Mrs King was not caring properly for her children, the terms of the report included the elder boy from her first marriage as well. Mr King was out of work and living with his parents when he made his application. He had been separated for two months.

The enquiry: the welfare officers' story

The welfare enquiry was undertaken by a man and a woman (from the IMS and the Divorce Unit respectively). The report spanned three months, with the bulk of the work concentrated in a four-week period. One or more members of the family were seen on six separate occasions, representing six hours of time spent in direct contact with parents and children. Reports were obtained from a school, and an educational welfare officer was consulted. Both parents attended an appointment at the Divorce Unit to read the welfare report which endorsed an agreement proposing joint custody, care, and control to Mrs King, and reasonable access to Mr King. Six weeks later they were both present in court to hear the agreement ratified in law.

In order to clarify the issues which divided them, and to assess their potential to work at these together, the two welfare officers invited Mr and Mrs King to a joint meeting at the office. Mrs King telephoned to say she was uneasy about a joint appointment because she and her husband did not get on when they were together; she did, however, agree to keep to the original plan. Part of the process of that interview, in which the problem about capable parenting was redefined in terms of Mr King's reluctance to relinquish the marriage, has been described earlier (see pp. 84–8). Three interesting developments occurred in that interview. In the first place, there was a quite unpremeditated division of labour between the welfare officers. The female officer addressed the child-care issues in the case and offered to explore these with Mrs King in order that her husband might be reassured that his son was being well looked after. The male officer related more to Mr King's reluctance to give up his marriage, and offered to see him on his own to discuss his feelings about divorce in private. Second, the parents became less angry towards and suspicious of each other and their officers; there was a degree of accessibility between all those in the room which had not been present at the start of the interview. Finally, the support given to Mr King (as a spurned partner as well as a parent), and the reassurance Mrs King obtained from not being pressured into taking her husband back, was followed by an agreement. We believed these three developments were causally related.

Unlike most of the cases in the core sample, it was possible with the Kings to empower them to take responsibility for the enquiry and to make use of it for their own ends to effect change. Hearing Mr King's anxiety (rather than blame), it was Mrs King who proposed that we could 'make a social welfare arrangement for someone to come round and see me, to prove to Mr King that those children are being looked after properly', to which Mr King replied 'if they're looked after properly I'd be more easy'. The management of the rest of the enquiry was discussed and planned with the parents present. There was a degree of party control over the enquiry which was lacking in most other cases.

The work which followed underpinned the position which had been reached at the first meeting. Subsequent appointments were arranged weekly in order to keep the momentum going. Mr King saw the male officer to share his regrets about the marriage ending, to talk about the problems he faced by having no job or home of his own, and to discuss the significance of his son for him in these circumstances. By the end of the interview he had accepted that his application for custody had been prompted more by passion than reason. The welfare officers met the children in the course of a home visit, and were introduced to Mrs King's new partner. Satisfied that the children were receiving adequate care, the female officer saw Mr King to give him the reassurance he had asked for.

The next joint meeting was spent checking how access was going and planning the court report. Mr and Mrs King were chatting together when they came into the room and the change for the better between them was plain to see. The original agreement was confirmed. A proposal that custody should be shared supported Mr King in feeling that his position as a parent was being given formal recognition without raising Mrs King's fears that she was opening the door for him to return into her life. They came to the office on one further occasion to read the completed welfare report before it was filed with the court.

Although the children were seen, the focus of attention in this enquiry was principally upon the relationship between two parents. An alienating pattern of interaction had followed from Mrs King's decision to shed the marriage in order to make room for a new man in her life. Mr King's behaviour had then been organized around getting back to and at a woman who had cut him out of the family. This in turn threatened Mrs King, causing her to retreat further and so aggravate the cycle. When Mrs King was reassured about her divorce, and Mr King was reinstated as a parent, they were able to have the kind of relationship appropriate to their circumstances.

The welfare officers considered they had done a good job in this case and had contributed towards a successful outcome. They had witnessed substantial changes in the way the parents saw the custody dispute and in the way they related to each other. As a consequence of these shifts it had been possible to help them reach agreement. The agreement was thought to have been connected with the process of distinguishing between feelings of hurt and anger which were the result of the failed marriage, and feelings of anxious concern for the future well-being of the children, which were appropriate to the couple as parents. So long as this distinction remained blurred, the battle about divorce was in danger of being fought out in the nursery.

The task of distinguishing between and attending to the separate issues was made easier by two welfare officers working together. When the enquiry was completed they predicted that 'the improvement will hold, and Mr King will keep up his interest in [his son], although not in the elder boy in whom he has always shown less interest'.

The enquiry: the parents' story

His view   The Kings were approached for a follow-up interview eight months after the report had been filed and six months after the court decision. Mr King failed to respond to the appointment letter and was not available on the telephone; he was therefore not seen. Mrs King later explained that he was no longer living with his parents, but was vague about his current whereabouts. It was learned indirectly that Mr King had been ejected from his parents' home and was moving from hostel to hostel in search of temporary accommodation. There were other signs of decline, a fate befalling a substantial number of men in the core sample.

Only one piece of feedback came directly from Mr King and this was given to the female officer during the course of the enquiry. When he had met her to hear the outcome of the home visit he had looked positively spruce, and had said he felt much better after his talk with 'that young fellow'. A little earlier, that same officer had met Mrs King in a supermarket. She had said that her husband was behaving much better towards her, concluding that 'somebody must have spoken to him'.

Her view   Mrs King accepted the invitation to be visited at home for a follow-up. She said she had valued the advice she had received from her welfare officers and found them 'helpful' and 'fair': 'It helped. Right at the beginning we flew at one another. It did a lot of good. My ex-husband realized what he was doing to stop me getting a divorce. He'd been awkward.' She compared this experience favourably with the welfare report which had been prepared when her first marriage had failed. This time round the enquiry had 'cleared the air'. Having two welfare officers had assisted in this process: 'She was more for me and my side, and he was for helping Mr King. He saw him a couple of times to help him break off the marriage. He didn't want to give up his son.'

Unfortunately, success in instigating access had brought a new set of problems in its wake. After the court decision, Mrs King married again. She subsequently found that her youngest son's visits to his father had become increasingly unsettling for her and the family. He had become more difficult to control:

> 'He's getting really out of hand because of his dad [who] goes round to the school playground, gives him sweets, tells him things . . . is seeing him more . . . he comes home full of what his dad has promised and said, and it cuts across other family arrangements or outings. . . . We've got nothing to punish him with. He gets away with things. I often threaten him with he won't see his father.'

The boy's allegiance to his father was experienced by Mrs King as a threat to the position and authority of her new husband. This was a second source of discomfort:

> 'It's these last weeks. He comes in cheeky, shows off about his dad in front of Bill [her new husband] and hurts him. . . . It's upsetting now, especially for Bill. He didn't really agree with access at all. He wanted a clean break from [Mr King]. Perhaps I should have done that. I don't want anything more to do with him.'

It was Bill, the new husband, who pointed out a third source of difficulty: 'There's another thing. He comes back and talks about his dad, and that might upset the other one who hasn't seen his father – doesn't even know his father.' To which Mrs King added: 'Now, all of a sudden, I've got [the elder boy] wanting to see his father after nine years.'

The researcher found herself drawn into a counselling role, pointing out that it sounded as if Mrs King had things to discuss with her former husband, and suggesting she might contact her welfare officer again for some voluntary help. Mrs King is known not to have taken up the latter suggestion. The researcher tried to speak to the boy who had access to his father but this was made impossible by him and the adults present. There was therefore no opportunity of saying whether he had been helped by the enquiry or not. Gaining access to children was as difficult in this instance as it can be for welfare officers who have to make an assessment for the courts.

Comment

A brief, concentrated piece of work effectively separated feelings resulting from a failed partnership from questions which concerned future patterns of involvement between parents and children. This allowed the Kings to work together as parents to enable access between father and son to take place successfully.

On the face of it, this case lends support to the commonly held view that negotiations between parents about future patterns of parenting are most successful when conducted soon after separation, and certainly before attitudes harden and positions become entrenched. We could, however, cite other cases in which the rawness of a recently broken marriage made discussion between parents quite impossible because of their sense of inflicted injury. The Kings were accessible to an intervention that addressed the different aspects of their problem and they were capable of responding. It was clear at the very first interview that they could be flexible and that an agreement between them was feasible.

However, circumstances change. One might guess that Mrs King's decision to remarry so shortly after her separation and divorce inflamed a still open wound for her former husband and his son. There was an emotional motive for each of them to unsettle, if not sabotage, the new partnership. In many of the core sample cases the remarriage of one partner was capable of reawakening feelings in the other which may have been dormant for years, and not just for months as in the King's case. Sometimes these feelings were strong enough to trigger applications to courts, as happened in the next case to be described. Even without a new marriage to contend with, a successful access arrangement between father and son might have been expected to unsettle the family system by generating envy in the elder boy who also wanted a father to visit and spoil him.

It could be argued that we, as welfare officers, might have anticipated some of the knock-on effects of successful access, and countered these by recommending a supervision order. This would have provided extended support through a potentially stressful period of change. Because these parents had unhappy memories of past social work intervention we might have known it would not be easy for them to come back for further help on their own initiative. However, extended help would have required a change in the nature and primary task of the Divorce

Unit. Although resources to fund action of this kind would be well justified in terms of preventing future stress in the family, predicting events and estimating their effects is a skilled and chancy business. The Kings' experience suggests that some families would benefit from extended support and counselling, and perhaps this is particularly indicated when they are close in time to the final separation in a marriage. Many more supervision orders would be recommended if welfare officers were in a position to play safe in this respect. Yet barriers might still remain between them and families because of their primary task and official status. An alternative approach would involve creating centres which were accessible and easy to use for people who might be least inclined to tangle with officialdom and the authority associated with it. To prevent the breakdown of yet another marriage, the Kings may well have required help, support, and resources over and above what the Divorce Unit was in a position to supply at that time.

Cluedo: the Hood/Ham enquiry

Cluedo is a game for detective investigators. A crime has been committed, and by a process of elimination the culprit is discovered. There were four players in the Hood/Ham enquiry. For Mr Hood the offence was Mr and Mrs Ham's attempt to deny him as a father. For Mr and Mrs Ham the offence was Mr Hood's unwarranted intrusion into their lives. Neither side was under any doubt about the identity of the culprit. The fourth player was the welfare officer. He was unclear who had committed what offence. Caught between two totally discrepant accounts, he only knew that someone was lying. At first he joined the game in the hope of discovering the truth, but very soon he gave up and suggested a different kind of game – say, 'Kiss and Tell'? Sadly, the three other players refused to play.

Mr Hood and Mrs Ham had been separated for six years when the current dispute surfaced. Fifteen months after marrying again, Mrs Ham and her new husband applied to adopt the eight-year-old twins of her marriage to Mr Hood. Mr Hood countered this application with one of his own, applying to the same court for reasonable access to his sons. The registrar ordered that an adoption and welfare enquiry should be carried out concurrently, and that both applications should be heard together when the reports were completed. The adoption enquiry was assigned to a social worker from the social services department who acted as guardian ad litem.

The enquiry: the welfare officer's story

This was one of seven enquiries in the core sample not to have been co-worked. The welfare officer was a member of the IMS team, and this was the first case he took on. The report spanned nine months, including a break of three months when Mrs Ham gave birth to a baby. The active reporting period was no more than five months. One or more members of the family were seen on twelve separate occasions, involving 15 hours of interviewing time. There was a substantial amount of contact with the social worker preparing the adoption report, and an enquiry was registered with the Criminal Records Office. The report submitted to the court endorsed an agreement, albeit reluctantly arrived at, in which the twins were to have reasonable access to their father subject to certain considerations of detail. The adoption application was withdrawn. The welfare report recommendation was endorsed by the court, but seven months later (one month after the follow-up interviews were conducted) the matter returned to court because the arrangements were not working satisfactorily. At this second hearing, the conditions of access were defined and a warning was given to the parents that a further welfare report would be ordered if the new arrangement failed to work out.

Having heard from the social worker that the parents had not spoken directly to each other for at least a year, and that their accounts were very discrepant, the welfare officer chose what he considered to be the manageable option of beginning the enquiry by seeing each parent separately. His naive assumption was that he might learn where the truth lay from these separate meetings.

At the first meeting, Mr Hood said he had enjoyed relaxed and fairly frequent contact with his sons (and, incidentally, with his former wife) until Mrs Ham remarried. He had last seen them shortly before their most recent birthday, but since then he had been denied access. At her interview, Mrs Ham said there had been no contact between father and sons for six years and claimed they would not recognize their father. Moreover, she said the twins had grown up to regard Mr Ham as their father and Mr Hood would be a complete stranger to them. The welfare officer found both parents very convincing, which made life rather difficult for him. Totally discrepant accounts can have the effect of driving the listener mad, and expedite the search for a view, if not the truth. He was faced with the choice of organizing the enquiry around proving one parent to be a liar (which, if it were possible, would not necessarily guarantee an improved outcome for the children), or doing something else.

He chose to concentrate his efforts on working with Mr and Mrs Ham. As his starting point he picked up Mrs Ham's assertion that the twins did not know who their real father was, and discussed, first with her and later with her husband, the reasons why they had not been told. He hoped to encourage disclosure of this vital information as a first step in the enquiry. While supporting this approach, his Divorce Unit senior advised him to check out the stories further.

As discussions proceeded, the issue of 'telling the twins' receded, making way for an implicit acknowledgement that they already knew that Mr Ham was not their father. The Hams conceded that Mr Hood's mother had, until recently, seen a lot of her grandsons, and this was a substantial crack in their presentation. The twins were seen twice on their own at home, but seemed anxious to deflect attention away from themselves while the adults sorted out their differences. They spent the whole of the first contact talking about and demonstrating their toys. At the second meeting they drew a family tree with the welfare officer, completely excluding the father's side of the family until told that their mother had talked about granny's visits to their house. She was then drawn in. The welfare officer used the opportunity to tell the boys he had visited their granny and that she missed them and hoped to see them soon.

By this time the welfare officer mistrusted what the Hams were telling him, and impelled by his senior who also thought they were stalling, he took them to task for not having 'been told the half of it'. Mr Ham, as the spokesman, was outraged that Mr Hood had applied for access 'out of the blue' and without consulting them first. His wife was concerned that the bid for access undermined their attempts to build a new family unit, and that it was placing them under intolerable strain, especially when she had only recently given birth to another child. They wanted to integrate their new family, including the twins, whereas Mr Hood was seen as wanting to dismantle it, taking them out. At this point the social worker and welfare officer took up different positions. The social worker argued that priority should be given to supporting the position of Mr Ham in the new family unit; the welfare officer argued that the chief priority was not to deprive the twins of their real father. They reflected the conflict between the Hams and Mr Hood.

The report then developed into a struggle to convene a joint meeting. This involved working with Mrs Ham's divided loyalties (which became ever clearer when she was seen on her own) and her fears that the boys would grow up like their father and would be seduced by 'fast cars and big presents'. It also involved discussing with Mr Hood why he had acted through the courts rather than presenting his request informally, and alerting him to the need to be reliable and consistent if access were to be reintroduced. Mr Hood said he had been angry about being 'shut out', and had gone straight to his solicitor because he could not trust his temper when he felt strongly about things. He thought they were 'getting away with it', and said that given the opportunity he could offer himself as a friendly, worldly-wise uncle to his sons.

A joint meeting between Mrs Ham and Mr Hood was eventually convened. There was more than a hint of blackmail in the negotiations between the parents, and the welfare officer struggled to keep them away from making allegations in order to encourage them to air their fears about the consequences of an adverse court decision. At the end of the interview Mrs Ham traded access for financial support, a condition Mr Hood accepted until he consulted his solicitor and was advised to revoke the offer. This reneging on an agreement enraged Mr Ham who complained about the unjustness of an enquiry process which favoured 'the least accountable person'. He accused the welfare officer of 'fence-sitting', and was all for having the 'battle' in open court.

The battle was averted by an informal meeting between Mr Hood and Mrs Ham, a meeting of which the welfare officer knew nothing until later. This allowed the access agreement to stand. The report was then written, and discussed with Mr and Mrs Ham. Mr Ham described it as 'tepid', and said that from then on he was going to 'keep his cards close to his chest' and 'play the system'. Mr Hood did not see the report. He failed to respond to a letter and did not keep an appointment made by telephone.

The welfare officer, while cautious about making any claim to have facilitated access, thought – with a touching sense of optimism – that he had been instrumental in restoring the balance that had been disturbed by the adoption application. He wrote in his summary:

> 'With hindsight it is easy to say that results would have been more quickly achieved by seeing the parents together from the outset. But it is also possible that in view of what was at stake (in terms of secrets) the same resistance would have been encountered. Perhaps it took time to establish sufficient trust, sense of safety, and time for negotiation . . . before the joint meeting could come up with a suggestion everyone could stomach. I would predict that when the follow-up is carried out, apart from delivering a Christmas present Mr Hood will have seen the twins on no more than one, possibly two, occasions. It would not surprise me if the right to access had not been taken up.'

The enquiry: the parents' story

The prediction that access would not take place turned out to be right, but for reasons different from those suggested in the summary. Mr Hood claimed he was being prevented from visiting his sons. He had made another application to court, and this was heard a month after the follow-up interview took place. The application extended to nine years the period in which the judicial system had been involved with the Hood/Hams over divorce-related issues.

His view   Mr Hood was very critical of the enquiry. It had taken too long, he was 'back to square one'; 'exactly in the same position', and Mrs Ham had made a mockery of the welfare service (something he secretly admired in her):

> 'Well, I told you on the 'phone, I didn't think much of it . . . I don't know whether he was too young or inexperienced, but I don't think he knew what he was talking about half the time. Nothing wrong with him, but my wife walked round and over him . . . I got what I wanted, but I could have got that without all the two and a half years it took to get there . . . It hasn't worked out because my wife is still refusing access . . . She said to me, "There's nothing you can do. They won't put me

in prison for refusing to let you see them", and that's true. No way I could see them unless I snatched them, and that's not in my nature. You see as far as all that divorce welfare was concerned, I knew that he [the welfare officer] was being conned. She's very, very good my wife – we've both worked in night clubs, and there's far more psychology goes on there than there ever will be in college or school.'

About the joint negotiating meeting between him and Mrs Ham he had this to say:

'We had one. It just ended up in an angry scene because she was denying she ever had money from me, and when his back was turned she smiled and smirked at me. She knew she was getting one over him and it was just boiling me up. After that meeting my brother was in a pub, and we all went over to the pub, and in there we were laughing that she put one over him. And I was laughing! I could do that. I don't love her but I do like her, and I understand that she's trying to get the best for herself as much as she can, which is what every human being does. We had a better meeting in the pub – she, me and my brother – than we ever did with him.'

The contest looked set to continue. Mr Hood had been advised by his solicitor to keep a record of his dealings with Mrs Ham to build up a case for when they returned to court. In his search for justice Mr Hood concluded:

'I am a fascist in my thinking. Courts are too lenient. Courts should enforce a penal penalty. I wouldn't like it to be applied, but just to frighten, scare. We all know now in London that if you mug an old lady all you get is a slap on the wrist – plead that you're an underprivileged child. All the welfare services are being conned regularly . . . People just laugh at the law now. Even I laugh at it . . . I don't think there's a lot anyone can do for me now unless we have Enoch Powell back and a fascist law, so people can't get away with it.'

Her view   In fact it was Mr Ham who dominated the follow-up interview, and his wife seemed content to let him speak for her:

'We should have chucked the summons in the waste paper

basket. We're now back at square one. It upset her and cost us a lot . . . if he had tried to contact me before he took legal action we might have been able to talk. But we couldn't talk then and we can't talk now. My view of the service is that we were very dissatisfied with it. The approach wasn't suitable for our circumstances. We were interviewed nine times; my wife was pregnant; we went to the office. Mr Hood was only seen once. We thought he [the welfare officer] did not have a correct view of the whole picture . . . He wanted to show a high-profile involvement. Mr Hood would have been satisfied with less if [the welfare officer] had not got in on it . . . We thought we could resolve things by the three of us talking, but he and the solicitors wanted to be involved . . . We were intelligent enough to weigh up the situation. We weren't a couple of lost sheep going to him for guidance. We knew what was what . . . [he should have asked]: Are the boys unhappy here, unfulfilled here? Are they missing their father? Why didn't he report on this house and compare it with how Mr Hood lives and apply the same criteria? But he would not.'

Mrs Ham joined the interview and endorsed what her husband had said:

'Intervention has done nothing. We wanted to adopt, but that wasn't to be. We've given up now. It was very important two years ago . . . he's depriving our sons while not being willing to bring them up . . . we should never have got into the legal process . . . it is better outside a compulsory system. If we had not panicked and 'phoned a solicitor we could have 'phoned social services or some such.'

The only thread of comfort to be drawn for the welfare officer was added as a rider to her assessment that nothing had changed.

'All the investigation made no difference, didn't change anything. [The welfare officer] was very persuasive. If it hadn't been for him I would never have met Bob [Mr Hood] again. I suppose it helped us [Mr and Mrs Ham] to talk about what had happened a lot more.'

The overwhelming criticism was that the welfare officer was out of line and out of his depth. Perhaps the parents had picked up that he was operating in a subculture very different from and alien to his own. But they were also reacting to a situation which was unchanged and unchanging.

Comment

We will never know if a more experienced officer, adopting a different approach, might have achieved a more satisfactory outcome in this case. As things are, the Hood/Hams stand for the small proportion of parents who seem set upon preserving something unresolved, and who prefer contest to co-operation, litigation to agreement, and the triumph of securing a conviction over the depressive experience of accepting a share of responsibility for arrangements not working out. The culture of their worlds may well have a part in reinforcing this approach to settling disputes.

It was our view that there were also powerful unconscious forces at work in this enquiry. They were connected with a secret wish to preserve something between the three – and possibly all four – 'players' in the match. The sexual rivalry between Mr Hood and Mr Ham was allowed to run unchecked by Mrs Ham, for whom it might have served to express her own conflicts about the man with whom she most wanted to be. A lot of energy and excitement, as well as anger and deeply-felt injustice, were attached to the stag fight between the men and denigrating the authorities (here represented by another man).

While the psychology of such intransigence has to remain speculative, a lengthy antecedent history of divorce-associated litigation, plus very discrepant accounts of events, as well as the avoidance of direct communication between parents over a prolonged period of time, may serve as indications that efforts to promote agreement through negotiation are likely at best to be extremely time-consuming and at worst, a complete waste of time.

In this, as in some other enquiries, an issue which has been hotly debated at a national level became central to the relationship between the two professionals involved in the enquiry. This concerned whether or not the claims of the 'psychological parent' should take precedence over blood ties. The welfare officer and social worker were in agreement that children should not be brought up in ignorance of their blood parentage. Beyond that, they differed as to the weight that should be given to blood ties and ties of affinity. For them, the question was whether the interests of two children would best be served by supporting the family in which they were currently being brought up, or by preserving ties outside the family that connected them with their history and by defining 'family' in more generous, realistic, and complicated ways. On this question they differed.

Blind Man's Buff: the Robin enquiry

Blind Man's Buff is a party game in which an unlimited number of people can take part. One person is blindfolded and sent out unseeing into the darkness to catch as many people as he can in the time allowed. He relies upon senses other than sight to detect where the other players are, and they – longing for the excitement of a chase – both attract attention to their whereabouts and run for it when they are in danger of being caught.

The Robin family were one of 10 'satisfaction' enquiries in the Divorce Unit sample of 140 cases. Mr and Mrs Robin had lived apart for two years, Mrs Robin looking after her 6-year-old daughter and Mr Robin looking after their 5- and 8-year-old sons. They were in agreement about applying for a divorce under the two-year separation clause, and proposed that the existing arrangements for their children should continue. The judge called for a welfare report because he was uneasy about the children being brought up separately. As far as the welfare officers were aware there were no signals other than a breach of convention which attracted attention to their case. Apart from being informed that the Robins had proposed an unusual arrangement, their welfare officers were in the dark about what they were looking for.

The enquiry: the welfare officers' story

The welfare enquiry was carried out by a man and a woman (from the IMS and the Divorce Unit respectively). The report period was six weeks, although there was only one interview with the Robin family which lasted for just an hour. Schools were contacted for reports. The outcome was a very brief report which endorsed the parents' agreement and the arrangement which had by then been operating for nearly two-and-a-half years. Two months later the court endorsed the recommendation.

The Robins were offered a family interview so that the welfare officers could see, as well as hear about, the extent of any difficulties. Both parents seemed surprised that a welfare report had been called for and unclear about its purpose. This was particularly true for Mrs Robin who had not been at court on the day the order was made. With the welfare officers, the parents went through the details of their arrangements, how the day-to-day responsibilities of child care were managed, and the feelings each had about the children spending alternate weekends together with one or other parent. Mr Robin explained on behalf of them both that this pattern of care preserved each parent's active involvement with the children, as well as making sure that their sons and daughter saw a lot of each other.

The welfare officers were struck by the relaxed and easy relationship between all the members of the family, who sat closely together in the room. As the interview proceeded they became increasingly uneasy about probing for cracks in arrangements which appeared to be working well. They decided to restrict further enquiries to obtaining reports from the schools, saying they would submit a brief report supporting existing arrangements if all was well there. That is what happened. In their profile report they wrote:

'We would predict that the arrangements will continue to work well – and flexibly – to respond to the developing needs and interests of the children. This was an unusual report prompted by unusual arrangements – departing from a principle that children of one family ought not to be living in separate households. In this case – is it a new generation? – the arrangement helped not to divide the family.'

The enquiry: the parents' story

His view The female researcher who interviewed the Robins eight months after the enquiry had been completed was more than a little surprised by what she discovered. She was impressed by the decor of Mr Robin's home, the style of his dress, and his fastidious neatness. He confided to her that there was 'a lot of woman' in him, and that his marriage had been atypical in that it had been broken up by a woman with whom his wife – and not he – had become involved. The researcher formed the impression that there was some ambiguity about the sexual orientation of both parents, an impression which strengthened the more detail

Mr Robin supplied. He talked at length about his marriage and present circumstances, and seemed to appreciate an audience. In connection with the welfare enquiry Mr Robin had been in two minds, half wanting his contribution to be appreciated by a full enquiry but settling for concocting a story which discouraged further attention:

> 'We put our story together. She [Mrs Robin] asked me to do the talking and they took our story at face value . . . they never came to see my home [a complaint Mr Robin repeated more than once, implying that he would have wished the welfare officers to have seen and admired his well kept home]. I could have been telling them a pack of lies . . . the kids were there . . . but it was difficult for them to say anything other than OK . . . I did not want the boat rocked. My wife and I had a story which avoided nastiness and unpleasantness . . . if they looked any further, it might have upset things. It was for the best . . . I was desperate for my divorce, and it was better for it to go through like that.'

He then went on to talk about Mrs Robin and their relationship as parents in terms which would have galvanized a full enquiry had they been used with the welfare officers:

> 'Well, we presented it as equal but it wasn't really. I do all the running about; I do all that's needed. She's not really interested. She's a rather neglectful mother. Nicole is often grubby and shabby. Her knickers are not changed and she has holes in her shoes . . . [wrinkling his nose] the boys come home smelling of the dog and such like . . . I do rather more of the caring. I have them more often and do the fetching and carrying . . . I think she might not have wanted any of the children but I thought "why should she get away with that?" '

Her view When the research interviewer visited Mrs Robin's home, where she was living with another man, she was surprised by its appearance after the denigrating observations made by her former husband. Her home was, in fact, neat and newly decorated, nowhere near as untidy as she had been led to expect, even if not as obsessively tidy as Mr Robin's house.

The researcher found it difficult at this interview to elicit any views from Mrs Robin about the enquiry. She would say 'I can't

remember', or 'it's all such a long time ago', or 'I'm starting a
new life now', and especially 'I don't think much about things'.
There was therefore little to counteract or confirm Mr Robin's
view of what had been and was then happening between them.
Her flat recollection of the enquiry was in these terms:

> 'We were only there three-quarters of an hour. They seemed a
> bit taken aback. I remember them saying they were used to
> quarrelling couples, whereas we had made up our minds and it
> had been working well for about a couple of years. The woman
> was more dominating. She asked more questions. I thought
> what she asked the children was strange, but I can't now
> remember what the questions were. My "ex" can talk much
> better than me, so he explained and I agreed with what he
> said.'

About the report she recalled that 'it said what we said. It was
fair'. The subsequent court hearing had been 'over in two
minutes; it was an anti-climax'.

Comment

The Robin enquiry vividly highlights a question of central
importance for this book. Are the best interests of children better
promoted and safeguarded by accepting and building upon
whatever potential there might be between parents for agreement, or are there people who are better able than parents to
propose and put into effect alternative arrangements? The
question does not have to be answered in either/or terms. Yet it
does raise an issue of crucial importance about the boundaries
between public and private responsibilities, and the effects of
their interplay upon each other.

The welfare officers were not given sight of the picture that
emerged at the follow-up interview with Mr Robin. Had they
been they might well have proceeded to a full investigation. As it
was they noted parents who were in agreement, children who saw
each other frequently, and an arrangement which had been in
operation, satisfactorily by all accounts, for over two years. The
influence of the conciliation movement on welfare practice is well
illustrated by this case. Given no warning bells there was a wish
to respond to the agreement of parents and to support their
proposals. In retrospect it can be said that the welfare officers

were offered a blindfold which they accepted and in that sense
entered unwittingly into collusion with the Robins. Provided
with no overt evidence that anything was amiss, they decided to
do no more than write to the schools for a report. While the
Robins told them that the judge 'had been in a grumpy mood'
when he ordered the report, the welfare officers concluded that
the parents had 'unwittingly got caught up in the clutches of the
legal process'.

The judge appeared to have responded to a traditional unease
about divided arrangements for children by ordering a report.
But would it have helped him to know what the researcher found
out? Personal values might have complicated even more than
usually considerations about what was in the children's best
interests. Had the welfare officers visited the parents at home
would they have learned any more than they heard at the office?
The researcher met the Robins in a neutral context and not in the
course of a welfare enquiry. No account of their discussions was
to be forwarded to the court. That must have had a freeing effect
upon what could be said.

This case generated a lively debate in the Unit about whether
secret and unsettling issues can and should be revealed and
explored during an enquiry when parents have agreed to their
own solution. In this case, the Robins succeeded in pulling the
shutters down and concealing aspects of their lives which they
did not want exposed to the public gaze. There were other
enquiries in the core sample where parental agreements did not
terminate the investigation process. Why the agreement did so in
this case and not in others must, one might guess, be related to
the nature of the interaction between the parents and the welfare
officers involved. The welfare officers did not conceive of their
role in a paternalistic way and were not made anxious enough to
conduct a full enquiry. That may all have been for the best.
Investigation may not add to knowledge. A little knowledge can
cause a lot of distress.

On their private account the Robins' case deserves a second
look. Mrs Robin was hoping for something more from the court
appearance and Mr Robin was explicit about his disappointment
about the response of the official world. We suspect that neither
conciliation services nor welfare enquiries would have provided
the kind of response they were searching for. The absence of a
dispute between the parents would not have made them obvious
candidates for conciliation. The constraints of investigation did

not provide the conditions of safety and confidence for discussing personal agendas. He wanted to be able to talk about feeling ill-treated as a partner and a parent, to discuss questions that divorce had raised for him personally, and to be appreciated for the efforts he had made. She wanted the end of their marriage to be marked in a less peremptory fashion than it had been thus far. While the benefits from opportunities of this kind may not accrue directly to children, benefits there are likely to be. As with the Sheens and the Kings, a third kind of response was called for which provided for counselling support free of stigma and the risk of inviting unwelcome attention. Perhaps, too, there was a plea for ritual to mark the significant changes brought about by divorce.

Note

1   The legal advice they received was that a joint custody order could be made without specifying care and control.

7
UNDER THE MICROSCOPE

'It was like being put under a microscope for the whole time.'

A mother

'Microscope', 'magnifying glass', 'goldfish bowl' – all these images were used by parents to convey their experience of being reported upon. They were under no illusions about the purpose of the welfare officer's presence. However much they valued support offered in the course of an enquiry, or respected the fairness with which they were treated, parents were aware that they were under observation and therefore vulnerable to the conclusions drawn by 'strangers' about matters that were often felt to be of life and death importance to them. The emotional lability of vulnerable parents, combined with the power vested in the role of the reporter, made the enquiry an uneasy and sometimes volatile experience for both sides. This will be apparent from the preceding descriptions of the four courier cases. In this chapter, we have assembled the comments of parents from the core sample as a whole in order to build up a general picture of the enquiry experience. The next chapter will consider the investigative process from the welfare officers' point of view.

We have relied upon the retrospective accounts of parents who were followed up for the pictures of the enquiry process presented here. While they register important issues, and frequently make vivid reading, it is impossible for them fully to portray or explain the experiences to which they relate. Words require a context to take on meaning; different contexts can radically alter the meaning of the same words. What is said about one person may be intended for others. Language may articulate thought imprecisely, and be misunderstood or misconstrued by the listener. It may also be used to conceal feelings and to accommodate what is thought to be expected rather than what has been experienced. Moreover, the listener introduces his or here own bias in the way words are edited and presented.

Four points need to be borne in mind when considering the consumer reports recorded here. In the first place, not all the parents in our core sample of 30 enquiries were seen for a follow-up meeting. Out of a possible 60 parents, 11 fathers and 6 mothers were not interviewed. Of the 11 fathers, 6 failed to respond to a letter of invitation and a subsequent telephone call or visit (4 were believed to have moved away without leaving a forwarding address). The remaining 5 responded but refused to be seen. If they gave a reason at all, it was along the lines of one man who wrote 'now that my divorce is all over I do not wish to see anyone'. Of the 6 mothers, 2 refused to be seen (one because she wanted no further reminders of the past and the other because matters were still sub-judice) while the remaining 4 had changed their addresses and were untraceable.

Such messages as there were from parents who were not seen for a follow-up interview indicated that they wished to leave a painful episode in their lives well behind them. How far refusals were linked with feelings towards welfare officers, or about the enquiry experience, was unclear. While the letters of invitation (which were sent to all the parents in the core sample) made it clear that the follow-up interviews were research orientated and quite separate from the welfare enquiries, certain ambiguities remained. For example, the interviews were offered either at home or on Divorce Unit premises, and the invitations bore the letter heading of the Divorce Unit and not the IMS.

In the same way that it was important to ask why some parents opted out of the follow-ups, it is equally important to ask why those who chose to involve themselves did so. The reason we gave for approaching parents for their views was that consumer reports could improve services to divorcing families. No doubt many parents considered this sufficient reason for reliving a painful episode in their lives. Other reasons became apparent during the interviews. The motives for participating in this piece of consumer research constitute a second factor relevant to the interpretation of what was said.

The distress of reliving painful experiences weighed as heavily for those who agreed to be seen as we surmised it did for those who declined. Five parents gave their consent only after they had been contacted by telephone, and on the condition that no face to face interview was involved. Three parents (2 men and 1 woman) talked to us by telephone and 2 (a man and a woman) agreed to complete an open-ended questionnaire (a hastily devised substitute for the interview). All 5 said they would find a personal interview too distressing.

The 19 men and 24 women who *were* followed up conveyed their reasons for agreeing to be seen by the way they used their interviews. For the majority, the interviews provided an opportunity to air grievances which had abated little, if at all, since the welfare report was prepared (about eight months previously in the majority of cases). Some hoped to perpetuate unrelinquished fights, and wanted interviewers to convey messages about former partners to their welfare officers. Others wished for their dissatisfaction with a report or court outcome to be made public in the hope that an enquiry might be reopened. One man threatened to expose his welfare officer to the national press unless he retracted what had been written in the report. While welfare officers (or courts and solicitors) might be denigrated if they were seen as responsible for thwarting parents in the pursuit of their objectives, parents also provided perspectives on the enquiry experience which we were sometimes in danger of forgetting, protected as we and our welfare officer colleagues were by familiarity with court procedures, the distance afforded by mutual reinforcement of our professional identity and purpose, and the busy-ness which sometimes dulled thinking in favour of applying established procedures.

The interviews were also used to express appreciation and gratitude. A substantial minority of parents felt they had been helped and supported by welfare officers through the enquiry period. They recognized the difficulties inherent in the reporting role, and were anxious to distinguish between person and role when they had adverse comments to make. Moreover, it was very seldom that a court report was considered to be unfair. With some distance from what, overall, had been a harrowing period in their lives, one or two parents were able to look back on the enquiry and remark on how badly they had behaved at the time.

We judged that 12 men and 12 women were motivated to participate in the follow-ups primarily to register their dissatisfaction with the enquiry process, and 5 men and 6 women to express their appreciation for what had happened. Four women did not appear to be strongly motivated either way and we judged their agreement to see us as compliance. A further 2 men and 2 women were tacitly asking for help. Assessing the balance of satisfaction with the enquiry process overall, we judged from the follow-up reports that the ratio of complaint to appreciation was in the order of 2:1. Thirteen women and 14 men were more dissatisfied than satisfied with the enquiry process as a whole, whereas the position was reversed for 11 women and 5 men. While women were marginally more dissatisfied than satisfied, the discrepancy was much greater for men – a point to which we shall return later. The reactions of most parents were mixed, resulting in their comments being registered on both positive and negative sides of the satisfaction ledger.

A third qualification concerns the blurring of the edges between what belonged to the enquiry experience and what belonged to the experience of divorce as a whole. Because we most wanted to learn about how parents experienced the enquiry we approached them eight months after reports had been filed with the courts (or the enquiry dropped). We hoped memories would remain fresh in that time, and we were not to be disappointed. The timescale also fitted the budgetary constraints of the project, a consideration of some importance for us. The drawback of this timescale was that experiences of divorce remained raw for many parents, making it more than usually difficult to distinguish between what belonged to the enquiry and what belonged to their experience of divorce as a whole. No doubt the remembered interventions of welfare officers provided a focus for feelings generated by a whole range of factors associated with divorce. We believe this to be a major constraint on how far what was said can be taken at face value, although it is possible that there is an element of rationalization on our part in adopting this view. We were frequently hurt by what we read in the follow-up reports, and sometimes it was as if we and the parents we had seen had been party to quite separate enquiries. On other occasions we recognized the truth of their observations. With time, our personal anger and hurt – even shame – were dulled by a sense of inevitability, and we managed the feelings generated by consumer reports with some humour.

A final consideration to be borne in mind is the part we, as researchers, played in the follow-up interviews. In the way they were conducted we directed the attention of parents to three broad areas about which we wanted feedback. First, and most important, we wanted to know how the interventions of welfare officers had been experienced. Second, we were interested in the reactions of parents to solicitors and the courts. Third, we wanted to know how the original circumstances which led to the welfare report were regarded at the time of follow-up, taking into account the influence of the enquiry and the decisions of the court.

The interviews were conducted in an open-ended and unstructured manner, allowing parents to determine the priorities accorded to different issues and the order in which they came up. It was not always possible to cover all three areas; parents occasionally refused to be diverted from their own agendas, and our preoccupation with obtaining feedback about the enquiry process sometimes obscured other areas. Where possible, interviews were tape-recorded, although some parents refused. Detailed reports on the follow-ups were always made by the interviews soon after they had been completed.

Parents' experiences of the enquiry process

The effects of being observed

Once past the initial shock and confusion that sometimes accompanied hearing that a court had ordered a welfare report, parents were under no illusions about the investigative role of welfare officers. They were there to write a report. Even before they met the individuals in role they were forming their own ideas about what an enquiry might involve and where it might lead. Because of their influence with the courts, welfare officers were to be resented, feared, persuaded, or manipulated, but never ignored. When they were experienced as assessors and judges their presence was inhibiting: 'I was worried that I was saying the wrong thing to them when I was with the children. Maybe I shouldn't tell them off in front of them 'cos they'll know that I'm a child batterer – you know? – and all things like this.' If they spoke to children on their own, or listened privately to allegations made by the other parent, their interventions could be immensely threatening, undermining a parent's sense of control and personal security. If they convened a joint meeting the experience could be even worse:

'I felt I had to justify, justify, justify, all the way along the line.

And anything he said, you felt you had to say something else, because you felt "those two are sitting in judgement, and are assessing my character and assessing his character – are going to decide the future of my child".'

Sometimes there seemed to be disappointment that an enquiry was not rigorous enough. This disappointment may have been with an agency which was seen to have offered half to help and half to report, in the end falling between two stools:

'I felt we had a really hard struggle that wasn't appreciated. And when I said at the end of the interview "When will you be seeing us again?" he said he had enough for his report. There is not a lot you can tell from one office interview and one home visit on such an important issue. I would have called at least once unexpectedly. Then a week or two later he 'phoned and said I would have to bring my daughter to the office for an interview with her and her father. I thought he had been to see my husband, or had an interview with his supervisor or something, and decided it would have to be done. . . . There was pressure of an unwarranted sort, really. In the end I consulted the solicitor, who said I should do what they wanted. If I did otherwise it would look as if I were being obstructive.'

Expecting to meet an inquisitor, the efforts of welfare officers to initiate a different kind of relationship – one in which parents might be encouraged to arrive at their own settlements – could be perplexing:

'I didn't quite get the basic concept of what they were trying to do, to attain. Now, looking back on it, I can perhaps look at it in a different light. What they were trying to do was to get us to come to some form of agreement in a more amicable way, so we could part on really good terms, and there'd be no tension caused to upset the children. But the situation wasn't that way, so it just didn't work.'

For some parents, encouragement to meet and negotiate with a former spouse was more persecuting than the idea of an enquiry. It was as if black and white distinctions had to be preserved in order for them to survive, and the paraphernalia of investigation

played neatly into confirming a view that no-one on the outside
was to be trusted:

'I found it the most harrowing experience. I don't like
impositions, and that is one [pointing to the tape recorder].
That was the one thing that really upset me at the interview
[the tape], and they also wanted to take a video of it. I said no,
and asked why. And they said "Because we want to study your
reactions"! When you've got a tape recorder, let alone a video,
you do think twice before saying anything because you're
worried it's going to be used.'

For others, the first meeting provided some reassurance against
the worst fears of what an enquiry might entail:

'You go with a big well of things and think "Crikey, what's
going to happen to me, and what's he going to ask for, and
what am I going to get?". But the first thing they said you
knew that wasn't going to happen. They said "Hello", and
who they were, and would you mind if the interview was taped
for later purposes. They started it off on a nice even footing,
and we progressed with our news from there. It was quite nice
. . . a slow pace, no-one was rushed. The subject of Bronwen
was broached later on.'

The welfare officers' methods

Joint interviews

In the attempt to promote settlements it was the rule, rather than
the exception, for parents to be invited together for the first
meeting with their welfare officers, a meeting to which their
children might also be invited. This practice attracted much
adverse comment: 'All we did was argue'; 'We just bickered and
got nowhere – I walked out'; 'An hour of sitting and getting
slagged off'. The great majority of women who commented about
being seen with their former partner (and women objected more
than men) felt the outcome to have been destructive:

'I 'phoned and said "You don't seem to know there has been
an abortive attempt [at conciliation] through the judge, and I
don't think it's good to have all three of us because it's going to

put her [their daughter] through it". Neither were there when I rang. I had to say it to a secretary who said "That's how things are done". We got there and it was absolute murder. She was rocking back and forth, clearly in great distress. I behaved like a complete harridan – screamed the place down. He was delighted, and said "She's been rehearsing this for weeks", and the whole thing was a complete fiasco.'

'I found it helped the children more when he wasn't there. They expressed their own opinions. In the same room we were all tensed up . . . I disagreed with us all being together in one room because we couldn't really talk. Every time I used to say something my husband used to cross-examine me; and every time he used to say something it was exactly the same. And the children used to butt in . . . It ought to be like they did it the second and third time [when they were seen separately] and when they visited here.'

Mothers particularly appreciated being seen on their own. Their association of separate meetings with separate status sometimes resulted in their harbouring suspicions that welfare officers wished, by arranging joint appointments, to coerce them back into marriages from which they had resolved to escape.

In the eyes of some women, then, an unintended consequence of trying to engage both parents was to forge an alliance between welfare officers and fathers who wished to be reinstated as husbands. This raised a dilemma for us and our colleagues, since we wished to preserve our neutrality and to encourage parents to work together in order to promote communication and agreement between them (as well as to assess for the purposes of the court report how able they were to co-operate as parents). The use of two officers extended our range of possibilities, sometimes allowing for a constructive balance to be sustained between conflicting sets of needs:

'We agreed in the end, but we didn't actually talk about it together. Basically, one was working with him and the other with me, and I think it was the last but one meeting: he was in that office, I was in another office, and we were trying to come to some agreement . . . and they said "John's agreed to joint custody with you having care and control" – and it was a relief, you know, thank God for that.'

It may have been that the views and feelings of parents about the overall purposes and potential of the enquiry encounter (especially when they differed from their welfare officers) found expression in attitudes towards joint meetings. While welfare officers proposed straight talking between parents in the hope of bringing about an agreement which would remove the need to usurp their positions, parents responded to the investigative purpose of the relationship and the threat posed by a former spouse. Their experience was of meeting under conditions in which they felt in danger of having something precious taken away from them. It was an open question as to whether the threat originated primarily from us, as welfare officers, or from the parent who had triggered the enquiry process in the first place.

For some, our attempts to do more than furnish the courts with reports was like sighing for the moon, or pursuing an ideal image of 'happy families' which served only to underline a sense of failure:

> 'You get this letter which says "and bring your son with you". That really infuriated me. I thought, "how can they be so blind – people who are meant to be trained in that field – how can you be so blind as to think, oh yeah, bring your son along, and dad, let them all meet up". It doesn't work like that. I know everyone would like to think that you'd get happy little units everywhere – mummy, daddy, and one or two children – but it doesn't work out like that.'

> 'I know the object of the lesson is to get parents on speaking terms so access can be organized between everybody in the future without outside interference, but I don't think we've got a hope in hell of that happening here. I don't want to get in touch with him. I don't want to speak to him. Least of all do I want to pay for the privilege. I'm living on handouts, he's not. So that's it. I don't want him near me or on my property.'

For others, it was just the response they needed, and they only regretted that no-one was available to help sustain the progress that had been made during the enquiry:

> 'We needed someone to help us with the problem we had because the grown-ups weren't communicating. We needed someone from outside to say: "Right, let's sit down and talk

about this. What do you want to do? What have you got to offer Carol? What's best for her future?" It just helped a great deal. . . . we felt as though we were helped up until the court case, and then there has been a year's gap when we've been stranded – no one to turn to.'

Two workers

A prominent feature of our approach to the core sample enquiries was allocating two workers to each case, an approach taken in 23 of the 30 enquiries. There was no doubt in our minds that a co-worker had a freeing and supporting effect on the work undertaken, and those enquiries that we believed had resulted in successful outcomes (in terms of securing negotiated agreements) were all ones in which a pair of workers was involved. When it worked successfully in the eyes of parents, it was because of the equitable effects of having someone separately available for each partner. Men, in particular, were likely to value a male welfare officer, because they felt intrinsically disadvantaged by their gender in pursuing claims as parents. As one man remarked about his two female officers:

'Both the officers knew that the girls would be better off with me, yet they did their utmost to explain or tell me that their mother needed them more than I (sic). Being women, and having motherly instincts, I would say it was almost impossible for them to be completely unbiased . . . I think divorce, however amicable or otherwise, would benefit from male involvement in divorce welfare – male officers for fathers and female officers for wives – to provide a more balanced and effective service. The welfare of each parent must be as important as that of the children.'

Having a male officer did not necessarily result in a satisfactory enquiry experience for fathers, although this arrangement was clearly appreciated by some. One father complained that while his male officer had appeared sympathetic towards him when they talked on their own, in company with his former wife and his female colleague he became a 'yes man'. Support was valued, and though this was not always forthcoming it was more readily available from two officers than from one. This was largely because there was less concern about compromising a position of neutrality when there were resources for an officer to support each parent. While support might be experienced as having come from the officer of the same sex, this was not always the case.

With two welfare officers there were also opportunities for parents to contrast one with the other. Sometimes it seemed to us that such contrasts were purposeful, serving to provide an outlet for conflicting feelings which might be externalized and targeted upon one or other officer, thus creating a black-and-white world of allies and enemies. One man described his woman officer as 'brilliant', adding that he 'wouldn't do her job for all the tea in China'. In contrast, her male colleague was slated: 'What he said is total lies. He twisted things; he twisted words.' The fact that the two officers worked together and accepted joint responsibility for the report was disregarded in the process of dispensing blame and absolution. Splitting of this kind was harder to detect and to be sure about when distinctions were drawn on the basis of age, sex, and personal characteristics:

'I liked a man and a woman. That's good. But not the woman I had. He was very good – quiet, just listening . . . But to keep interrupting, as the lady did, and to take an obvious stand which I then have to agree with or argue with is not helpful. They should be neutral. I don't know whether they were married, either of them – and I don't want to know – but I think they would do a better job if they were married . . . I think it's easier to talk to an older person . . . Not their fault that they're younger, but I think older people need older workers . . . I think you want an older person who can bring a little wisdom and sympathy to the interview. As you must be aware she put my back up, which is not what she ought to have been doing, she should have been like the other chap. I got the impression that he thought "There but for the grace of God go I, anyone can go through this, whoever you are". Whereas she was thinking "There's something wrong with him", which is not right.'

Many parents came away from the enquiries feeling there was no justice. This was particularly true of the men, who were less likely than women to succeed in their applications. Their comments at follow up demonstrated how sensitive they were to anything which might indicate that welfare officers were not being impartial in their enquiries. So it was expected that parents should be seen on an equal number of occasions and in comparable situations, especially when children were to be present. There was an implicit assumption that enquirer and subject needed to be the same if the enquiry was to be carried out equably. Hence it was thought to be preferable for welfare officers to be parents, to be married, to come from a similar social, ethnic, and educational background, as well as to be of the same sex as the parents under investigation. This last condition – laid down by both men and women, but more vociferously by men – led some fathers to prescribe positive discrimination as the remedy to the injustices of an intrinsically unbalanced contest:

'I can understand your people's point of view, really, if you're trying to take the middle of the road and trying to be fair to both sides. In a way, to be fair you've got to lean a lot on the man's side and try to put his point of view forward, because everybody's concept of it is "Oh, the woman's point of view is first considered as being the more suitable parent".'

For others – mothers – this was a recipe for another kind of injustice:

'He wanted a change of social workers, just as he had changed solicitors three times because of his dissatisfaction with the outcome. . . . The social workers had an impossible job, an awfully depressing job. They leaned over backwards for my husband because he was being so awkward. That rather got on my nerves.'

Home or away?

By and large, parents valued an informal approach to the enquiry, and this could mean that they were more at ease in the familiarity of their home surroundings than in the offices of the Divorce Unit. However, home visits were sometimes experienced as an intrusion, or an invasion of privacy. Mrs Sheen, of the nominal group of divorces, said to her welfare officer that she preferred being seen at her home, and part of her preference was to do with feeling there was more time available for her during home visits than at office interviews. Yet when she was followed up by a researcher she said she bitterly resented the intrusion of home visits. It could well have been that her ambivalence about the territory on which the enquiry was carried out reflected her ambivalence about the enquiry process as a whole.

The association of territory with feeling in or out of control of events made the home or away question an important one. While many parents preferred to be seen on their own and in the familiarity of their home surroundings, there is no doubt that we, as welfare officers, preferred to meet them on *our* home ground (the office) and on what we hoped would be neutral territory as between two parents who were living apart. No doubt we were also influenced by being more interested in working with parents towards a negotiated settlement than in inspecting bedrooms and bathrooms, although this came into the investigative remit. No unequivocal answer was given by parents to the question of where they preferred to be seen, although we discerned a presumption in favour of home contacts. When office visits were arranged, there was evidence that people were very sensitive to surroundings and atmosphere:

'[When you arrive] you get offered a cup of tea, and you sit there in the warm, and you have magazines to look at, and you kind of relax a bit. By the time you come to talk to everybody it's not so bad. [The room] was just armchairs – it was obviously an office – there were a lot of books and a desk, lots of plants, all welcoming. I'd had to sit outside with my ex-husband. I think the first meeting was with him. They were both sitting there, but we weren't arranged in rows. We were kind of all around the room. We took our tea in with us . . . it was like a conversation rather than question and answer.'

Approaching children

It is perhaps not surprising that the way children were included in the investigative process was a sensitive area. Here, welfare officers intruded directly upon the domain of parents. Professional views about what was best for children (for example, that they should have regular contact with the parent who was not living with them, and they should be told about what was going on) sometimes conflicted with the views of parents who feared, or had to live with the consequences of implementing suggestions that welfare officers might make. Parting briefly from a child, so that a welfare officer might hear his or her views in private, could be immensely threatening, as if it heralded separation of a more permanent kind. The younger the children, the more anxious about welfare practice were the parents:

'I was claiming custody of the three, and he was claiming custody of one – the eldest, but they saw fit to see all three children anyway, which I didn't agree with . . . I thought that was totally out of order. At the time my little girl was five . . . I really can't understand it with the younger children. I can't see what they get out of the interview. It's just like before you go in their daddy buys his little girl a bar of chocolate, and then they'll say "Well, do you love your daddy?" She'll say "Yes, of course I do, daddy's just bought me a bar of chocolate". Now, I mean, what on earth can they get out of that? . . . the elder boy, I will say that, they got the truth out of him.'

Some custodial parents believed the enquiry to have heightened the level of uncertainty with which their children were living, and they were anxious to expedite a settlement. Pursuing negotiations with the non-resident parent threatened to delay matters further. Moreover, there was a risk that their children might acquiesce with, or become interested in proposals to initiate contact with him or her. When this happened it was common to hear the complaint that welfare officers had 'manipulated' or 'brainwashed' children, and by so doing had made the lot of the custodial parent that much more difficult:

'I have told the welfare officers that I believe they have manipulated Helen by putting it into her head that she would like to see her dad. . . . She does attempt to pull rank on me – a real little madam – she's very clever at playing him off against me, and I don't think it's been of any benefit to her other than satisfying her curiosity as to what he looks like. . . . I can't say [the enquiry] has been a waste of time. No. But I don't really think it's got us anywhere either. We've talked, we've gone from why did I think the marriage broke down onwards. To a degree that was useful. . . . We've had heated discussions. I've cried. I've said to him that whatever decisions are made in that court they affect my life and the children's lives, and I don't like other people making my decisions. And I don't really feel that they fully understand just how much I've got on my plate.'

The investigative role of the welfare officer was at its most undisguised when children were seen apart from their parents. Not only did they fear what might be said out of their hearing, they feared that children might be exposed to the full burden of the distress of a broken marriage:

> 'I never tell Derek anything that's going on [about the divorce] ever. He's never ever heard anything, because if they hear snatches they get hold of the wrong end of the stick and their minds start working. . . . I tell you what did upset me. I was waiting for my husband to turn up, and waiting out in that corridor, and there was a woman sitting on the bench seat and two boys, if I remember rightly. And the boys had gone off somewhere. And all I remember was one of them coming back, and she said "What did they say?". And he said "Oh, they want to see dad next". Oh – I could never take Derek there and be in that situation! There was something about it which utterly repelled me. I could almost feel the sadness there, and I thought "No way are they doing that to me and Derek". What do they say to these children? My mind was working overtime.'

It is true to say that at times we, too, felt uncomfortable when interviewing children in the course of preparing reports. Some of us were less adept at it than our welfare officer colleagues. Yet on balance we felt satisfied that the enquiry offered an opportunity for children to talk, sometimes for the first time, about feelings connected with the breakdown of their parents' marriages. With young children we had to rely upon drawing and play, as well as words, to encourage communication. Even then it could be hard for children to speak without feeling disloyal to one or other parent. At follow up, we were permitted to speak to children from six of the core sample cases about their experience of the enquiry, and most were non-commital. One 9-year-old girl expressed her present dilemma and her feeling of loss in terms which indicated some of the problems she and her welfare officer faced in managing the purpose of their meeting. It also suggests the high level of skill required to help children communicate about their feelings in an enquiry context:

> 'Mummy's still sort of worried about how I feel because I just say "Well, it's yes and no" [to the welfare officer] because I'm

too scared to say what the truth is. I'm afraid she might say "Oh you go with him, I don't want you here", and [the welfare officer] might say "Well go with him, your mum doesn't want you here anymore, so go". I'm scared, but I would tell the truth. When I was in my mum's tum, and [her elder sister] was a baby, all things were alright then. I was only a month old then, and it's sort of nice because we went everywhere we wanted and got everything we wanted. Now we're not very rich because he's got all the money. Did you know he took the cassette? Well, we were really upset by that. [Interviewer asks her about being in her mum's tummy.] No, it was when I was a month old. It was all nice then. But when I became about five this all started, and I just got confused by what was all happening. It was so confusing. I can't remember anything. I just don't know what I'm talking about. I do, really.'

Some parents approved of the way their children had been treated during the enquiry. Those who were appreciative generally thought that it had provided an opportunity for children to 'get things off their chest'. One mother remarked how apprehensive her children had been about seeing the welfare officer, one of them refusing to go. She added that after the experience 'They did not seem to mind being interviewed, and George withdrew his objections.' But the real contribution the welfare officers could make to children was to end a period of uncertainty. As one little girl recalled, 'It all began to feel better when I knew who I was living with.'

The balance of satisfaction

From our assessment of the comments parents made at follow up we estimated the ratio of complaint to appreciation to be in the region of two to one. It was clear that some parents felt their welfare officers had made a positive contribution towards easing the tensions associated with the dispute which had brought them to court. They felt they had been helped to communicate with their former partners, listened to, supported, and contained. One man referred to his female officer as a 'lifeboatman', while another described his male officer as 'a breath of fresh air' in a process which had left him feeling stifled and exploited. Several parents commented that they had valued the breathing space which the enquiry had created when they had otherwise been feeling under pressure. These parents were likely to see welfare officers as fair and impartial, but also caring and wishing to help: 'I felt they were trying to help us sort it all out. It was a very relaxed atmosphere, quite nice, and the children didn't mind going at first. I felt they genuinely wanted to help.'

Appreciation was not necessarily dependent upon the 'success' of the welfare officers' interventions; their interest and concern could be a consolation in the face of intractable circumstances:

'On the whole they have done their best. They couldn't have done more. In fact she [the welfare officer] put more effort into it than she needed to, really, or was required to by law – I mean by the times she went to see Bronwen, and the time when we were at the office which ended up rather late. . . . Although I didn't get what I wanted, I don't think they could have tried any harder.'

'They helped me to get a lot of things off my chest, but didn't help to sort out the dispute . . . they took me back to when the marriage was breaking down. I hadn't spoken to anyone about it. It helped me to say how I felt . . . but whatever I said made no difference. No way was he going to change his mind.'

'It was a totally unnecessary operation, but given that it had to be gone through – once my husband had alarmed the judge – it proved a helpful and clarifying experience. Both welfare officers were tactful and sensitive. Going over the history was helpful. I think we talked about things we might otherwise have avoided.'

However, the balance of satisfaction with the enquiry process was usually dependent upon a case having been heard and support having been won. Parents were most likely to be satisfied when reports were in their favour (*Table 14*, Appendix I) and when children were living with them (*Table 15*, Appendix I). The following illustration demonstrates the struggle one woman had to obtain a hearing from welfare officers who were trying to preserve their neutrality and independence of action:

'I'd written things down, got my case prepared as it were, trying to show how John was behaving. It was terrible, but I had done it and what I wanted was someone to come to my house [to interviewer] like you are today, and talk to me and listen to what I feel. It took me ages to get them to do that. They just wanted to do things their way. They would ask me *their* questions. I used to come away terribly distressed after the first few meetings. Every time I started she would interrupt and say "How do you feel about that?" – and I felt as if she was some sort of psychiatrist asking me some unnecessary question. I was crying. She could see. Why didn't she just let me spill it all out and stop interrupting me, making me feel worse and churning me up? I just wanted to say my piece, but it took a lot of shrieking on my part to get this done. 'Phoning – two hour 'phone calls! – pleading just to be listened to; don't ask questions.

Then, having said that, I thought them tremendously helpful. Their presence, just being there, was amazingly helpful. I thought she was actually a very nice woman, and had I not met her in these circumstances – if I'd met her at a party – we might have been friends. I actually liked her very much. I felt as if I'd said my piece. They made it clear why they didn't want to listen to my tapes – used in a bad way before – so, tapes away . . . They were really good referees – which was all I wanted – and they took the heat out the situation. What helped was that I *really* felt they were on my side, and I suppose that's not what they're supposed to do . . . I felt she was backing me up. She told me how I was playing into his hands with all my emotional outbursts. I felt "That's great; she's seen through John. She's on my side." '

A favourable recommendation in the final report was definitive evidence of that support and public vindication of a parent's position. Women were generally more satisfied than men with the enquiry (see *Table 14*). For them, satisfaction was always associated with a favourable report recommendation, whereas for men this was not necessarily the case.

Reports were prepared in 27 of the 30 core sample enquiries. In 2 cases (both access applications) fathers withdrew their applications, and in a further case an interim arrangement between the parents was sufficiently satisfactory for the enquiry to be placed in abeyance. Since report recommendations were broadly in line with court decisions in all 22 of the cases which had come back to court one year after the completion of fieldwork, satisfaction with the enquiry was also associated, as one might expect, with a favourable court decision. While parents tended to be dissatisfied with the enquiry process overall, most parents were satisfied with the content and fairness of their reports. Many produced copies to show to their interviewer. Even so, there was often doubt expressed about how much an enquiry could really discover about complex family relationships, and sometimes a sense of shock was registered about seeing oneself in print:

> 'I thought the report was very fair although, like any report, they can only skim basically over the outside of things. Unless you actually live in a house with people, you can't say "Well, that person should have the child, or, that person should definitely have her", because you don't know people that personally.'

> 'I read [the report] and everything in it was fair. Sometimes things look so awful when written down in black and white . . . when I saw it written down, it looked quite shocking. But there was nothing in it that was unfair.'

Despite being offered the opportunity to read the report before a copy was sent to the court, several parents had not seen it before their solicitor received a copy. Some declined the invitation to come to the Divorce Unit for that purpose; others came, but complained about having to do so:

> 'I am very busy. I asked for the report to be sent. They refused. I went to the office and was kept waiting half an hour. I sat and read it, said "Fine", returned it and left. I could have done that at home. Parking was difficult. The whole thing took one and a half hours – to read a report they could have put in the post.'

It sometimes seemed as if unconditional support and absolute understanding were the prerequisities for feeling satisfied with other aspects of the reporting process. The comments made about welfare officers (which were mixed) and their reports (generally favourable) usually focused, when they were adverse, upon personal incompatibilities and failures fully to appreciate individual circumstances. Criticism might be about youthfulness, inexperience, lack of qualification for the job (usually specified in terms of not being married and having no children), selective reporting, manipulation, ineffectiveness, personal antagonism, bias, authoritarianism, or irrelevance. Whether or not the criticisms were justified, these were the subjective experiences of parents who identified aspects of the reporting process with which they felt dissatisfied, and which can be expected to have affected how they responded to the settlements that finally resulted.

It sometimes felt to us as if those parents who had no part in initiating the welfare enquiry always resented what followed as an intrusion and a destructive influence in their lives, whereas those who had been instrumental in setting it up were bound to end up disappointed and disillusioned. This is not an accurate representation of how things were, but demonstrates the disheartening effects the follow-up interviews could have upon our morale, and their ability to undermine other memories and experiences of the enquiry process. To be fair, parents did not always attach blame to welfare officers for what they recognized as their own impossible and intractable circumstances. More likely, they would view their endeavours as misguided, naive, or hopelessly out of touch. No doubt repeated disappointments had hardened many of the parents against hope, and having become wedded to their dissatisfactions they were not anxious to run the risks of being seduced back into a vulnerable situation. In so far as the interventions of welfare officers offered the hope of change, there might be good reasons for resisting olive branches offered during the enquiry process and then decrying their failure. The reasons have to do with the politics of survival.

Nevertheless, comments like 'a complete waste of time and effort', 'a waste of public money', 'the whole experience was useless – worse than useless' and 'should be abolished', set the tone for not a few follow-up interviews, especially with men, and one would have to be extremely blinkered to explain such reactions solely in terms of the psychopathology of the parents in our sample. To do so would be to confirm the views of one man who had 'come to the conclusion that social workers are all out to misunderstand things'.

There was little doubt in our minds that many parents felt shamed and humiliated by the public exposure that followed from their failure to settle privately upon suitable arrangements for their children. However hard we might try to counteract their humiliation, our presence was sometimes perceived as an intrusion by unqualified people into 'intimate and private matters'. Again, it was the men who expressed their feelings about this most strongly:

> 'They may have degrees in sociology, but they don't know the experience of going through a divorce'.

> 'We had to go to a strange room in a strange place and talk to these strangers. And she had to talk about who she wanted to be with – as if it was any of their business. I also felt that I was spoken to on the lowest common denominator. It was a patronising attitude which I took offence to from people with probably poor degrees who have fallen into that little line of work. Perhaps a lot of the people they deal with, in poor circumstances, are not adequately educated.'

An obvious criticism of the enquiry process, and one more likely to be made by women than by men, was that it delayed divorce proceedings and deferred the date by which they might be released in law from their marriages. In our core sample of cases, the time spent interviewing family members ranged from one to neary 30 hours per enquiry. Most enquiries took between 5 and 15 hours. These figures do not include the considerable amount of additional time spent on the telephone, in court, writing letters and reports, keeping case records up to date, and conferring about work in hand, nor do they double up the hours when two officers were interviewing together. No attempt was made to estimate the time spent on these back-up activities, but it was thought to be well in excess of that spent in direct contact with families. Interestingly, the *nominal* cases (10½ and 29½ hours) and the *long-lease* cases (both 15 hours) took proportionally more interviewing time than the *shot-gun* cases (which ranged between 2½ and 22 hours, most falling in the 5 to 15 hour range). The cases in the fourth group (5) all took 4 hours or less.

Taking the interval between allocating and filing a report as the duration of the enquiry, core sample cases had a longer timespan than enquiries in the one-year sample: 76 per cent of the core sample enquiries were completed in under six months as compared with 83 per cent of the one-year sample. Shortening the timescale further, 23 per cent of the core sample enquiries were completed in under three months as compared with 49 per cent of the one year sample. No figures for interviewing times were kept for the one-year sample.

The greater amount of time spent on the core sample cases, and the longer timespan embraced by them probably reflect our having expended more time and effort on these cases than is usual, and the practical consequences of our having been available for appointments on only one day a week. While the period between allocating and filing reports provides a good measure of the time span of the enquiry from the welfare officers' perspective, it seriously understates the deferment of proceedings for parents. Normally, there was little delay between a report being ordered and the Divorce Unit receiving notification of this. Documents took two weeks or less to pass from the referring court to the Divorce Unit in three quarters of the Divorce Unit sample of enquiries. In only 7 of the 140 cases did it take longer than six weeks. However, there were frequently long delays between the filing of a report and the case returning to court to be heard.

For many of those parents who did return to court, delays in fixing a date of hearing effectively doubled the length of the enquiry, and with it the period of uncertainty for children. A return to court was likely to be delayed when the recommendations of a report suited neither parent, or when there was no pressure to obtain a decree absolute, and interim arrangements were considered to be working satisfactorily or better than they might following a return to court. Delays occasionally resulted from administrative inefficiency, but more usually they were of the parents' (or their legal advisors') making. Eight of the core sample of enquiries (27 per cent) and 18 per cent of the one-year sample had not returned to court 12 months after the fieldwork ended.

Solicitors and the courts

While the main purpose of the follow-up interviews was to obtain feedback about how enquiries were experienced by their subjects, many comments made by parents concerned their experience of judicial procedures as a whole. Welfare officers were part of the judicial system, and were sometimes inseparable from it in the eyes of parents. So it was that some of the criticisms about delays, about surrendering parental responsibility, about bias, and the stigmatizing effects of court proceedings, were repeated in connections with solicitors and the courts.

'It all took far too long and has cost me a small fortune. I think a lot of time and money was wasted. It could have been settled a lot quicker than it was. Four years it dragged on – far too long, a very bitter battle indeed. The courts took far too long. The solicitors make everything worse . . . and we end up the losers.'

For parents, the outcome of the court hearing was a gamble. It was as if once sucked into the judicial system, parental responsibility was surrendered to the fates. Good fortune, aided by a good solicitor, were the key determining factors:

'You've been a parent for 15 years, and all of a sudden it can be the judge's decision, or the Divorce Unit's, whether you keep your child or not. It just depends on who's got the stronger solicitor. It's out of your hands. It's not your divorce the minute you go into it . . . you pay your deposit and it becomes a whirlpool, and you are in the middle of it, and you are praying that you are going to come up from it and you are not going to drown.'

Many men assumed that the odds were stacked against them, and that the court bias was of more significance than that of welfare officers:

'I have been to court 11 times and have never gained anything out of any hearing. The judge does not even listen to the man. It's heavily prejudiced towards women – the solicitors tell you that. There's no deviation. . . . I was in court once about an upset over the children, and before the judge heard anything do you know what his remark was in open court? "Oh God, not another father trying to be a mother." What chance do I have?'

The stigma of the court proceedings was directly linked by some parents to being 'made to feel like a criminal'. This was particularly acute for those parents who had a criminal record – 'it was as if I was on trial that day . . . the judge looked on me as a criminal' – but could be equally uncomfortable for those who were unfamiliar with courts: 'It was all, I dunno, it was like a dream, like it wasn't me it was happening to because, as I say, I've never ever been to court. I've never done anything like that before, and it was as if it wasn't me doing it.' Generally speaking, solicitors received a divided press – as many favourable comments as unfavourable. In contrast, the courts tended only to be mentioned when complaints were being made:

'My solicitor was extremely good, both to me and in his work. He made himself available to me at all times and I could not fault him. The court, on the other hand, I found rather inefficient – once losing my divorce application for four weeks (their admitted mistake) prolonging the agony even further. Then they gave me the wrong court instructions with regard to maintenance for the children, causing a further four weeks' delay.'

Other parents felt they faced defeat from the outset, experiencing a sense of exploitation, even by those who were employed to represent their interests. Solicitors were portrayed by these dissatisfied parents as only being in the job for the money, prepared to escalate conflict either out of financial interest or in the misguided pursuit of their client's interests, biased in favour of women, and almost always unavailable when wanted on the telephone. Divorce was the 'gravy train which [solicitors] jump off when they see there's no money left'; 'I have the impression that if I'd had more money I'd have had more help.' In one case, the perceived lack of support from a solicitor came from a woman who believed that as a 'real heavy churchgoer' the solicitor censured her behaviour on moral grounds. In all these cases it is impossible to know what actually happened. The women last described had, as it happened, been personally supported by her solicitor well beyond the call of professional duty.

Indications of change

It was no part of our research design to evaluate the effects of the enquiry process, or to estimate the impact of judicial procedures upon outcomes for the parents and children in our sample. This would have been a complex and demanding exercise. As its starting point a decision would have needed to be taken about what constituted the best interests of children and how these might be assessed – both subjective and highly contentious areas. However, parents expressed their views about whether or not they thought there had been an improvement or deterioration in their situation, and we have selected some of their assessments to conclude this account of the client's experience of the enquiry process.

It is interesting that those who thought their circumstances had changed for the better were usually women; few of the men were positive in their evaluations. Because the two parties to the dispute frequently evaluated their experiences very differently, we have selected in addition to the evaluations of the four courier cases described in Chapter 6 six further pairs of appraisals, each pair referring to one enquiry.

Him   'I am extremely happy in my work, which is a great help. I have recently remarried and want to be left alone to get on with my new life.'

Her   'I think it was too quick for him. He was so bitter about me leaving; he still is. He won't come in. He still stands at the door. It's all over as far as I'm concerned. If he wants to be friends I'll be friends for the children's sake. There's things I'd like to discuss with him – secondary school – but he's reverted to the old John, not interested . . . I'm happy as I am now. I'm still going out with the same fella and I like it as it is. I like my independence. I've given up work so things are a bit tight, but I like being at home and having time with the children because I've never had time with the children, I've always had to work. I think I'm coping well with it considering what I went through.'

Him   'We still have a lot of problems . . . an attitude of mind has got a lot to do with it, but things do seem to look a bit better.'

Her   'I feel so much bitterness now towards him. I honestly feel if there was any chance of making some sort of go of anything left the only way it would have happened is if the court ordered him to go – not by the welfare department.'

Him   'At the end of the day I'm out, so I don't think there's anything good come out of it as far as I'm concerned. . . . If a person wants [the marriage] to end, end it will. As far as that's concerned I won't say [the enquiry's] an absolute waste of time, but it doesn't do any good.'

Her   'Now at last I have what I always wanted – Johnny and me living together in peace. Since Frank left, life is at last beginning for Johnny and me. We get on all right, and

Johnny is beginning to grow up, stand on his own feet a little bit. . . . Johnny seems to get on better with his father just lately. He used to be a bit uptight about visiting him and would come home a bit umpy, but now it seems a lot better and he looks forward to seeing him – and I am glad.'

Him 'We are perfectly civil when we meet. We don't want anything to do with each other. The children are happy; we are; I see the kids two or three times a week; access is absolutely free – but my financial position is terrible.'

Her 'I've never regretted our decision to part. It's the best thing we ever did. We've all benefited. I feel much better. The children are happier. We were destroying each other. Our youngest never knew his parents other than quarrelling and unhappy and it's had its effect.'

Him 'I had to go out of town to work, so my daughter was spending more time with her mother, and I could only see her weekends and half-term. It turned out quite well because her mother had then calmed down a bit, and since then we've jogged along from there. I bite my lip and make arrangements from day to day and week to week. Our daughter really has two homes . . . One feels like an unpaid au pair. It's laughable really.'

Her 'He was forced to look at things as they were . . . He had to treat me with a bit more respect. If custody is joint we must consult. I had been doing this; he had been spiriting her off. He stopped behaving like that, and I think they [the welfare officers] are the ones who did it – I'm sure they did it. He suddenly changed his attitude during the months as this thing went on, and fortunately it still stays.'

Him 'Access was going fine until [the welfare] mucked it up. After he had sided with my wife, matters went from bad to worse. . . . I have won before and I will win again.'

Her 'Well, he's applying for custody again. . . . It's been going on for years, yet we were divorced within three months. He won't ever stop. It's the only way he can get at me. . . . The judge said access every third Sunday from 10 till 5. Well, when it came to it the children just would not go. They screamed, cried and were ill; they would not go. So now he's trying to do me for contempt of court.

What am I supposed to do? Force them out screaming and crying?'

On the whole, we felt rather gloomy about how much had changed as a result of welfare intervention. Many parents remained entrenched in battles that appeared relentless. If truce there was, the peace which followed often seemed to be an uneasy one. However, we were seeing parents close on the heels of the enquiry, and very close in time to the decisions of the court in some cases. We were not seeing their children, who may have benefited. Moreover, we ourselves were close to the enquiry experience. Perhaps our doubts about whether or not there had been any change were, more accurately, reflections of our experience of divorce court welfare work. It is to this experience that we now turn.

8
ON A ROLLER COASTER

'It just seems we're on a permanent roller coaster in this Unit.'
A welfare officer

The image of life in the Divorce Unit as a never-ending roller-coaster ride caught our imagination. It conveyed the sense of relentless pressure, of fluctuating mood and morale, and of the need for something substantial to hang on to which we came to associate with the experience of divorce court enquiry work during the fieldwork life of the research.

As practitioner researchers we contributed to, and were a part of the turbulence in the Unit between October 1982 and April 1985. Moreover, we wrote this account of what it was like to work as a welfare officer in that period. In some respects we were least qualified to write the account, being neither welfare officers nor full-time workers in the Unit. The impact of the work upon us as outsiders will have affected the picture we describe. However, not being part of the Unit carried certain advantages. One of them was the freedom to record experiences without the dulling of sensitivity which comes from repeated exposure to distressing events. Another was the release from being unduly constrained by professional interests within the probation service. Nevertheless, this chapter is concerned with subjective realities. Whether these realities belong more to us than to our welfare officer colleagues will be for the reader to judge.

We describe an episode in the life of an agency striving for a new identity. Although it is a piece of history, written by those who had a part in making it, we believe it has something to say about the effects upon individuals of operating in a changing professional climate with a clientele who were themselves undergoing stressful transitions. The Unit that exists today is different from the Unit we joined in 1982. The world in which it operates has also moved on. Like other organizations, it cannot stand still.

This chapter presents something of the experience of what it was like to be a divorce court welfare officer – and a research practitioner – in a particular specialist Divorce Unit, during a period in which a government interdepartmental committee reported on conciliation, a committee on court procedures in matrimonial causes took evidence and produced a consultative document, the Solicitors' Family Law Association came into being, the National Family Conciliation Council was set up, the Home Office produced a Statement of National Objectives for the Probation Service, and Family Courts once again became a subject for serious discussion.

In writing about a period in the Divorce Unit's history we became aware, as did our welfare officer colleagues, of the parallels between the research we were doing and the enquiries they (and we) were undertaking into the ways families functioned. In certain respects our presence changed the Unit and the way it went about its business, much as being the subject of a welfare enquiry changes the behaviour of individuals within a family. The discovery did little to make an intrinsically uneasy relationship more comfortable. 'Sometimes it's like reading a welfare report on yourself', remarked one welfare officer when describing how exposed she felt on seeing her words written down in a 'black and white, out there, minuted way'. We were one of several influences affecting the operations of the civil arm of the HPS at the time of the project. Other pressures from within and outside the probation service also contributed to the roller coaster experience.

For the duration of the fieldwork period we attended, recorded, and participated in the weekly staff meetings of the Divorce Unit. By and large these meetings alternated between case discussions and business agendas, there being some flexibility to meet the contingencies of a busy unit. Every six months or so, a half day was put aside for a meeting of the staff, the research team, the Assistant Chief Officer responsible for the Unit, and the Chief Officer of the HPS. These meetings monitored the progress and experiences generated by the research, and later provided a forum in which the draft and final chapters of this book were discussed. From all these meetings we have attempted to distil recurring themes which affected practice and management in the Unit, and which had important implications for the settlement-seeking aspirations of the staff in conducting their investigative role.

The agenda

The records of 35 business meetings and 45 case discussions, plus some internal memoranda, constitute an agency diary for the two-and-a-half years of research fieldwork. They point up the context in which staff were carrying out their duties, and highlight major pressure points which affected their day-to-day work. Outwardly, the Unit remained relatively fixed and unchanging. The staff group stayed intact for most of the period, the range of their tasks changed little until the point of our departure, and offices, furnishings, and letter-headings remained the same. While the public face of the Unit was constant, its internal life, as demonstrated by discussions at the weekly staff meetings, was in a state of flux.

On the agenda of the first business meeting we attended were three items: office security, the Divorce Unit 'roadshow', and IMS research. These items delineated three areas which defined the context of welfare operations during the life of the project: relationships with clients, relationships within the Unit's professional network, and relationships with the IMS team. The three areas affected and overlapped each other.

The Divorce Unit and its clients

Violence

The agenda item 'office security' concerned the decision to add a glass panel to one of the interviewing rooms in response to concern in the HPS as a whole about the risks to probation officers from violent clients. There had, some time earlier, been an attack on one of the officers in the probation team which shared the same premises as the Divorce Unit. Protection for secretarial staff, proposals for an alarm system connected to the neighbouring police station, and measures for safeguarding officers who interviewed clients in the evenings or on unattended premises all received serious attention in the early business meetings.

While the impetus for this agenda item came from the criminal arm of the probation service, it resonated with the experiences of officers working in the Divorce Unit, and certainly made an impact on us researchers as we joined the team. At the time, one of the welfare officers was receiving police protection following a threat, taken seriously by the service, to kill her. This, while very unusual, demonstrated the emotional battering and verbal abuse which was a part of divorce court welfare work, and the risks attached to interviewing people who are in a state of emotional distress and psychological disturbance. Conscious decisions would sometimes be taken to see parents at the office, during the day, and when other people were in the building, solely on the grounds of anticipated violence.

Violence was very much part of the divorce experience of many of the parents in the core sample. Some had initiated and been victims of actual assault. The incidence of applications for ouster injunctions and non-molestation orders underlined the fear of violence which was expressed by many parents in the course of our enquiries – women in particular. Men, too, experienced these same applications as violent body blows delivered by the law on behalf of an erstwhile spouse. The physical, emotional, and social decline that often followed divorce was frequently experienced by men as an assault on their former state of being. It is not surprising, therefore, that welfare officers should be prey to verbal and emotional abuse when stepping into the arena of their clients' troubled lives.

The verbal violence was not all located in the Unit's clients. We, and our welfare officer colleagues, were capable of becoming incensed by the treatment meted out by some parents to children, to former partners, and to ourselves. While overt hostility and physical violence was very much more evident in the behaviour of men, women also were quite capable of evoking considerable hostility in their partners and their welfare officers: 'While I was listening to her, being very calm, and restraining myself from telling her what an evil, monstrous baggage she was, I sat and shook for about an hour . . . I was so angry . . . you do go away feeling quite ill.' This welfare officer described driving home in a state of shock and disorientation, and had difficulty remembering what had transpired in the interview. She thought the experience had produced the effect of placing her in the father's shoes, and it had allowed her to appreciate the full weight of his burden of powerlessness, making his violent protests understandable. The first nine months of the project witnessed three car accidents among Divorce Unit staff, construed by the welfare officers as being directly linked with the stress of their job. Later in the project, sickness rates were talked about in the same way.

While levels of verbal abuse from clients did not vary much during the life of the project, our response, and that of the Divorce Unit team, did. We had joined a recently formed and recruited team who, like us, were more vulnerable to the impact of the work in 1982 than they were in 1985. One year into the project an IMS researcher commented upon her experience in these terms:

'Well, the thing that hit me was the degree of violence. I had three cases in a row where there were injunctions against the husband for having beaten up his wife . . . it's always more complicated when you get into it, but the degree of violence as well as verbal abuse – I feel it quite distressing; especially the degree of ruthlessness when children are being used as pawns. The thing is, my defences must be working better or something. I'm not as uncomfortable about it. They're either working better or protecting me better.'

Our surprise early on in the project at hearing the firm, raised voices of our colleagues used with parents over the telephone was replaced later on by an appreciation of the justification for behaving in that way. Our own interviewing and telephoning manners were gradually overtaken by a wariness and directness which was unusual for us. We became more active and assertive than we were before the project began. Mattinson (1975) has written about this sort of mirroring behaviour between clients and workers and the unconscious purposes served by such reflections. Uncontrolled behaviour can elicit authoritative responses, and sometimes these are necessary for people who feel in danger of destroying others or of going to pieces themselves. Sometimes, of course, they indicate the needs of workers more than those of clients.

Establishing a thick enough skin to withstand the buffeting of enquiry work was necessary for survival in role. At times, parents came close to penetrating defences, and then added efforts were necessary to keep them out. One such time was when the clients' views of the enquiry experience percolated into the Unit. This challenge to the working assumptions of the Unit resulted in we and they closing ranks to keep out the intrusion. One IMS member remarked that he had yet to meet a client he actually liked. Lending support to him a welfare colleague said she had 'grown generally indifferent. It's so repetitive you begin to see the ploys they use, a regular pattern, you say "here we go again".' Another commented 'you can't please both of [the parents] so you're bound to get stick'. 'If I had to contemplate a lifetime of this I would be in total despair', commented a third member of the Unit in an attempt to console. 'Never expect your client to be grateful' was a piece of advice proffered to one of the research team early on in the project. It lodged in our memories to counteract the impact of disappointment about our actual achievements and abused offers of help.

In the same way that parents may not be able to afford gratitude, or to become beholden to others when trying to preserve their own integrity, welfare officers also had to survive in order to keep going. Disappointment had to be managed, and a jaundiced sense of realism was one device. Such realism failed to do justice to the very real attempts made by welfare officers to engage their clients and to avoid hiding behind their reporting role. It concealed distress about feeling ill-treated and sabotaged when the intent was to offer constructive help and advice.

Intransigence

Intransigence was as discouraging as abuse, and closely connected to it. As we have described earlier, both the Divorce Unit and IMS staff had aspirations towards helping parents reach agreements, so obviating the need for courts to do more than ratify arrangements which had been worked out between the parents themselves. These aspirations were thwarted when parents were unable to reach and sustain agreement, and when they were determined to coerce welfare officers into accepting the responsibility for whatever transpired.

A sense of impasse was frequently given as the reason for bringing a case for discussion to the team meeting. 'Is this a lost cause or can more be done?' 'Deadlock dividing the workers.' 'How to gain access in a closed, heavily defended system which has operated for years?' 'Needing more equipment to break the deadlock.' 'Where am I going?' 'Can you create a father from an immature man?' 'Total confusion as to what to do next. Feeling imprisoned in a destructive process and unable to get free – with real anxieties as to what is happening to the child.' These were some of the questions and comments written on the team meeting forms (see Appendix II) specifying why a case had been brought for discussion.

Looking at the progress of the team meeting records during the course of the project there was a noticeable shift from hope to disillusionment in the research team's and resident staff's feelings towards work with clients. Never was this more marked than just over halfway into the project when the first follow-up results were becoming available. These were some of the responses from ourselves and the Unit staff:

'Not one client has been pleased, or liked what we have offered.'

'The really depressing thing is that some of the cases are back at square one. Intervention has not changed a thing, and the fight continues.'

'I haven't got over the gap between what I thought I had offered and how they experienced it.'

'The reality is that parents in possession have the whip hand – irrespective of the court decision. What we go through becomes a ritual in some cases.'

The impact of the consumer view was in the threat it constituted to the professional social work identity of welfare officers. The senior officer of the Divorce Unit circulated a paper to her staff which spelt out the dilemma for them very clearly:

'The follow-ups are showing that there is an inescapable divergence between client and worker perceptions and needs during the divorce/conciliation process. Clients, on the whole, want to be allowed to separate, do not want to regard themselves as still a family, want a period of lengthy emotional and practical support, want vindication and justification, and seem either bemused by what we offer, or feel "manipulated", "pressurized", etc. into negotiation and compromise. Welfare officers, on the whole, want to hold parents together, consider them as a reconstituted family, stay for a short period alongside them, offer little if any practical advice, and want it all to be about negotiation and compromise.

Given such a basic divergence, there has to be an inescapable baseline question for workers about how much anything "therapeutic", in the most general sense of the word, can be attempted, and how much social work principles can be utilized. Ironically, it may be that the old DCWOs' style more matched clients' expectations and left them less dissatisfied.'

Corporately, the team recovered from the body blows dealt by consumer feedback, and established a case for constructive management which left them in a less jaundiced mood about the value of their work than the consumer reports had initially produced. One officer put the situation succinctly in the course of a case discussion: 'Let's face it, these two parents are not going to agree, so how do you manage an imposed solution?' Case discussions focused upon supporting the welfare officer to survive and to manage enquiries in progress. That survival was aided by understanding why people were behaving as they were. Particularly important was an appreciation of the cumulative effects of present and past losses on behaviour which helped us to modify our expectations. In that sense, understanding was a valuable ally in withstanding the onslaught of clients and their feelings.

Trust

It is endemic to the experience of divorce that the capacity of former partners to trust each other is severely taxed. A climate of mistrust and suspicion is the rule rather than the exception when arrangements necessitated by marital breakdown are being worked out. Not surprisingly, this climate affects how welfare officers regard the parents they see and influences their behaviour. One of the culture shocks for the IMS team working in a welfare setting was to encounter barefaced lying. Accustomed to tolerating and valuing the different perceptions and different realities that generate conflict between partners in a current marriage, the discrepant accounts given to us by many parents on the way out of marriage were difficult to relate to in other than a mistrustful and pejorative way. We feared, as a result of our investigative role and responsibilities, having the wool pulled over our eyes.

Reflecting on his experience halfway through the project, one of the IMS team described the problem in terms which must echo the thoughts and feelings of some parents:

'I think, by the very nature of the job, as soon as you do an enquiry about children you are walking into the crossfire between two parties – so that if somebody actually holds their fire you're suspicious about their motives. You can't really trust any nice gestures that are made. . . . Alternatively, of course, if you cross these people, you feel they're gunning for you . . . they'll want to take things to pieces – notably, of course, the report at the end.'

One of his colleagues had jested early on in the project that an essential piece of equipment for any welfare officer was a lie detector: 'Lying is very important – there is a fight for survival here. Sometimes I feel quite mad trying to put two different stories together.' Situations of this kind were not uncommon, and undermined confidence in any joint enterprise with parents, particularly for those of us who had come from an agency offering therapy: 'Two essential ingredients of a therapeutic alliance are a common task and a degree of trust. These are more often absent here than not. So what does the client/worker relationship amount to?' While there was an inclination to attribute the constraints upon settlement-seeking to parents, we were later to appreciate how our survival needs closed us off from them in the same way we felt they were closed off from us. We were also to appreciate the constraints of agency context upon what could and could not be achieved.

Context

So far we have presented a predominantly negative view of the clients of the Divorce Unit in explaining that welfare officers had to protect their own boundaries and come to terms with disappointed professional aspirations. It would be misleading to leave the story there. We and our welfare officer colleagues liked and enjoyed some of the parents we met, and we thought of them as 'parents' and 'people' rather than 'clients'. We were moved by their distress, identified with their predicaments, and sometimes felt tempted to champion their causes. Moreover, these parents made a bid to be heard, were capable of gratitude, and wanted support and help. Their needs, although often ambivalently expressed, synchronized with the professional social work aspirations of their welfare officers. These needs were seldom fully met. Two reasons for this stemmed from the fact that welfare officers worked in an agency whose primary task was to investigate and report to the courts.

The first, and most obvious, consequence of this fact was that we and they felt under pressure to appear, as well as to be, neutral and objective in our involvements with parents. In order to produce a report which had some chance of being acceptable to the subjects, as well as to the courts, a tightrope had to be walked between the two sides. Even when we felt more sympathy with one parent – indeed, especially when this was the case – we would try to conceal this, and represent the other parent's viewpoint so that he or she might come to accept the position as it was seen by the enquiring officer. Very often, however, in so far as views were often formed early on in an enquiry, welfare officers felt that their neutrality was a myth. While they would use their influence to balance the effects of the final court outcome the need to preserve impartiality inevitably distanced welfare officers from parents who, above all else, were searching for a dependable ally.

The second consequence of the reporting function was that the welfare officer's client was properly the court, not the parents. Courts initiated a steady stream of enquiries to which the Divorce Unit had to respond. There was pressure to maintain a steady turnover of reports so that a backlog would not build up. Time and again it was noted at team case discussions that families required protracted help if they were to overcome the difficulties to which court applications had drawn attention, but the agency had neither the time nor the resources to respond. Enquiries uncovered needs which had to be left unattended because the agency's primary objective was to furnish the courts with reports, rather than to provide a social work service for the families concerned. Judicial action could be very effective in relieving uncertainty and putting an end to protracted fighting. In that respect, welfare officers could be instrumental in meeting some pressing needs. Yet except by making matrimonial supervision orders, courts were unable to provide the long-term help that some parents intimated they needed, and which we were convinced was necessary.

In the core sample of cases, supervision orders were made on only two occasions. In one of these it was assigned to the local social services department, in line with existing policy. We would urge parents to contact the Divorce Unit if they ran into difficulties in the future, and sometimes this offer was written into the conclusion of a report. Our motives for this were mixed.

On one hand, we tended to believe that the 'real' work of adapting to changed circumstances could only follow the certainty of a court decision. We also held the view that we would be on a firmer footing with parents if our services were sought out rather than imposed. On the other hand, long-term work sat uneasily with the reporting rhythm of the Unit, and threatened to clog up the works. There is no doubt that as well as formally signalling to parents that their services would be available in the future should they be required, the practice of mentioning the voluntary offer of help in the concluding section of a report was also intended to deter judges from making supervision orders when there were fears that they might otherwise be tempted to do so. Informal offers of help were seldom taken up, and because of the demands on resources there was usually little regret about this.

While the court-related context of welfare operations had its drawbacks, it was also a source of authority that created opportunities as well as constraints. 'Enough is enough' was a phrase that recurred frequently at team case discussions, drawing attention to the importance of curtailing fights. An early return to court was one means of checking behaviour. Parents and welfare officers were well aware of the power they had to present their cases to the courts in a favourable or unfavourable light, and this spur to good behaviour could have a controlling effect in potentially volatile situations. Moreover, that power could be used to balance out some of the unevenly distributed advantages that parents felt they had, or lacked, in relation to each other. In short, the welfare role had a regulating and policing influence in a potentially anarchic world. Moreover, the discipline of writing a report in a way that represented both parents' views, and that attempted to account for the difficulties and differences they were experiencing could, in itself, have beneficial effects. At best, an outside view carried authority; at the very least it had to be taken into account, providing the possibility that it might affect the views and positions of parents.

Satisfactions

Given the impact of clients upon welfare officers we searched for the satisfactions the job provided. In the context of the relationship between welfare officers and their clients, satisfaction came from three main sources.

In the first place, and despite the intransigence of many parents, there was satisfaction when some level of agreement was reached. Against the subjective impressions described so far, welfare officers (again including ourselves) were surprisingly optimistic about the outcome of enquiries in their reports to the courts. In 16 out of 27 reports (59 per cent) full agreement was reported between the parents, and reports endorsed these agreements in their recommendations. Differences remained between parents for the remaining 11 enquiries, although some measure of agreement was reached on some issues in some cases. Nevertheless, courts were required to adjudicate in these cases in the absence of parental agreement.

Of the 16 cases that reached agreement, 5 sets of parents had agreed before they met their welfare officers and a further 2 agreements were uneasy, reflecting situations where children were unhappy about, or refusing to see the non-resident parent. These parents were reluctant to press their claim against the children's wishes, and we, who had also been unable to overcome the resistance to access, also considered that coercion would be counter-productive. This left 9 cases where agreements were arrived at in the course of, and presumably as a result of, work during the enquiry itself. These were the cases in which we believed, mistakenly or not, that some change had been brought about. The arrangements themselves changed little. What was achieved was frequently in the nature of a change in attitude towards the way things were.

While agreements were reported to the courts in 59 per cent of the core sample of cases, the registered figure on the questionnaire was higher. Of 28 questionnaire assessments (the 2 not registered were among the first enquiries to be taken on, when procedures had not been fully worked out) 20 (71.4 per cent) estimated that parents were nearer agreement at termination of the enquiry than at first interview. These estimates were made by welfare officers at the close of an enquiry. They were an improvement on the 56 per cent judged to be nearer agreement in the one-year sample of case questionnaires. Two of the core sample agreements represented one partner giving up a claim, leaving 18 enquiries (64.3 per cent) where the chances of joint parenting were thought to have improved. However, in only a small handful of cases (four or five) were welfare officers confident that agreements would hold without further outside help or control. Quite often there was a suspicion that agreements

were reached to quieten the enquiry officer while nothing
changed substantially in the behaviour of parents towards each
other and their children. These qualifications took away some of
the edge of satisfaction that might otherwise have come from
claiming an agreed outcome.

It the second place, welfare officers derived satisfaction from
their involvement with children. The staff of the Unit frequently
saw them as the unsung heroes of divorce, and believed that if, by
stepping into the firing line, they could take some of the pressure
and burden of responsibility from children, then it was all
worthwhile. In a discussion about the feelings welfare officers
had for family members children came out top in terms of
popularity, and were the family members with whom welfare
officers most identified.

'Children are by far and away the most likeable . . . their sense
of social justice and decency is far in advance of their parents.'

'You get allied with the child in the middle, inevitably.'

'I feel in bleak moments that parents may hate me for ever
more, but some satisfaction is gained from allowing the
children an opportunity to speak.'

Several welfare officers were very skilled in their dealings with
children. Supplies of paper, felt-tip pens, pencils, dolls and a
dolls' house not only provided children with something to do, but
also gave them a means of expressing themselves. Their drawings
festooned the walls of the offices and went some way towards
reducing the formality of a modern purpose-built office. Children
were seldom the object of humour or criticism in team case
discussions; even when their part in exacerbating conflict
between their parents was acknowledged and discussed, they
always received concerned attention. Our welfare colleagues
pointed out to us that a serious failing of the follow-up interviews
was that the views of children were seldom heard. The hope was
that had they been able to speak, they would have vindicated the
efforts of the welfare service. The most inflammatory kind of
remark a parent could make to a welfare officer was of the type
actually made by a parent during a difficult attempt to restore
access: 'Do you like upsetting children? Do you enjoy your job?'

The third source of satisfaction stemmed from the report-writing process. At one level, the report marked the end of what was sometimes an uncomfortable, even stormy, relationship. But the satisfaction of report writing was of more fundamental significance than 'getting out', or 'forming a nicely turned sentence', although both of these could satisfy. What was raised as a question by one of the IMS staff during the course of the project became a point of view: 'Is the satisfaction about having attained a view? . . . The most important thing is to have a story you can live with.'

The process of report writing was an integrative one for welfare officers, allowing them to represent discrepant views and to provide explanations. In an emotionally fragmented and conflict-ridden climate, attaining a point of view was important for the sanity of the investigator. It represented a kind of debriefing, in which a story was told and an explanation provided for the behaviour of the parties in the enquiry. The story told by one (or two) of the participants (the welfare officers) often focused upon the enquiry process itself. From that limited experience conclusions were drawn about how parents might be expected to behave in the future. The story was told diplomatically, and the subjects of the report were always represented in the best possible light. In this, we and our welfare colleagues were sometimes false to our feelings but true to our purposes. As well as informing the judge, the report was intended to act as a balm to injured parties in the hope that it might have some healing effects. The report, then, was a diplomatic document which tried to honour the views of both sides and to save face for all concerned in the interests of securing a peace.

From the point of view of the welfare officer's experience, the report was important because it formulated a credible and coherent perspective. We, like the parents we saw, desperately needed a story of events that we could live with, and one which exonerated our behaviour. We, like the parents we saw, strongly resisted attempts to unpick that story because our own coherence depended upon its staying intact. One of the IMS researchers talked about the satisfaction 'of being able to tie a bow on the reports and send them off into the blue'. 'Until you find the bow is untied' interrupted one of the Divorce Unit team; 'yes, and the resistance to having the bow untied is enormous'.

An attempt was always made to meet parents to allow them to read the report before it was despatched to the court, and in most cases this was successful. These meetings were always anxious events for both sides. The metaphor of legal brief and bow stayed with us, and one of the IMS staff talked about his despair when the report failed to signal the end of an involvement with a difficult set of parents whose case repeatedly came back to court. He described:

'An increasing despair as the year went on about the degree of intractable problems. Chris was talking about tying a bow on cases. I had one which I thought was beautifully sewn up, and lo and behold it's come back again. The rest have been attempts at tying up a package.'

The art, not the purpose, of report writing was less to give an objective account of the situation in which parents found themselves (although the situation would be represented accurately as the welfare officer saw it) than to achieve a balance through telling a story to which all the parties to the enquiry (children, parents, welfare officers, and the courts) could subscribe.

Secretarial support

It would be remiss to ignore the secretarial role in the Divorce Unit when considering its relations with clients. The secretaries took all the incoming calls. If welfare officers were unavailable they had to deal with the enquiries themselves. They performed an essential gate-keeping function for the Unit, regulating the inflow of messages to officers and representing their availability to clients. From both quarters they were in a potentially vulnerable position. The welfare staff were aware of the pressures upon them as a note from the Unit's senior to headquarters staff made clear:

'Secretaries in the Divorce Unit face a great deal of verbal abuse and violence from clients, both in person and over the telephone. This is one of the greatest stresses that a welfare officer has to live with, and must be even more so for secretaries who have not received any professional training in handling it. It is a standing joke amongst welfare officers that you cannot even relax for a five minute 'phone call, and have to remain constantly alert to the possible implications of what is being said. The same applies to secretaries who may be less immediately aware of the manipulations taking place, less knowledgeable about official policy, and worried that having faced a barrage from an irate client they will then face an irritated officer who tells them they have done the wrong thing! . . . It is also clear that clients will frequently take it out on a secretary, because it is safer to do that, and will subsequently be pleasantness itself to the officer concerned. In addition to all of the above, on most days there is a continuous heavy flow of 'phone calls which come into the Unit without pause and fragment the secretaries' concentration. At the end of a day of heavy work they are frequently left feeling they have achieved little.'

The same document, which requested extra secretarial resources, referred to the burden of typing lengthy and emotive reports and case records, the degree of direct contact the secretaries had with clients (often acting as childminders), and the personal nature of the work which was as taxing for secretaries as it was for welfare officers. She might have added to the list the extra secretarial burden arising out of our research presence in the Unit. On top of all this, an often tired group of officers would assemble in the secretaries' room for tea and sympathy. Not surprisingly, the relationship between welfare and secretarial staff was sometimes strained. This relationship was one barometer of the emotional climate within the unit.

The Divorce Unit and its network

The work of the Divorce Unit brought its officers into contact with a wide range of professionals: judges, solicitors, social workers, police, other probation officers, housing officers, head teachers, voluntary workers, and, of course, welfare officers from other areas. Within this professional network, three relationships featured prominently: relations with management and other teams in the local probation service; relations with the courts; and relations with the conciliation service which started operations shortly after the project began.

Relationships within the probation service

At the first business meeting we attended, a suggestion was put forward that the Divorce Unit team should go 'on the road', visiting other probation teams in the area to explain the work it was doing to improve working relationships. The Unit, it will be remembered, had only recently been established as a specialist enterprise and the 'roadshow' was conceived out of a wish to be recognized as a part of the local probation service and to share some of the enthusiasm generated by the launch.

At this stage in the project morale was high, partly because of a Home Office inspection which had reported very favourably on the Unit, and partly because of the excitement of being in at the beginning of a development inside the probation service which was relevant to the national debate about the best ways of managing divorce.

The picture changed as the project proceeded. The impact of the job took its toll on staff. The early optimism about what might be achieved from a specialist base was tempered by experience. At low points it could feel as if civil work was the least popular area of work in the service. By the end of the project there were signs that probation officers working in the mainstream of the organization's activities were envied because their work was valued, their conditions were stable, and a court report signalled the beginning of a helping relationship rather than the end of an enquiry.

Management support was affected by adversity. In the first year of the project both the Chief Probation Officer, who had been instrumental in setting up the specialist unit, and an Assistant Chief Officer with special responsibility for the Divorce Unit were unavailable for a long period because of illness. The Unit reacted as if it had been bereaved of parents, sensing itself to be more of an orphan in the probation service than before. Its working assumptions could no longer be assumed to be taken as read, and energy had to be channelled towards inducting another Assistant Chief Officer, who extended his brief from the criminal work of the service. The induction went well. 'I've already picked up not to talk about how many reports you've got but how many bits of work are on hand, because the report is only a vehicle', he commented at one team meeting. Joined by the Chief Probation Officer on her return to health, they were able to reaffirm some of the values which were not universally held within the service as a whole, and by so doing restore a sense of institutional security for a Unit which felt on the periphery of the mainline activities of their colleagues in criminal work.

The level of perceived support from management was also

affected by two initiatives about which the Divorce Unit was ambivalent. Both were logical consequences of the move towards specialization yet both were experienced as unsettling by a Unit which felt it was not being allowed sufficient time to establish itself. The first was the proposal that the Divorce Unit should move to new, self-contained premises, near the centre of the HPS catchment area, and in the same town as the county court from which most orders for reports originated. The second was that the Unit should extend its operations to handle all the civil work in the area (serving magistrates' courts as well as county courts, and undertaking adoption enquiries along with divorce court welfare enquiries).

The proposals generated a certain amount of excitement. The proposed change of address, in particular, occupied much staff time and generated fantasies about the kind of residence that would be suitable: an old house with a garden, kitchen facilities, and play room, which was attractively situated but in reach of the shops and public transport facilities. The sense of tranquillity and contented family life conjured up by the way the new premises were imagined (there was a telling confusion about how the address of one strong contender should be spelt – Bridle or Bridal Close!) was far removed from the reality of enquiry work as it featured in case discussions. It was as if an idealized home was created in the minds of the staff to sustain hope and to protect against the painful realities of the job, a phenomenon we considered relevant to the ways some divorcing parents served by the Unit managed their own predicaments. These dreams were not lightly to be disturbed, and the problem of finding suitable premises was as predictable as one might expect in the circumstances.

Commenting on the unsettling effects of the proposals upon the Unit, its senior officer referred to a 'golden age' (correspond- ing with the first nine months of the project's life) when the staff were confident, well regarded, and on top of their work. In a paper to the Assistant Chief Officer responsible for the Unit at that time she wrote:

'I am trying to understand why there is a large gap between the organization's and the team's perceptions of what is happening at the moment. The organization feels that it is making positive decisions on our behalf which will help both ourselves and the area; the team feels that it has wandered into some kind of punishing nightmare which may end in effectively sabotaging our good operation.'

In particular she noted that the Unit's priorities were concerned with 'sharpening our thinking and practice about different models of conciliation' and with its 'commitment to the IMS and their research project'. These were different from the priorities of headquarters staff, which focused on implementing the transition to a civil work unit by a change of accommodation and provision of extra staff. Reflecting her feelings of alienation she wrote that she felt: 'The SPO feels forced to make some kind of choice about priorities which are not "real" to the Unit at this point in time and may, in addition, seem to threaten the Unit's own choice of priorities which are real to them.'

We were tempted to speculate about parallels between the feelings of Divorce Unit staff in relation to their management, and feelings of parents towards welfare officers whose interventions might undermine their sense of making a free and unpressured choice. In both contexts, pressure applied from the best of motives could have alienating effects.

The Unit also felt decreasingly supported by developments outside the local operations of the Service. In 1984 the Home Office produced a Statement of National Objectives for the Probation Service. Civil work was accorded a low priority and was not seen as an area into which additional resources were likely to be channelled. The document made a substantial impact on the probation service as a whole, and while approving the trend towards specialism in civil work it mooted the possibility that this area of work might be jettisoned at some time in the future. Divorce court welfare officers, it seemed, were facing the risk of being disowned by their parent service.

It certainly appeared to us that there was a fundamental anomaly in the status accorded to a small specialist unit whose priorities were increasingly parting company with Home Office priorities. It had a bearing on job satisfaction, in so far as that derived from an identification with the Probation Service. That identification was increasingly being tested.

Another significant development came from the deliberations of the Booth Committee (1985). As it become clear that this Committee would recommend in favour of making an absolute distinction between conciliation and reporting activities, the Unit was forced to define its own position. While some members felt the distinction was helpful and clarifying, others felt that it changed the nature of their job and threatened their professional commitment towards effecting settlements between parents within the context of an investigative relationship.

By the end of the project there was considerable disheartenment and division within the Unit, which was at first concealed from us. The 'roller coaster' experience was taking its toll on staff. Anxiety was expressed about the extent of overtime and weekend working, and about levels of sickness within the Unit. In prospect was the retirement of the Chief Probation Officer, the departure of the IMS research team, arrivals of newcomers to the staff group, and a change of accommodation, title, and function for the Unit as a whole.

Relationships with the courts

The one stable point in this changing environment was the relationship that welfare officers had with judges, registrars, and court staff. Formally, the courts were the Unit's clients, and considerable satisfaction was obtained from servicing them with competent reports, and from the high regard in which they were held by satisfied judges. By and large, welfare officers felt that their reports were closely attended to and valued, and that they had a considerable influence upon the decisions ultimately reached at court. Of the 22 cases in the core sample that had returned to court for adjudication by May 1986 (one year after the project ended), in 15 the welfare officers' recommendations matched the decisions of the court exactly, and in the remaining 7 cases they matched in all but a few details. The widest fluctuation between adjudication and recommendation was when a court ordered sole custody to a mother rather than the recommended joint custody (the child was in the care and control of the mother), and made an order for reasonable as opposed to defined access. In this case there had been a significant change in the father's circumstances between the filing of the report and the court hearing. Formal contacts with judges were supported and underpinned by occasional informal meetings, allowing welfare officers to feel that their views and predicaments were, by and large, adequately understood by the courts.

The importance of the courts to welfare officers, and welfare officers to the courts, does create conditions in which collusive alliances might arise. There is nothing original in the suggestion that welfare officers might anticipate a judge's decisions and tailor their report recommendations accordingly. There is no doubt that the likely reactions of a judge were carefully weighed up when we and they were writing reports, but in our experience that did not prevent us from following our convictions when making recommendations, even when these were thought likely to be in conflict with 'second guesses' about how a judge might decide.

There were occasions when a judge's ruling or treatment of a welfare officer generated friction. 'Some reports are not read by the judge' commented one officer in the context of a judgment which undermined an agreement that had been reached by and with one set of parents. Dissatisfaction was seldom with local courts; it was more likely to result from dealings with other areas. In one instance it led the senior officer for the Unit to suggest that there was a need for welfare officers to be represented in court. In another, it resulted in a letter of protest to a court liaison officer about the punitive tone of a standardized letter ordering a welfare officer to attend court.

Two substantial changes took place in the Unit's dealings with courts towards the end of the project's lifetime. An in-court conciliation scheme was started at the local county court and staffed by the Divorce Unit, and the move to become a Family Courts Unit (made after the research was completed) raised the prospect of a new set of relationships with magistrates' courts in the area.

By and large, however, the relationship between welfare officers and the courts was satisfying and relatively unchanging. Conflict about the time taken in preparing reports, when it did occur, was more likely to be with the legal representative of one of the parents than with the courts. The courts represented a fixed point in the Unit's changing world. Perhaps for this reason a breakdown in communication, when it did occur, was felt very keenly.

The local conciliation service

Before moving to the third area of turbulence in the Divorce Unit's environment, mention must be made of the voluntary, out-of-court conciliation service which, with the help of the probation service, the Divorce Unit, and a member of the IMS team, established itself while the project was under way. The Chief

Probation Officer had offered encouragement and practical support to the enterprise, and with the senior officer from the Divorce Unit (and an IMS member of staff) sat on the working party and sub-group that helped to set it up. Perceived, in part, as its own progeny, considerable help was provided by the probation service in setting up the service and training its staff.

A relationship that began in a spirit of generosity ran into difficulties as time went by. The pressures on Unit resources left little spare capacity for the needs of a new service. Moreover, as the conciliation service began to establish itself, a degree of rivalry developed between the two bodies. Divorce Unit staff feared losing rewarding areas of their work and being left with the heavy end of the business. Conciliation service staff felt the Divorce Unit was restricting the scope of their potential usefulness. Matters came to a head (and were resolved in favour of the Divorce Unit) when both services made a bid for staffing the in-court conciliation scheme.

This development would be of local interest only were it not for the manoeuvrings taking place on the national landscape over the appropriate boundaries between conciliation and welfare services. The conciliation movement steadily gathered momentum in the first half of the 1980s, attracting widespread interest and support. With the publication of the Booth Report (1985) and, later, the statement of the President of the Family Division (Arnold 1985), a clear demarcation line was drawn between conciliation services and the activities of welfare officers. For the welfare services, there was a prospect of being relegated to the second division, left to report only on those parents who had failed to reach agreement and who were therefore likely to be, to quote one IMS member of staff, 'the knacker's yard end of the conciliation movement'. It also opened the way for the development of a separate conciliation service in Britain. While this was to be welcomed, the threatened removal of potentially satisfying activities which were in tune with the professional identity of welfare officers constituted a further source of stress for a Unit which had to work out its position in relation to these new developments.

The Divorce Unit and the research

It was an act of considerable courage for a recently established Unit to invite research into its operations. At a time when five welfare officers were starting to band together as a specialist team, and to work out a corporate response to the challenge of enquiry work, we were trying to establish a research presence in the Unit. The influx of three additional people, with little or no first-hand experience of divorce court welfare work, into a small and relatively unestablished working group, for one day a week, was a source of additional worry and work for the welfare and secretarial staff of the Divorce Unit.

The logistical complexities of housing the project will be apparent enough. We had to be accredited as probation volunteers to legitimate our direct involvement with the clients of the Unit. We had to be accommodated in an office and provided with secretarial support. There had to be cover for the enquiry work in which we were involved during the time we were not at the office. We had to be inducted into the ways of the Unit and the context in which the service operated. We needed supervision and surveillance so that the Unit discharged its professional responsibilities properly. While we reduced the number of enquiries undertaken by the resident staff, there can be little doubt that we increased their workload. The burden of our presence fell upon the senior welfare officer in particular: 'I can remember the first few Thursdays. I have never felt so knackered in my life. I didn't think I was physically going to survive it if it went on being that exhausting. It took me to the Monday to recover.' The emotional burden of our presence was as taxing as the physical burden. In the eyes of the Unit we represented a disconcerting blend of expertise and ignorance. Three members of the Unit's staff had been on courses run by the IMS, and our competence as marital therapists was not called into question. However, we were transparently naive about the welfare context in which the research was to take place:

'It is a very bizarre thing to have to supervise people who combine two totally conflicting extremes. On the one hand, when you come in on a Thursday it is like supervising the newest of new officers immediately off training; whilst at the same time it is supervising extremely experienced, sophisticated therapists who have been my teachers.'

Early fantasies about IMS wizardry both undermined the confidence of the resident staff and provided every inducement to relegate the relevance of their experience to the ivory towers of Tavistocktonia:

'It can be very hard for members of my team to believe they
are experts in any sense, in any way whatever in this
co-working relationship . . . [They have] fluctuating confidence in terms of their degree of idealization of the IMS, in
terms of feeling they can stand up to them, in terms of not
often understanding the words that are used.'

The research brought additional burdens. We came armed
with questionnaires and forms which we wanted welfare officers
to complete. We asked questions, questioned procedures, and
raised doubts. We also brought into the Unit the results of the
follow-up interviews, and exposed staff to consumer views of
their activities. Fears about the potentially damaging consequences of the research were expressed in these terms: 'We are
going to hear a lot more in the next year than we want to hear . . .
I feel you will leave us at the end of the day in a worse state than
we were before . . . I steel myself for the inevitable.'

Perhaps most difficult of all for the staff of the Divorce Unit
was that we proposed to be not only 'outside' researchers but also
'inside' practitioners. The participant observer stance we tried to
maintain throughout the project created uncertainty about
whether we were in the Unit or out of it. The uncertainty was as
much in us as in the welfare team. At the beginning of the project
we proposed that the IMS team worked in isolation with the core
sample of enquiries in order to build up a distinctive experience
which would inform our dialogue with the Unit. The anxiety
which lay behind this proposal was that co-working with welfare
officers on enquiries would 'contaminate' us, and that we might
be sucked into the practices and procedures of the agency in a
way which would deaden our critical faculties. It took the divorce
court welfare staff to point out that we would not then be
researching the work of a specialist unit.

While we sometimes felt frustrated by not being able to engage
the team in the research enterprise as much as we would have
liked, they frequently expressed their dissatisfaction – and sense
of personal hurt and rejection – arising out of our dual role. Our
preoccupation with maintaining an appropriate boundary could
seem stand-offish, especially when, at other times, we were fully
involved with the team and shared the roller coaster experience of
life in the Unit with them:

'You're doing an odd dance of coming towards us then backing off . . . so that we feel sometimes that we lose you when we've established something . . . you're here and then gone again, and it's not the same . . . We feel warmth one minute, and the next there's those little symbolic phrases – like when Chris was at a meeting without the others and I said "Wasn't our meeting a good one this morning?", and you said "Is it our meeting?" '

Our concern to preserve an 'outside' view made life difficult for us, too. One of the research team commented, 'We are caught between a sense of gratitude in being here and the need to protect our time and function.' Our guilt resulted in taking in some small part of the Unit's work which was outside our research brief.

Within a year of the project starting we had agreed that it was nonsense for us to do other than partner our welfare officer colleagues in undertaking enquiries, and this relieved much of the tension about the collaborative nature of the research and our accountability to the service for the work we did. 'We're more of a group since co-working, instead of two little separate groups', commented one of the welfare staff.

However, co-working brought with it a new set of difficulties. Nearly half way into the project there was a blow-up in one of the co-worked enquiries which all of us remember as having been the most difficult crisis in the research relationship. The crisis occurred not between parents, but between the welfare officers doing the enquiry, and its impact made it difficult to reflect upon possible overlaps between these two systems. Had that been possible it might have made the heated conflict intelligible in terms of the work which in turn would have made the crisis more manageable.

This case, perhaps more than any other, demonstrated to us what a complex business it was to disentangle interlocking patterns of relationships in order to arrive at an explanation of behaviour. What took us all by surprise was the ferocity of the emotional impact upon the Unit and IMS staff. It emphasized for us how crucial it was to have a containing structure if welfare officers were to survive the persecutory anxiety which we came to associate with welfare enquiry work and which could surface in working relationships. It also emphasized for us how difficult it was to provide explanations that were at all adequate to the phenomenon we both witnessed and were a part of. In short, fully knowing about and experiencing the subject of our enquiry made us unreliable reporters. Distance would have retained our sense of perspective, but could we then have so fully experienced what was at stake for those upon whom we reported?

The dual nature of the research relationship created an experience that was uncomfortably close to the phenomenon of divorce court enquiry work. As researchers, we placed the activities of the Divorce Unit under scrutiny and reported upon them. The Unit then felt like a parent whose capacity to care for her children was subject to outside review. As practitioners from the IMS and the Divorce Unit we 'co-parented' the 'children' (i.e. the families) of the Divorce Unit, and on occasions experienced how difficult that could be. Both experiences were illuminating, but they were an additional stress factor for a Unit which already felt under pressure from other directions.

If the research relationship presented the Unit with difficulties, it also had its rewards. Joint working was beneficial as well as costly. The core sample of cases received more attention (in terms of time given over to discussion and thought, if not hours of direct contact) and were rated more optimistically on completion of the report than were the one-year sample for the Unit as a whole; 64 per cent of core sample questionnaires indicated that welfare officers thought parents were nearer agreement at the end of the enquiry as compared with the beginning (71 per cent when one parent withdrawing a claim was included in the same category), as compared with 56 per cent for the one-year sample. Having two officers available for each enquiry could reduce (as well as increase) the stress of the work. Some division of labour allowed skills to be deployed differentially, as we saw in the case of Mr and Mrs King. In difficult cases it was recognized that 'two heads are better than one', and in several cases explicit acknowledgement was made of the value of having a man and a woman involved in the same enquiry.

The response of the Divorce Unit

We have suggested that the 'roller coaster' experience of working in the Divorce Unit during the fieldwork life of the project can be understood by looking at the relationships between the Unit and its clients, its parent organization, its relevant professional network, and the IMS research team. These relationships interlocked to create a climate that was at first challenging and stimulating, but which became increasingly threatening. We witnessed, and were a part of, a process of disillusionment.

Conceived in a climate where conciliation promised to unlock the secret of procuring rational if not amicable settlements in divorce proceedings, the Divorce Unit began life with high hopes of facilitating agreement between disputing parents. As time went by, the realization grew that many of the parents who appeared on the doorstep of the Unit's office were unlikely to be able to reach agreement, and were arguing about very much more than what appeared on their court applications. Attendance at conciliation conferences confirmed the impression that we, and they, were dealing with a different client group, and operating in very different circumstances from the fast-developing out-of-court services. Within the probation service the Unit felt increasingly isolated (an isolation which was partly welcomed), while the wider debate about the relationship between concili-ation and investigation threatened to rob them of work to which they felt professionally committed. How were they to respond?

From our outside perspective we were, at first, surprised by the amount of time which was spent on internal meetings. Substantial resources were spent on the training and equipping of staff, and discussing practice, developing appropriate family therapy skills, and attending courses organized outside the service. The hunger for training was understandable in a field of work which was new, and in a Unit which had only recently been formed. 'If only I had that I could do this, but I haven't and I can't,' said one officer describing the allure of extra training at that time. Another, when trying to put her finger on the rewards of the job, said 'I don't get satisfaction from the court or from children . . . my satisfaction comes from what can be created with my colleagues and in my own thinking'. We came to view these self-sustaining activities as having a similar function to the *necessary narcissism* we have described in connection with the behaviour of parents. They aimed to develop a sense of internal cohesion to withstand the pressures from outside.

We noticed a change in ourselves, and in our welfare colleagues, as the project proceeded. The therapeutic intent to effect change gave place to managing what was not going to change. This did not occur without a struggle. However, the shift in emphasis emerged clearly from the notes kept on team meeting case discussions. A debate about the technique of reframing negative statements made by parents in positive terms led one officer to comment 'I think the IFT [where she had learned the technique] would have kittens if they saw some of our cases'. We, too, encountered a growing resistance within ourselves to understanding what was going on in the cases discussed (despite this being our stock in trade) in preference for seeking out a management solution, as if the two activities were separate. Understanding requires sufficient protected space to stand back and reflect, a necessary counterbalance to up-front intervention-ist strategies which are sometimes compelled by reacting to events because of the feelings they generate.

After the team meetings, presenters noted on a form what they had found helpful from the discussions. The kinds of comments on these forms made it clear that 'sharing the load' was an important function of the meetings. When the team became 'partisan and heated' discussions were of less value. 'Accepting what cannot be changed', 'recognition of no magic', 'support for not picking up the stone and finding all sorts of things crawling out', all indicated a process of coming to terms with what was not possible. We and our colleagues used the discussions to tolerate 'being used differently by clients and not being split as workers', to provide protection against 'being sucked in' to client systems, and to obtain 'help in getting out' of intractable situations. The meetings were also used to 'rehearse and test arguments for the report', and to secure 'help in predicting the effects of recommendations'. Despite our fear that therapeutic understanding was sometimes lost in the process, we were surprised by how frequently understanding was cited as important for the process of case management.

While expectations were being revised about what might realistically be accomplished in the context of the Divorce Unit, a picture began to emerge of the opportunities and constraints associated with the enquiry role. On the positive side, the authority of the courts was thought to have a restraining influence upon parents, and it provided welfare officers with access to those who would not otherwise have come into contact with each other, or with the front-line agencies. The contact provided an opportunity to meet the children of divorcing parents and to give them an opportunity to express their feelings and views. It also gave welfare officers power to call a halt to ill-treatment by making veiled threats – often not so veiled – referring to the powers of the courts. As one parent commented: '[They tried to] wear us down . . . it was better to reach an agreement than to leave it to [the judge] . . . different judges have different feelings and views on these divided issues.' The welfare report was in itself considered to be a powerful means of trying to reflect back to parents what was happening between them and to their children. It provided an opportunity to write down, in acceptable language, what might not adequately have been heard in the course of the enquiry.

On the negative side, we and our colleagues felt the enquiry role restricted our access to what people really thought and felt. The pressure of time meant that contacts had to be relatively brief, and even if it was considered prudent to maintain them beyond the date of a court hearing, there was resistance to doing so because of the toll on resources needed by the Unit to carry out its primary task effectively. Moreover, parents were generally unenthusiastic about being brought together to hammer out an agreement, and could experience such attempts as persecution. They threatened to upset a worked-out view of why things were as they were, and on which they depended for psychological survival.

For the Divorce Unit staff, meetings, training days, and team retreats served to bind together a staff who were competent but vulnerable, given the uncertain and often hostile environment in which they practised. There was, in our view, a powerful unconscious preoccupation with creating a 'good' climate inside the Unit as protection against the 'bad' world outside. Surviving as a welfare officer inside the Unit required that differences were handled tactfully. There was a wish that the staff might be 'at one', if not 'as one'. The discomfort with the research presence can partly be understood in these terms. It was as if we had to choose between being uncritical friends on the inside, or unfriendly critics on the outside. Considerable energy was expended by the staff in maintaining their integrity against the fragmentation outside. The polarization that could result from surviving in this way ran the risk of making staff less accessible to parents than might have been the case in less threatening circumstances. In so far as this defence replicated those deployed by parents against each other, welfare officers were contending with the internal worlds of their clients and had to do better than they to respond effectively. The struggle to resist lapsing into defensive behaviour was part of the welfare officer's lot, as it is with all social workers.

Being present at the team meetings on a Thursday morning frequently felt like sitting round a tribal camp fire while stories were told of exploits in the hostile territory of the surrounding jungle. The staff of the Unit were good raconteurs, telling their tales with humour and a light touch. The stories were reassuring because they united the group and provided a buffer against the sometimes miserable predicaments of the families they saw. Coffee was provided at the beginning of the meeting, and the large dog belonging to one of the officers was often touched and stroked as she sprawled on the floor.

No doubt the subjects of our stories would have told their tales in a different way, with different villains and victims. When the major concern is to survive a turbulent passage, an explanation for what is happening, and an account of the journey taken so far, are indispensable aids for coming through safely to the other side. The explanation and the story do not have to be correct, only hold together the besieged psyche. Perhaps this is as true of welfare officers (ourselves included) as it is of the parents they see in the course of their work. The welfare report, even at its best, cannot be an objective statement of how things are because that will never fully be known. In reporting the truth as the welfare officer sees it, the report strives to be a diplomatic document to which it is hoped all the parties concerned can subscribe without feeling their integrity has been damaged. Welfare officers need to be able to venture into their clients' worlds sufficiently to enable the different stories to be told and heard. If necessary, they have to be in a position to write a different account, a third story, to which all those concerned can say 'good enough'.

9

FACTS AND FICTIONS

'Man – let me offer you a definition – is the story-telling animal. Wherever he goes he wants to leave behind not a chaotic wake, not an empty space, but the comforting marker-buoys and trail-signs of stories. He has to go on telling stories. He has to keep on making them up. As long as there's a story, it's all right. Even in his last moment, it's said, in the split second of a fatal fall – or when he's about to drown – he sees, passing rapidly before him, the story of his whole life.'

Graham Swift
Waterland

Divorce is a fact of life. Following a sharp increase in the 1970s the divorce rate has now reached a high plateau. The confidence of those who regard marriage as a life-long partnership has been shaken; private and public interests have been threatened. The consequences of divorce, actual and potential, have become the subject of intense debate. Here, fact merges with fiction. For some, divorce represents a hazard to the social and moral fabric of society. For others, it represents a release from oppression and a recognition that not all marriages can be expected to work.

At a personal level, most people would accept that divorce can have devastating consequences, at least in the short term. The social, emotional, and material costs can be high. Particular concern is registered about the 150,000 or so children affected each year. However poor their parents' marriage, there are strong indications that the wishes of children, if not their interests, come into conflict with those of parents over the decision to divorce. Most children will be extremely unsettled by seeing parents go their separate ways. Some will suffer long-term consequences, the most serious of which may be the burden of a forfeited childhood. Divorce constitutes a potentially serious physical and mental health hazard for parents and children alike. The way it is managed, and the social and legal processes that carry people through this transition, are therefore of vital importance to the health of a community.

Traditionally, the judicial system has acted as the guardian of public and private interests when marriage breaks down. The welfare of children has been defined as the crossroads at which these interests intersect. Section 41 of the 1973 Matrimonial Causes Act is the legislative statement of the paramountcy of childrens' interests when their parents divorce. It has guided the behaviour of judges in relation to family breakdown for more than a century, although 'welfare' has meant different things to different people at different times.

As social attitudes towards divorce have changed, the judicial system has been called upon to respond. There has been unease from inside legal circles about whether the welfare principle is being effectively applied in practice. The Law Commission's review of custody arrangements in family law (1986) concluded that the courts' procedure of approving arrangements for children before making final a divorce had 'not been successful in any of its declared aims' (4.10). Noting that the Booth Committee (1985) had made proposals which would allow such arrangements to be considered in more detail at an earlier stage in the proceedings than at present, the Commission went on to suggest that courts might also do more to put parents in touch with whatever services (counselling, conciliation, and social services) were available locally on the basis that 'improving upon the indirect effects of the court's duty would appear a more effective use of the resources available than strengthening its investigative functions' (4.13).

That such a suggestion could be made is a mark of the developments which have been taking place outside the court-room in the past ten years. Conciliation services have been set up in many parts of the country to offer an alternative to litigation for resolving disputes. A chorus of approval has greeted the philosophy of assisting parents to manage their own affairs in as uncontentious a manner as possible when marriage ends. As a result, conciliation services have been introduced within the precincts of the court as well as outside.

Occupying ground somewhere between parents, courts, and conciliators are probation officers who work as divorce court welfare officers. Their workload has grown rapidly in the past fifteen years. By statute their role is to investigate the circumstances of divorcing families and to report to the courts. By training they are social workers inclined towards helping those whose needs warrant attention. By aspiration many are conciliators working in and out of court.

This is the climate of change and review in which the project described in this book was conceived and executed. Staff from the Institute of Marital Studies and a specialist Divorce Unit joined forces to explore the feasibility of encouraging privately ordered settlements while preparing welfare reports for the courts. Behind the venture was a wish to explore the operational boundaries between conciliation and investigative practice, and to make a contribution to the debate about how disputes might best be settled for those subject to welfare reports. The contradictions inherent in the excercise were not, in prospect, unduly daunting for a service accustomed to working with the conflict between authority and autonomy. In retrospect we were less sanguine about what might be achieved.

For two-and-a-half years we worked with a group of welfare officers at their Divorce Unit, monitoring the clients who came and went, attending team meetings, and preparing reports for the courts. From this experience we collected facts and fictions which we have assembled into our own story. As a story it has limitations. It is drawn from the experience of a particular group of parents and children. It is drawn from the experience of a particular group of practitioners (ourselves included). Yet from the attempts to bridge gaps between and within these two groups, the story has important things to say about practice and policy.

The predicament of parents

It may be considered a weakness of our story that parents feature more prominently than their children. This may have something to do with being marital therapists; welfare officers telling the same story might highlight the parts played by children. But parents occupied the centre stage of our enquiries for two reasons. First, they put themselves forward. They compelled our attention, they tried to upstage each other, and they were reluctant to draw their children in from the wings. Second, we regarded parents as holding the key which could unlock the door to their children's well-being. Propositions which discounted their importance were not considered practical except in very extreme circumstances.

The parents seen by welfare officers are only a small proportion of the divorcing population as a whole. They are seen in a context where a certain amount of paranoia is healthy. Few allow others ready access to the secrets of family life, especially when they have the power to introduce unwelcome change. The clients of the Divorce Unit were similar to other divorcees in that they were weighted towards the lower and disadvantaged end of the social spectrum. Wives were more likely than husbands to have petitioned for divorce, and mothers were more likely than fathers to have care of their children. However, there were two areas in which important differences were apparent.

The first of these was that the Divorce Unit saw a high proportion of parents for whom the 'behaviour' clause had been used to establish the breakdown of their marriage. Unreasonable behaviour was cited as the grounds for divorce in 55 per cent of the one-year sample and 74 per cent of the core sample, as compared with 36 per cent of cases nationally in 1982. The use of this clause in divorce proceedings has been associated with high levels of conflict and contest. In contrast, the two-year consent clause for divorce was used in 4 per cent of the one-year sample and 7 per cent of the core sample, as compared with 25 per cent nationally in 1982. Taken at face value, then, the Divorce Unit (and the researchers in particular) saw an exceptionally contentious group of parents.

This statistical impression was confirmed from first-hand experience with the core sample of cases. In many of these cases separation came as a shock to one partner (usually the man). Litigation followed closely behind. About a third of the one-year and core sample parents had instituted legal proceedings within six months of separating, a substantially higher proportion than even Murch's (1980) court welfare sample. These parents tended to act first and talk later, much later for those who were reluctant to talk to a former spouse at all. Pressure was applied to make far-reaching decisions in haste and at a time when passions were running high. The breathing space potentially afforded by the welfare enquiry was frequently ignored because of negative associations to the investigative process and a sense that the enquiry constituted an obstacle to expediting the judicial process. Uncertainty also threatened to undermine vulnerable psyches; those who managed their hurt feelings by projecting blame onto others were anxious not to be disturbed by alternative interpretations of their circumstances.

In three-quarters of the core sample the decision to divorce had been taken by one partner unilaterally, and against the wishes of the other. These circumstances have been associated elsewhere with high levels of conflict and poor adjustment to divorce. We estimated that one or both partners had been unable to accept the ending of their marriage in 83 per cent of the enquiries in which we were involved, and that this formed a very important part of the emotional context in which child custody and access disputes took place. In some cases it is reasonable to view applications to courts on these matters as being akin to contesting a petition for divorce.

The distressing short-term consequences of divorce noted in other studies was well supported, and even amplified by the experience of parents and children in the core sample. Emotional stress, ill-health, financial hardship, and social isolation were no strangers to them. Men, in particular, were frequently locked into a downward spiral of cumulative loss, as one by one, links with spouse, home, work, friends, family, and children were severed. An image developed in our minds of a man and woman on a see-saw. Marriage was a weight which upset the balance, depressing the woman; divorce was the weight which worked with the same effect for the man. While separation succeeded in freeing some women from an oppressive and stultifying relationship, it could strike men with the force of an Exocet missile coming out of a clear blue sky.

Psychological survival was at stake for these parents. A petition for divorce could have the impact of a declaration of war, following upon which the world was divided into friends and foes. Divisions of this kind served to buttress beleaguered parents, although at a cost to their health and emotional equilibrium. Children had to find a place in this world, and acted as allies and arbiters when they were not keeping their heads down to avoid the crossfire. The prevailing climate of persecutory anxiety encouraged splitting, a psychological process designed to protect the self from self-knowledge when it challenged the acceptable fabric of identity. The temptation, consciously and unconsciously offered, to attribute all that was blameworthy and reprehensible to others could be irresistible. Financial resources, physical effort, emotional energy, and social influence were sometimes expended as if there were no tomorrow. They were directed towards constructing and maintaining stories about why things were as they were, and how they had come to be that way, which were capable of sustaining vulnerable and threatened identities. The more parents had suffered from losses in the past, the more vulnerable and inflexible they were in the present. They, even less than others, could afford to depart from their familiar scripts. The narcissistic preoccupation of parents, necessary for their survival at that time and in those circumstances, frequently left little in the way of dispassionate concern for the often competing interests of their children.

An adversarial judicial system is peculiarly well matched to the desires of parents who feel persecuted, besieged, or deeply wronged. Litigation is one means of constructing and conveying a story, and of imposing it on others. The purpose of the story is to convict others and to vindicate the self. Court decisions can be received as a form of public absolution, an acquittal, or a life sentence. In the nightmare world of villains and monsters to which divorcing parents may sometimes temporarily regress, the concept of matrimonial offence is eminently more comprehensible than that of irretrievable breakdown. Similarly, adversarial procedures can seem to promise richer emotional rewards than processes which invite negotiation and appeal to reason. Indeed, testing reality by meeting, face to face, those who are held responsible for what is wrong can be a persecutory experience, not least because unconscious forces are at work to maintain ogres in the world outside as a defence against the pain of loss, guilt, and feelings of personal failure which might otherwise be experienced within.

Welfare officers have a place in this paranoid system. There is a fit between those who invite intrusion by the way they handle their divorce and those who intrude in order to safeguard the interests of children. There is a fit, too, between those who behave in ways which need to be checked and those who have the authority to provide a check. Not surprisingly, welfare officers are greeted with a mixture of suspicion and hope. As potential allies who have influence at court they are to be welcomed but with a degree of mistrust. As potential adversaries they are to be feared, criticized, and even pilloried, enthusiastically so when they behave in ways which support the paranoid assumptions of besieged individuals. When they bring parents together, their intentions may be misconstrued by partners anxious to escape from marriage. When their intentions are understood they may be regarded as naive. Either way, attempts by welfare officers to draw parents together may run counter to the expulsive and polarizing processes by which they try to ensure their psychological survival. Only if some headway can be made in distinguishing the role of parent from that of spouse is there a chance that the divisions between adults will become less essential to personal survival. The needs of children might then be invoked with considerable effect to mobilize the resources of a partnership between two parents.

The distinction between partner and parent is, at the best of times, a subtle one. Such niceties are easily overlooked in the heat of a divorce battle. In addition to having an exaggerated propensity to fight for survival, we believed that our sample differed from other divorcing populations in a second way, and one which made this distinction more than usually difficult to maintain.

In our view, the core sample of cases contained a high proportion of 'parental' as opposed to 'peer' marriages. Partners would talk of their marriages in terms which evoked images of mothers contending with difficult children, or fathers controlling rebellious daughters. We thought it likely that many of these parents had entered marriage in the hope that it would satisfy needs which had been unmet in their own families, or that it would provide a remedy for conflicts which remained unresolved from those earlier times. While such hopes of marriage are by no means unusual, the investment in creating a family and having children (as compared with enjoying a partnership and sharing parenthood) was exceptionally important for these parents. The decision to marry and have children coincided in two-thirds of the core sample cases, a high proportion which we did not feel was sufficiently explained by any cultural tendency to delay marriage until starting a family. When marital and parental roles have been fused at the outset of marriage, and little progress has been made in distinguishing between them during the course of marriage, it is not surprising that there are difficulties separating the roles when marriage ends. One parent's wish to make a clean break from the other will then influence attitudes towards access, as will her feelings about being left, sometimes literally, holding the baby. Another parent's wish to get back into a marriage, or back at a spouse, may be sufficient motive to contest the custody of a child or to enforce access. Either way, the confusion of issues will make the task of a welfare officer who wishes to bring about an agreed settlement a difficult one.

Even without the overlay of feeling about a broken partnership, bids made by parents for active involvement with their children (which were in tune with our aspirations to foster joint parenting after divorce) often had shaky foundations. It was as if parents sometimes wanted welfare officers to rewrite history, inflating the levels of their past involvements as parents and compensating them for all they had not enjoyed in those years. A future of being active as a parent was then being negotiated from a fictional basis of past experience. Even in the favourable environment of harmonious family life the burdens and rewards of parenting in our society are frequently unevenly divided between men and women. Leaving to one side the restrictions imposed by zoo opening times and the weather, the unfavourable environment following a broken marriage is not conducive to achieving what has only partially been achieved elsewhere. While divorce points up the uneven balance between parents in our culture, it is arguably the least favourable circumstance in which to try and introduce a remedy.

The predicament of welfare officers

The divorce court welfare services in this country are in a state of transition. Past identities and purposes are being reassessed. While the challenges this brings are usually welcomed, most welfare officers are likely to acknowledge that the process of review also involves tensions and conflicts.

Although closely associated with the criminal courts, the probation service has a history of working with families whose members have had no contact with the penal system. Until the 1960s the service offered an extensive marriage guidance service. In the last quarter of a century the civil work of the service has moved away from saving marriages towards saving children, and the role of the divorce court welfare officer has evolved in this context. While reporting on and supervising the circumstances in which children are growing up after their parents' separation, welfare officers have always had an eye to their professional social work identity in the way they have discharged their statutory obligations. The recent development of conciliation services, in which many probation officers have played an active part, has acted as a spur to considering how their role should develop in future.

   In the debate which has taken place about the relationship between welfare officers and conciliators they have sometimes seemed to be likened to two parents, one good and one bad. The qualities of conciliation, which support parents in maintaining control of concerns that are properly theirs, are favourably compared with those of investigation, which can seem intrusive when undertaken by powerful officials who may be depicted as seeking to wrest the responsibilities of parents away from them. Most commentators on the professional scene resist this polarized representation when considering the conflicts between the two activities. It is only when the activities of one are seen to encroach upon those of the other that feelings run high.

   Sensitive to the stigma that might attach to divorcing parents from being seen in an agency whose primary task is to provide a service to the criminal courts and communities, many welfare officers have specialized in their work and banded together a little apart from their parent organization. Some have staffed conciliation services which operate in the precincts of courts. Others have worked as conciliators in quite separate out-of-court schemes. This has brought in its train a new set of questions concerning the kind of institutional underpinning necessary for a stressful area of work no longer in the mainstream of probation activities.

   The Divorce Unit is a very good example of this trend in the probation service and its experience has drawn attention to the importance of having a secure base from which to work. The enthusiasm of the staff for specializing in work at one stage removed from their probation colleagues was tempered by concern about the security of their institutional base. Uncertainty about this was not conducive to withstanding the stresses of working with divorcing families. For this reason, if for no other, there is an urgency behind the need to clarify, in organizational terms, who is to carry responsibility for services to families appearing at county and divorce courts on family matters.

   A stable point in the changing world of the Divorce Unit was its relationship with the courts. Professional self-esteem and job satisfaction came from servicing the courts with reports which they knew were valued and appreciated. The setting up of an in-court conciliation service added to this satisfaction. Although too close to events to make a reliable judgement, we thought we detected a shift in the gravitational centre of the Unit during the lifetime of the project. Specialism, combined with a statement from the Home Office about future priorities for the probation service, moved the Divorce Unit into a wider orbit around its parent body where the pull of the judicial system could exert more influence than it had before. After the project ended the Divorce Unit extended its activities to include work from the domestic magistrates' courts, and changed its name to the Family Courts' Unit. We make no comment about whether this shift was desirable or not. The substantive point we wish to make is a general one: a secure professional and institutional base is essential to any service operating in the embattled world of divorce. Without it, staff are likely to be less accessible to families and will need to spend more resources on sustaining their own corporate viability. Whether or not a secure base will be provided by the Home Office or the Lord Chancellor's Department, or by some other body, the future will tell.

The movement from an individual specializing in divorce work to establishing specialist units which extend their brief to embrace the full range of civil work can be understood in different ways. There is a logic to a development which, if carried to its conclusion, will result in a quite separate service. A demanding area of work requires particular skills and resources which are more easily developed and maintained in a specialist setting than within a generic workload. But demanding areas of work can also generate stress. Specialisms are capable of creating hothouses in which pressures build up for which outlets must be found. Diversification then becomes an attractive option.

We have detailed the verbal abuse and emotional battering that can accompany welfare work, the intransigence that can frustrate professional aspirations, and the mistrustful and persecutory climate that can affect both parents and practitioners. We have described the demoralizing impact that consumer reports can have upon professionals who cannot reconcile the comments made by their clients with their own intentions and recollections. We have acknowledged the burden a research presence can be for staff and the distorting effects it can have upon the everyday operations of a service agency. These pressures can pull staff together in an alliance to withstand the onslaught of a demanding and potentially hostile world, and in ways which have echoes of the survival strategies used by parents. Team meetings and training programmes are necessary resources for self-sustenance, as well as for professional development. Exploits may there be described – and stories told – about the world outside and the world in here.

Persistent exposure to unhappiness, and to the burden of responsibility for making ethical and practical choices, takes a toll on its subjects. It may be that we, who were less seasoned than our welfare officer colleagues to the predicaments of their job, were unduly affected by our experience. Yet it was our impression that the nature of the work exacted a price from them as it did from us. Some relief from the relentless pressure of divorce court enquiry work seems to be essential for welfare officers to stay in touch with themselves as well as with the families they see. Providing educational programmes, social work services, and in-court conciliation schemes are all options that might be developed around the nexus of a family court as conceived by the Finer Committee more than a decade ago.

Seeking and settling

The aspirations of our colleagues and ourselves to facilitate agreements, as well as to prepare reports for the courts, may have accounted for some of the pressures we have described. In view of our downbeat description of the welfare officer's lot it may come as something of a surprise that a full agreement between parents was noted and endorsed in 59 per cent of the welfare reports in the core sample. Moreover, in 71 per cent of these cases (56 per cent in the one-year sample) parents were judged to have been nearer agreement at the end of an enquiry than they had been at the beginning.

These figures overstate the part we and our colleagues believed we played in effecting change, although a court order for a welfare report could have a deterrent effect upon disputing parents. Some agreements were effected before an enquiry began. Some which were arrived at later were designed to deflect unwelcome attention. Some were tentative and uneasy. Nevertheless, in a good one-third of the sample we and our colleagues believed we had been instrumental in securing a full agreement, and in a further third we had played some role in securing a partial agreement.

This optimism was dented as the results of the follow-up interviews became known. For example, the agreement reported in the Hood/Ham enquiry was shown to have been without foundation. So, too, was the marginal gain estimated in the Sheen enquiry. Other agreements, as in the Kings' case, led to new sets of difficulties which threatened to undermine the real progress that had been made during the enquiry. Nevertheless, we believed progress had been made towards reducing the intensity of disputes in a significant proportion of the cases, although we have no means of knowing if we were right. At the end of an enquiry we thought we had had some effect in between two-thirds and three-quarters of the cases; after reading the follow-up reports our optimism sagged to well below the halfway mark.

The gains that were made could not be measured in terms of changes introduced into living arrangements for children. They were more likely to be evident in the ways parents behaved towards each other, and in the process of coming to terms with what was not going to alter in their circumstances. Progress was usually hard-won, and the authority vested in the welfare officer's role was sometimes instrumental in calling a halt to destructive behaviour. These are perhaps more substantial achievements than conveyed by the tone in which they are described. Should this be the case, the depressive tone can be understood as reflecting the experience of the work from the IMS researchers' perspectives.

It may have been that we expected too much of ourselves and our beleaguered clients. It is interesting that we spent a much higher than average proportion of time with the prognostically least hopeful groups in our sample. The *nominal* group of divorces, illustrated by the Sheens, consisted of parents who remained ambivalently attached to each other, unable either to acknowledge their relationship as durable nor to implement a decision to part. Not knowing their own wishes, they pressed others to take the responsibilities that were theirs, and elicited a therapeutic response which could neither be sustained by welfare officers nor was appropriate to their role. Our experience led us to conclude that parents in this group were unable to reach agreement on post-divorce matters because neither partner had reached a stage in the divorce process where that was possible. Welfare officers could decide to accept the responsibility being passed to them on the basis that the burden of uncertainty for children was too heavy, or (perhaps and) encourage parents to consult those better placed to help partners who are undecided between marriage and divorce. Neither course guaranteed success in our situation.

At the other end of the spectrum were *long-lease* divorces, where the prognosis, as illustrated by the Hood/Ham enquiry, was equally poor. These parents remained distantly but chronically attached, as if they could never quite disengage from a sense of belonging together. A lengthy history of divorce-associated litigation, highly discrepant accounts of events, a determination and ability to play the system, plus a preference for bypassing direct communication, made these parents unlikely candidates for out-of-court assisted settlements.

More often than not, it was apparent in a first interview whether there was a prospect of parents reaching agreement with each other. This was true of the Kings, from the *shot-gun* group of divorces, and of other parents. The key indicator of a favourable prospect for agreement was a degree of accessibility in the way parents approached each other. This was partly determined by the situation existing between them at the time, and partly a product of the kind of opportunities and conditions of safety afforded by ourselves and the Divorce Unit staff. Accessibility implied a capacity, however limited, to hear what others were saying and to take it into account, to press for claims in an assertive but not self-defeating way, and to show a certain amount of flexibility towards the claims of others when the situation warranted it. Parents were most likely to be accessible when they were far enough from the trauma of separation not to feel that their lives were in pieces, but not so far that patterns of conflict had become entrenched and embittered.

The experience of simultaneously being reported upon and assisted to settle produced mixed reactions among parents. Some welcomed the opportunity to say some of the things which, until then, had remained unsaid, and felt they received a fair hearing. Feeling supported was the single most likely explanation for a satisfactory experience of the enquiry encounter, especially when it led to a favourable recommendation in the welfare report and the care and control of the children concerned. A favourable recommendation was not, however, sufficient explanation for a satisfied parent. The chance that both parents would feel satisfied with the experience increased when two officers were involved in the enquiry, and when there was sufficient similarity between practitioner and parent for the latter to feel understood. In particular, it helped for a man and a woman to undertake the enquiry so that male and female perspectives were represented. The need for two different points of view to receive separate attention made us wonder whether we were involved in conducting an out-of-court hearing for the parents we reported upon. In other words, we may have anticipated a court contest, but in anteroom conditions and informal circumstances, where the role of the final arbiter was pushed one stage further back. When both parents felt their point of view had been adequately heard they may have been more ready to settle, even when their predicaments remained substantially unchanged.

Co-working was also valued by us and our Divorce Unit colleagues. We felt less fragmented by working in pairs and better able to contain the stresses of the work. Having a colleague to confer with – and occasionally to fight with – helped preserve some balance between partisan interests. Agreements were more likely to be achieved when we worked in pairs than when we worked on our own.

We were concerned, however, about the absence of continuing support systems for parents who had managed to resolve their differences in the short term, but for whom an upset would easily throw the progress they had made into reverse. The Kings' case is a good illustration of the knock-on effects a successful agreement can have in a family which has been reconstituted after divorce. The primary task of divorce court welfare officers does not lend itself to extended involvements with families. Even when a matrimonial supervision order is made, the rhythm of enquiry work does not allow for the provision of long-term help. Sometimes a lengthy piece of work was carried out in the course of preparing a report, but there was usually a cost, in terms of pressure to complete, which came either from within the Unit because of an accumulating number of reports requiring attention, or from outside because of concern about undue delays. Moreover, some of the constraints that worked against client disclosure during the enquiry continued to apply once the enquiry was complete. Very few parents in the core sample chose to approach welfare officers for voluntary help once an enquiry was complete.

While parents valued some aspects of their relationships with welfare officers, others were disappointed and confused by their experience. We were criticized for being too intrusive, and for not being intrusive enough. Some parents would have welcomed help, but the investigative context of the relationship made them fearful that disclosure would be interpreted as failure, so lessening their chances of a successful outcome. Joint meetings were not popular with parents, and their purpose was sometimes misconstrued. In contrast, many parents appreciated the opportunity to have their say when their partner was not present. As with divorce itself, men and women tended to view these issues differently: men seldom objected to a joint meeting (although they could be critical of its failure to achieve what they wanted) whereas women were frequently anxious on this score. Men tended to be more dissatisfied with their experience than women, but then women generally had the upper hand. On balance, both men and women were dissatisfied with their experience.

It would be naive to pretend that welfare officers could always be capable of satisfying their clients if only they improved their service sufficiently. The interests of men and women, and parents and children, often diverge on divorce. The experience of divorce is frequently harrowing. Our wish to civilize and even sanitize the experience must, in part, reflect our own recoil from the pain of witnessing love turned sour. Parents bring to the enquiry relationship hopes and fears assembled from a lifetime's experience. Even in the most favourable circumstances it would not be possible to meet more than a small proportion of these. On occasions when we did engage the vulnerable and depressed feelings of parents, circumstances were not propitious for sustaining the work, and a small upset between them would result in violent recoil.

In these circumstances it is perhaps remarkable that very few parents had complaints to make about the reports eventually submitted to court, which were a blend of selected fact and opinion. While striving for objectivity they were also diplomatic documents designed to pour oil on troubled waters. They aimed to serve the interests of parents as well as those of children and the courts. When agreement had been possible the reports tended to be brief and to the point. When it had not, they were vehicles for publishing the stories of all parties to the dispute. The welfare officer's story was superimposed on the others in a way which it was hoped would allow for the maximum of consensus.

Arriving at a point of view, constructing a story to tell, these were the important processes for surviving in a world which had been fragmented by experience and was in danger of falling apart. Parents were engaged in rewriting their histories in order to ensure their future survival. Welfare officers, ourselves included, had access to them rather later than at the crucial time, but nevertheless exerted what influence they could to make discrepant stories compatible. The welfare report was the last ditch means of doing this. It was also a lifeline for the reporter. At the end of the day he or she, we and they, had to construct a reality from the often fragmented experience of conducting, in a conciliatory manner, the welfare enquiry. The process was cathartic in so far as it provided a means of putting ourselves back together again. Fact or fiction, we had a story to stand by.

Practices, procedures, and policy

It would have been cheering, no doubt, to close this account of our work with a happy ending, a series of positive recommendations for changing practices, procedures, and policies that might radically alter the face of divorce. To do so, however, would be to devalue some of the important observations we have drawn from our experience relating to the psychological constraints binding some parents and services at this time. There are those claiming access to whom access is impossible. There are those who are more concerned to secure control than to obtain custody. Practitioners must be able to withstand these pressures, and sometimes they will be unable to make contact however skilled, motivated, and experienced they may be.

It will be clear from the conclusions we have drawn from our experience of working as divorce court welfare officers that we believe there are limits to what can be achieved in terms of sustainable voluntary settlements, in that setting, with the particular families we saw. Our experience inclines us to the view that there will always be people who are unable to settle on their own account, and who need an authoritative intervention to contain the damaging consequences of unresolved conflict, if necessary, by taking matters out of their hands. Yet this book would be incomplete if it ended without asking whether there might be a better way of spending the considerable resources consumed by the existing systems and structures. Might the number of families who require welfare intervention be reduced by changes in the formal processes for managing divorce?

Whether contentious behaviour is somehow innate to the experience of divorce, or whether it is fashioned by the way society processes divorce is a question that is unlikely to be answered satisfactorily in either/or terms. Most likely, there is an interaction between the two. For those of us on the public side of the equation there are opportunities to mitigate some part of the damage and distress caused by divorce through the way we govern our own involvement. Welfare officers are part of the wider social and judicial system. What they are capable of doing depends, in part, upon what is happening elsewhere. Recent years have demonstrated how their role has changed in response to changes taking place around them.

We may be witnessing a change in the personal and social status of divorce from crisis to transition. The more commonly divorce is experienced, the less isolating and unpredictable the experience is likely to be. Change is always more manageable when there are opportunities to anticipate and rehearse what is to come than when it is introduced without warning. Those who have studied how change is best managed have drawn attention to the crucial role played by those who make up the social support system for individuals who are in a state of flux (for example, Caplan 1981). The value of resources which assist people to manage change on a cognitive level has been demonstrated in a wide range of psychosocial transitions.

To date, most of the resources for dealing with the aftermath of marriage breakdown have been vested in the judicial system. The first port of call for a person who wishes to leave a marriage is the solicitor's office. He, or more likely she, may have signalled an intent to leave to a doctor, a marriage guidance counsellor, or a worker at the Citizen's Advice Bureau, but very often the understood route out of marriage begins with legal advice. While recourse to the law is inevitable at some stage of divorce proceedings, and essential in terms of safeguarding personal interests, there is no absolute reason why solicitors, or any member of the judicial system, should be the first resort.

Some experiments are being conducted in attempts to explore alternative responses to separating families. In Holland, a local divorce centre has been set up in Groningen, on a time-limited experimental basis, to meet the needs of parents and children at all stages in the divorce process (MacGillavry and Bijkerk 1986). Special attention has been paid to bringing a range of expertise together under one roof, so that the diverse needs of parents and children who call on the centre can be met in an integrated way. Callers can select the kind of service they require. Whether they are looking for information, practical advice, counselling, or conciliation, the resources are on hand. When specialist advice is required, particularly in connection with points of law, appropriate referrals are made.

Early availability of information and advice has been found to counteract the impulse to take legal action in haste. The centre has found that since it was set up there have been more joint divorce petitions, and that these are often presented by one lawyer rather than two acting on behalf of both parties. Bearing in mind the sense of shock which accompanied the surprise separations in many of our core sample of enquiries, this development in the Netherlands offers much that is appealing.

To make informed choices about the future, children and parents need to know what is happening to them and the likely consequences of taking different courses of action. Perhaps it is early days to be suggesting evening classes on exercising choice in the family, although radio and television programmes are already opening up this area for discussion. Given the impact of divorce on physical and mental health, it is a highly relevant subject for public campaign. Organizations like the Health Education Council and MIND are well placed to act in this area. Some Divorce Experience courses are already being run in this country. The probation service in Leicester has been notable in this respect; their scheme has recently been extended to pay special attention to the needs of children as well as parents (Gordon 1986). So far, the scale of these developments has allowed only the tip of the iceberg to be touched.

As conciliation and divorce counselling services develop in this country it will become decreasingly likely that parents who have the potential to negotiate will become the subjects of welfare reports. The recommendations of the Booth Committee (1985) carve out a place for conciliation within the legal system, as well as recognizing its place outside. Providing administrative convenience does not take precedence over personal timescales the ground has been prepared for developments which may well snowball in the future.

The implications for the welfare service, as it is presently constituted, are mixed. In so far as they lead to more in-court conciliation work they are likely to increase job satisfaction for staff who are more interested in seeking agreements than investigating family circumstances. However, for those parents who still are unable to agree, the burden of enquiry work is likely to become more onerous than at present. For welfare officers to be able to survive the pressures of this work without the protection of cynicism or disengagement will require that they are not exposed to the burden unsupported and without the counterbalance of other more rewarding work.

There may be ways of relating to the hard core of welfare clients that remain unexplored. If pressures need to be brought to bear to settle the disputes in some families they might be found from within the divorcing community, as well as from within the judicial system. In California, success has been claimed for work done in groups with entrenched and embittered divorcing couples and their children (Campbell and Johnston 1985). The separate use of groups for men, women, and children, before mediation efforts begin, has been shown to be more successful than attempts to work with similar couples on their own.

Whatever services parents seek out or are directed towards, it is essential that purposes and procedures are explained as fully and clearly as possible, so that avoidable misunderstandings do not occur. Research suggests that practitioners and clients in therapeutic relationships can proceed with each other on the basis of quite separate sets of assumptions which never quite connect. Sometimes this is unavoidable. There are times and circumstances when people cannot afford to hear what they are being told. Yet that is no reason for neglecting dissemination of useful information. The manner in which a welfare enquiry is called for, the explanations given to both parents and welfare officers about the reasons for taking such a course of action, and the information that is made available about the processes involved, all contribute towards helping those involved in divorce proceedings to know what is happening to them. They are part of a process of supporting the resources of beleaguered parents to manage the situations confronting them. Welfare officers are in a position to prepare brochures about the ways in which they involve themselves with parents, and their reasons for behaving as they do, which might be of substantial help to their prospective clients. This would also provide an opportunity to draw attention to other services in the community relevant to their needs, even to compiling a list of the growing number of publications suitable for parents and children involved in divorce.

Ultimately the courts will always be involved in ending broken marriages. A contract which has been legally entered into must be legally terminated, especially when so many vital and conflicting interests are at stake. How far it is possible to assist in distinguishing between being a parent and being a spouse through the process of judicial procedures is beyond our competence to assess. To make divorce conditional upon satisfactory arrangements for children seems to be sensible from the point of view of protecting the children's interests, but it does little to assist parents to separate the two issues in their minds. This distinction is important if children are to have the best chance of retaining both parents after divorce, and anything that can be done to make it clear will be in their interests.

Pronouncing a marriage ended is a symbolic as well as a legal act. There are few formal rites of passage in our society, and those associated with family life show signs of being on the decrease. Yet several of the parents in our sample were disappointed with the perfunctory manner in which their marriages were ended. Divorce ceremonies may not fit the psychological needs of partners who are going their separate ways, but if as parents they are to begin a different way of relating for the sake of their children, perhaps there might be ways in which the courts, and other relevant institutions (for example, the Church), could help in the rituals they perform.

In 1974 the Finer Committee looked forward to a time when the courts dealing with family matters might be integrated. They envisaged a system which would combine informality of procedure with the resources and expertise relevant to divorce. How and when such a body will replace the courts of today remains to be seen. There is considerable support for taking this step, though financial resources and the weight of tradition act as brakes on implementing the changes. For countries like New Zealand, where family courts have operated since 1981, the new system is reported to be a vast improvement on the one it replaced (Hipgrave 1986). The high incidence of divorce in this country, and the range of needs which this generates, require a more flexible and broad-ranging response than the present system allows.

In looking ahead, there is always a danger of generating an illusion that if only services and procedures were different the pain and heartbreak of divorce could be abolished, and those affected by it would be freed to behave rationally and responsibly. This would, indeed, be to invent a fiction. The realities of divorce will continue to generate unhappiness and unreasonableness. Practices, procedures, and policy may have a mitigating effect, but they are unlikely to provide the cure to human misery and its sequelae. Experienced, imaginative, sensitive, and robust people will continue to be necessary to man the services currently available, and to plan for those which are yet to come. There are bridges to be built, and more stories to be told, if those who live in the shadow of an untenable past are to be assisted into the watery sunlight of ordinary living once more.

APPENDIX I
SAMPLE PROFILES
AND TABLES

Marriage separation and divorce

Most parents in the one-year and core samples were in the process of divorcing or, if not previously married (as in the case of 8 couples), establishing separate lives for themselves following a breakdown in their relationships. By the time welfare officers made contact with them they had usually separated, although 18 couples were still living together despite proceeding with their divorces.

The domestic circumstances of parents in both the one-year sample and the core sample are shown in *Table 1*. There are differences, although not statistically significant,[1] between the ways men and women had restructured their lives after the final separation. In both samples more mothers than fathers were living without a partner (though most of the mothers (*Table 12*) had day-to-day responsibility for their children). It is interesting to note that where there were new partners, as there were for 40 mothers and 38 fathers in both samples, more women than men chose to remarry. This corresponds with the finding of Ambrose, Harper, and Pemberton (1983) who found that men in their sample were eager to seek out another partner after divorce but were reluctant to enter a committed relationship and to remarry as readily as their former wives. However, these observations need to be qualified by the fact that domestic circumstances of a higher proportion of men than women went unrecorded in both samples. This difference is consistent with our impression that men were often reluctant, and sometimes ashamed, to describe their accommodation, having lost the tenancy of the matrimonial home and been forced to live in poorer surroundings.

As has been noted in other divorce court welfare studies, divorce proceedings and child applications were usually initiated soon after separation. Approximately a third of couples in the one-year and core samples (*Table 2*) started legal proceedings within six months of formally separating, significantly higher than the equivalent figure (7 per cent) in the group of couples not referred for reports in the Bristol study. This may indicate a greater tendency for parents in welfare samples to act precipitately.

Table 1 *Domestic circumstances of parents at first welfare interview*

	One-year sample (%)		Core sample (%)	
	Fathers (n=110)	Mothers (n=110)	Fathers (n=30)	Mothers (n=30)
Living alone	32	45	33	50
Remarried	7	11	4	10
Cohabiting	18	17	30	20
Living with former spouse (not separated)	13	13	13	13
Living with parents	9	8	13	4
Living with other relative	2	} 1		
Other arrangements	6			
Not known	13	5	7	4

Table 2 *Litigating in haste: The interval between final separation and decree nisi/first contact with a welfare officer*

	One-year sample (%) (n=96*)	Core sample (%) (n=26*)	Bristol petitioner sample (%) (Murch 1980) (n=10?)	Bristol DCWO sample (%) (Murch 1980) (n=41)
Under 6 months	34	31	7	22
6–12 months	23	23	16	17
1–2 years	26	23	19	22
3 years and more	13	15	59	34
Not known	4	8		5

*Couples living together have been excluded from the one-year and core samples.

The proportion of women who petitioned for divorce and the grounds used in establishing the breakdown of marriage suggest that, overall, the Divorce Unit encountered a group of particularly embittered and embattled divorcing couples, and that this trend was most marked in the core sample. A slightly higher proportion of women in the core sample petitioned for divorce, but this difference did not reach significance. However, in both the one-year and core samples the extent to which petitioners invoked the 'unreasonable behaviour' clause exceeded, at a significant level, the degree to which this clause is generally used. By way of contrast, the two-year separation clause with consent was used far less frequently than expected. Other studies (Murch 1980; Eekelaar et al. 1977) have reported similar findings and the Booth Report (1985), reflecting on the close association between contested child proceedings and the use of the unreasonable behaviour clause, observed that the bitterness and unhappiness of divorcing couples was frequently

Table 3   *Who petitioned?*

	One-year sample (%) (n=102)	Core sample (%) (n=27)	England and Wales 1982 (%) (OPCS 1985) (n=145802)
Wife	69	81	71
Husband	31	19	29

Table 4   *Grounds for divorce*

	One-year sample (%) (n=96)	Core sample (%) (n=27)	England and Wales 1982 (%) (OPCS 1985) (n=145198)
Adultery	34	19	30
Behaviour	55	74	36
Desertion	4		1
Separation after 2 years	4	7	25
Separation after 5 years	2		7

exacerbated and prolonged by the fault element in divorce and that this was particularly so when the fact relied upon was behaviour.

In trying to understand why some couples are at odds over their children post divorce and, as a result, are referred for welfare equiries, Murch (1980) drew attention to the fact that the families in his sample seen by welfare officers tended to be at a more advanced stage of the parenting cycle than other couples who divorce. Equating attachment to children with the length of time partners have been parents, he argued that fathers were more likely to fight for parental status when their children were older. He noted that the families of divorce court welfare clients tended to be larger than average.

In the Divorce Unit, welfare officers were also likely to encounter parents in their late thirties who had larger than average families (*Table 10*); most of their children would be of school age (*Table 11*). If our samples are representative, welfare officers are likely to be seeing a significantly high proportion of parents whose ages cluster in the thirties.

Compared with couples who divorced in England and Wales in 1982, parents in the one-year and core samples had fewer men and women than expected below 35 years and above 40 years. This is consistent with Murch's observation that divorce court welfare clients tend to be older than most parents who divorce. The relatively small number of parents over the age of 40 is because only parents with children under 16 years qualify for welfare reports by law.

While these figures are consistent with the idea that parents of the

Table 5 Ages of parents when first interviewed

| | One-year sample (%) | | Core sample (%) | | All divorcing couples England and Wales 1982 (%) (OPCS 1985) | |
	Fathers (n=110)	Mothers (n=110)	Fathers (n=30)	Mothers* (n=30)	Fathers (n=146654)	Mothers (n=146654)
Under 35 years	37	53	40	53	47	57
35–39 years	28	26	30	27	18	17
40 years and over	29	16	30	17	34	27
Not known	6	6		3		

*Including a mother substitute.

Divorce Unit tended to be advanced in the parenting cycle, it did not appear (as Murch's experience would have predicted) that they had been married longer than average. Although it was not possible to measure the *de jure* length of marriage (because most Divorce Unit couples were interviewed in the period between final separation and the completion of divorce proceedings) approximately a quarter of the couples in both samples had been together for less than five years, which was significantly higher than the equivalent figure in the Bristol question-naire sample. The length of *de facto* marriages is not recorded in official statistics, so that comparisons with contemporaries who divorced was not possible.

These comparisons (of parents seen 10 years apart) suggest that parents seen at the Divorce Unit had marriages of shorter duration than one might expect from the age of their children. This idea is supported by comparing their ages at marriage with those of other couples who divorced at the same time.

Table 6   *The duration of marriages/cohabitations measured by the time between the date of marriage/cohabitation and final separation*

	One-year sample (%) (n=96*)	Core sample (%) (n=25*)	Bristol DCWO sample (%) (Murch 1980) (n=41)
Less than 5 years	27	32	7
5–9 years	31	36	37
10–14 years	28	16	39
15–19 years	14	8	10
More than 20 years		8	7

*Parents still living together, and one core sample case where details were not known, have been excluded.

On average the Divorce Unit parents were significantly older when they married than other couples who divorced in 1982. Fewer couples in both samples married under 20 years of age, and more women married in the one-year sample between the ages of 25 and 30 than might have been expected from national figures. For men, the watershed was 25 years; fewer than might have been expected married below and more than expected above this age. The relatively late age at marriage was not adequately explained by one or both spouses marrying for a second time. There were only 19 remarriages (14 per cent), which compares with 13 per cent for all divorcing couples in 1982 (OPCS 1985).

Against the trend developing in the 1970s for married couples to delay parenthood, although compatible with their relatively late age at marriage, the Divorce Unit couples started their families soon after marriage or even before.

Table 7 *Age at marriage/cohabitation*

	One-year sample (%)		Core sample (%)		National Figures 1982 (%) (OPCS 1985)	
	Husbands (n=102)	Wives (n=101)	Husbands (n=29)	Wives (n=29)	Husbands (n=146698)	Wives (n=146698)
Under 20 years	4	28	4	31	12	37
20–24 years	48	50	48	41	52	43
25–29 years	29	18	31	24	21	11
30 years and over	19	5	17	4	15	9

In a substantial number of cases couples were impelled into marriage because of a pregnancy; in both samples approximately a third conceived their first child before marriage (almost twice the figure found by Haskey in his sample of divorcing couples) and a further third saw their first child born within the first two years of married life.

Table 8   *Date of marriage/cohabitation and birth of first child*

	One-year sample (%) (n=110)	Core sample (%) (n=30)	Haskey's representative sample of divorcing couples (%) (1984) (n=2164)
1st child's birth predates marriage	6		
1st child born within 9 months of marriage	25	33	17
1st child born between 9 months and 2 years of marriage	38	33	
1st child born 2 years or more after marriage	26	31	
Not known	5	3	

Children

Most disputes over children were custody disputes; just over a quarter of all cases were concerned with access alone. In both samples there was a total of 10 'satisfaction' enquiries; these are called for in situations where there is no necessary dispute between the parents but sufficient unease on the part of a judge or registrar to warrant investigation. There were 7 reports in both samples (one in the core sample) related to wardship proceedings under the Guardianship of Minors Act.

Table 9   *Grounds for ordering a welfare report*

	One-year sample (%) (n=110)	Core sample (%) (n=30)
Custody	59	57
Access	28	27
'Satisfaction'	7	10
Wardship and not known	7	6

Between them the couples in both samples had 281 children aged 16 years or younger. The average family size was 2.0 children, a figure slightly in excess of the national average of 1.9 for all married couples with dependent children in 1982 (Central Statistical Office 1984). In both samples there was a larger than average proportion of families with three children or more but very few families with more than this number, a fact which distinguishes our sample from divorce court welfare clients studied a decade earlier (Murch 1980; Eekelaar *et al.* 1977).

Table 10   *Family size*

	One-year sample (%) (n=109)	Core sample (%) (n=30)	Haskey's (1984) sample (%) (n=2164)	Oxford DCWO sample (Eekelaar et al. 1977 (%) (n=41)
1 child	34	40	} 87	20
2 children	36	43		32
3 children	21	17	} 13*	20
4 children	7			29
5 children	2			

*Haskey's figure of 13 per cent includes all children under 18 years and was the same figure for all couples who divorced in 1979.

Reliable figures on children's ages only emerged for the core sample. Distribution according to age shows that most of the children seen by welfare officers were at school and nearly a third were 12 years and over.

Table 11   *Age distribution of children in core samples*

	Core sample (%) (n=55)
Under 5 years	15
5 years and over	18
7 years and over	16
9 years and over	20
12 years and over	24
15 years and over	7

*For our purposes a child meant a boy or girl aged 16 years or younger living as a child of the family.

Our culture tends to assume that children are best cared for by mothers following marital breakdown. In most situations (between 70 per cent and 85 per cent of divorces) mothers retain care and control of their children (Richards 1982; James and Wilson 1984b). When fathers have care and control of their children, legal custody is more likely to be disputed and levels of conflict tend to be higher (Eekelaar 1982).

The degree to which a cultural preference for mothers as caretakers affects whether or not a report is called for is hard to establish. In three studies (Murch 1980; Eekelaar *et al.* 1977; and Maidment 1984) only Murch found an association between fathers exercising care and control and the likelihood of a welfare report being ordered. In his sample, a high proportion of fathers (32 per cent) and a low proportion of mothers (37 per cent) were looking after their children. The other two studies found no such association. In our samples, too, there was little firm evidence that fathers having care of their children was likely to trigger an order for welfare reports.

In only 15 per cent of cases in the one-year sample were children living with their fathers (10 per cent in Eekelaar's sample), and in a further 5 per cent care was divided between separated parents (Eekelaar 4 per cent; Murch 6 per cent). In none of the seven 'satisfaction' cases did fathers have sole responsibility for the care of their children. In both the one-year and core samples approximately two-thirds of the children were living with their mothers or a female substitute, although this figure is below the estimated range of 70–85 per cent for all divorcing couples. This difference may be partly accounted for by the unusually high proportion of couples in our sample (13 per cent) still living in the same house (7 per cent for Eekelaar).

Table 12   *Residence of children at point of first contact with a welfare officer*

	One-year sample (%) (n=110)	Core sample (%) (n=30)
With mother	64	67
With father	15	10
Shared (parents not separated)	13	13
Divided between parents	5	7
Other relative	2	3
In care	2	

While post-separation arrangements in Divorce Unit families did not seem to involve more fathers taking over the care and control of their children than would be expected from the practices of divorcing couples generally, it was more likely that courts had made an earlier order in cases where fathers had care of their children. This tends to support the conclusions of other studies that such arrangements tend to be more than usually contentious. Of the 19 cases where fathers were looking after their children in the Divorce Unit sample as a whole, 12 (63 per cent) were subject to a previous court order when the welfare report was requested as compared with 30 (33 per cent) of the cases where children were living with their mothers.

Socio-economic circumstances

The families seen at the Divorce Unit were less prosperous than the population of the HPS as a whole. The social class distribution of fathers was not significantly different from Haskey's (1984) representative sample of couples divorcing in 1979. The Divorce Unit samples are therefore consistent with the general observation that there is an inverse relationship between the divorce rate and social class, i.e. the divorce rate is highest for Social Class V and lowest for Social Class I.

Table 13 *Social class distribution by husband's occupation*

	One-year sample (%) (n=110)	Core sample (%) (n=30)	Haskey's sample (1984) (%) (n=2164)
Social Class I and II	24	23	19
Social Class III	46	50	42
Social Class IV and V	16	27	21
Not known and unclassified	14		19

While our sample was generally consistent with Haskey's, it did contain a very high rate of unemployment among men. Twenty-five men in the one-year sample were out of work at the point when they were first interviewed, representing an unemployment rate of 23 per cent. This was far in excess of the overall rate of male unemployment of between 6 and 7 per cent in the area at the time. The relationship between unemployment and family breakdown is complicated and has a 'chicken and egg' dimension to it. The risk of divorce for unemployed men is higher than that for employed men (Haskey 1984). Unemployment would therefore appear to be a factor predisposing some couples towards divorce. On the other hand, in the core sample of 30 cases, 6 fathers saw their unemployment as resulting directly from marital breakdown. For these men, unemployment was one of a cluster of losses (loss of the marriage, loss of the matrimonial home, loss of contact with the children) which seemed to produce a downward depressive spiral from which recovery was slow and difficult.

There was no evidence from the Divorce Unit sample as a whole to suggest that unemployment led fathers to increase the time they spent with their children; fathers in full-time work were more likely than they to have care and control of their children. Any assumption that unemployment creates opportunities for men to become more active as fathers receives no support from our experience, nor is there support for this assumption in other studies (for example, Jackson 1984).

The balance of satisfaction

More women than men were satisfied with their experience of the welfare enquiry, although the fact that children generally resided with their mothers may indicate that a child in residence, rather than the sex of a parent, may be the important factor. Closely related is the fact that satisfaction was always associated with a favourable report recommendation for women, although not necessarily so for men. The figures in *Table 14* relate only to the 43 parents followed up (out of the total of 60 in the core sample).

Table 14 *Satisfaction with enquiry and report recommendations – the core sample*

	Women	Men	(%)
Satisfied	11	5	37
Dissatisfied	13	14	63
	24	19	
Satisfied + favourable recommendation	10	3	
Satisfied + unfavourable recommendation	0	2	
Dissatisfied + favourable recommendation	6	5	
Dissatisfied + unfavourable recommendation	5	8	
Parents for whom no report submitted	3	1	
	24	19	

Note

1 Levels of statistical significance have been assessed at the 5 per cent level. In this appendix differences should not be assumed significant unless referred to explicitly.

APPENDIX II
RESEARCH AIDS

Questionnaire *Case ref. no:*

To be completed by DCWO/ Secretary

A. *Referral*

1. By whom

2. (a) Reason

   (b) Is this report requested by the Court in relation to an application to vary an earlier order?

   (c) If referred by a Court, under what statute are Court proceedings being brought in this case?

3. Date report ordered

4. Date received by Dept

5. Date report filed

6. Is this case held by Unit for action? Yes/No

7. If 'No' to 6 above, to which agency is case referred?

8. Internal allocation
   (a) Indicate criteria for internal allocation by ticking one or more of the following
   - (i) Next in line
   - (ii) Briefwork
   - (iii) Specialist or other interest of worker
   - (iv) Geographical consideration
   - (v) Priority case arising from pressure from the Court
   - (vi) Priority case arising from pressure from case
   - (vii) Priority case arising from delay in earlier allocation
   - (viii) Priority case arising from inter agency dimension

    (b) If above criteria do not apply, please describe alternative criteria

9. Worker(s) name(s)

10. *Court proceedings*
    (a) Who initiated Court proceedings to which this report refers?

    (b) Who requested a welfare report?

B. *General*

1. Composition of households at point of first contact with DCWO ('Mother' and 'father' refer to mother and father of children subject to dispute). If mother and father share same household, enter under Household I – mother's

Household I – mother's

1	Mother's d.o.b.

Indicate other members by entering dates of birth and relationship to mother

	d.o.b.	relationship to mother
2		
3		
4		
5		
6		
7		

Address of mother's household:

Household II – father's

1	Father's d.o.b.

Indicate members by entering dates of birth and relationship to father

	d.o.b.	relationship to father
2		
3		
4		
5		
6		
7		

Address of father's household:

If child(ren) are not living with father or mother indicate composition of household in which they do live. Enter date of birth and relationship to the child(ren)

Household III – other

disputed children			
	male/female	d.o.b. or age	relationship to disputing adults
1			
2			
3			
4			

other children			
	male/female	d.o.b. or age	relationship to disputed children
1			
2			
3			
4			

adults			
	male/female	d.o.b. or age	relationship to disputed children
1			
2			
3			
4			

Address of third household:

2. Domestic situation of spouses

Father   Mother

       Remarried
       Cohabiting
       No partner
       With relatives
       Continuing to share
        household with
        spouse
       Other

3. Father's occupation(s) at time of first contact or (if unemployed) last job
   (a) Job title(s)
   (b) Job descriptions(s)

4. Mother's occupation(s) at time of first contact
   (a) Job title(s)
   (b) Job descriptions(s)
   (including housewife/and mother if appropriate)

5. Date(s) and duration of couple's marriage(s) and/or cohabitation
   (Underline marriage/cohabitation which relates to current dispute)

   Father

	marriage/cohabitation	date began	date ended
1			
2			
3			
4			

   Mother

	marriage/cohabitation	date began	date ended
1			
2			
3			
4			

6. Date(s) of separation(s) between mother and father

7. Date of divorce
   (a) decree nisi
   (b) decree absolute

8. Grounds cited for irretrievable breakdown of marriage (please tick)
   (a) 'adultery'
   (b) 'behaviour'
   (c) 'desertion'
   (d) 2-year separation
   (e) 5-year separation

9. Children of marriage, subject to dispute

	boy/girl	d.o.b.
1		
2		
3		
4		
5		

10. Children(s) movements
   From the first separation until the time of first interview, what changes have there been in accommodation for the children?

	from	to
Change 1		
Change 2		
Change 3		
Change 4		

   From the time of first interview until the termination of intervention, what changes have there been in accommodation for the children?

	from	to
Change 1		
Change 2		
Change 3		
Change 4		

   From the first separation until the time of first interview, what changes have there been in the parental care of the children?

	from	to
Change 1		
Change 2		
Change 3		
Change 4		

   From the time of first interview until the termination of intervention, what changes have there been in parental care of the children?

	from	to
Change 1		
Change 2		
Change 3		
Change 4		

11. Contact with other agencies
    In the course of preparing a report, what contact has there been with other agencies? Indicate agency involved (GP, HV, school, SSD, Probation Service, hospital, voluntary agency etc) and briefly describe reason for contact.

12. Property and finance
    (a) At the point of first contact who of the contesting parties is living in the (former) matrimonial home?

    Husband
    Wife
    Husband and Wife
    Neither

    (b) Briefly outline the relationship if any in this case between issues of child care and ownership/tenure of property

C.   Methods and outcomes

1. Planning
   Was this case worked singly or with a co-worker?

   If a co-worker was involved in interviewing clients from the outset, please state reason(s).

   If a co-worker was involved at an intermediate stage of the work, please give reason(s).

   If the case was worked singly from choice, please give reasons.

   What was the plan regarding the first interviews? Please describe reasons for the choice.

2. Report
   Describe recommendation of report(s)

   How many reports (including brief notes) were submitted to the Court in relation to this enquiry?

   Did mother read report in the worker's presence? If not, why?

   Have the contents of the report been discussed with mother?

   Did father read report in the worker's presence? If not, why?

   Have the contents of the report been discussed with father?

At the termination of contact were the parties any nearer agreement on the matters under dispute than had been the case at the beginning of the contact?

Yes/No

If 'yes' to above question, describe in what ways.

In the worker's view, do you think that the level of agreement on disputed matters will hold, improve or deteriorate in the six months after the final contact?
Please tick predicted outcome:
  Arrangements will hold
  Arrangements will hold and strengthen
  Arrangements will deteriorate

Please describe briefly the reasons for your prediction.

Date of last contact with parents.

If contact continues beyond the Court hearing, on what basis will it rest?
  (a) Voluntary
  (b) Supervision order

3. Court hearing
   Date of hearing

   Did worker attend Court?

   Court decision (please describe)

Case profiles (Guidelines)

1. Fact sheet
   Name of case (use initials only):
   Court ref. no:
   Worker's name(s):
   Questionnaire ref:
   Age and sex of relevant children:
   Date request ordered and why:
   Total time spent on face to face or telephone contact with
   clients /other agencies:
   Date report filed:
   Follow-up due:

2. Flow diagram (append)
   Including relevant dates (marriage, separation, remarriage,
   illnesses, children, court hearings and other significant events/
   turning points as seen by the parties in their mat/divorce
   history):

3. Main features of the case
   Including why now? principal characters, working problems
   and impact on worker. Family diagram if helpful.

4. Opening gambits and first interview(s)

5. History of subsequent work
   Including contact with other figures and agencies (courts,
   police, solicitors) apart from the family where relevant. How
   often and over what time span are people seen?

6. Worker's perceptions
   Style of work, pressures, departures from 'normal' or intended
   practices; opportunities, constraints, frustrations. Contributions of supervision and co-working relationship.

7. Relationship (if any) between current dispute and past
   marriage

8. Other observations/hypotheses arising out of case

9. Assessment of work undertaken
   Is it complete? Value?
   Including recommendations in report and feelings about this.
   Will it hold? Predictions for next 6 months.

10. Worker's comments at time of follow up
    Including further information, details of court hearings, etc.

Team meeting case discussion

Part A   *Date:*

To be completed by presenters prior to case discussion (except question 7).

1. Name of worker(s)

2. Case ref. no (if allocated after 1.9.1982)

3. Client's initials:

4. Previously presented for discussion on:

5. Reason for presentation (including working problems):

6. Case summary
   (a) the main area(s) of dispute in the case

   (b) Significant interaction between principal characters

   (c) Method of work

7. Case discussion
   What did worker(s) find helpful in the discussion

Part B   *Date:*

To be completed by IMS

1. Main features of presentation

2. Impediments to reaching agreements
   (i) Explicit:

   (ii) Implicit:

3. Suggestions made concerning future work

4. Constraints affecting future work

5. Main discussion themes
   (a) Family-related
   (b) Worker-related
   (c) Agency-related
   (d) Team meeting related

REFERENCES

Alvarez, A. (1982) *Life after Marriage*. London: Macmillan.

Ambrose, P., Harper, T. and Pemberton, R. (1983) *Surviving Divorce: Men Beyond Marriage*. Brighton: Wheatsheaf Books.

Anthony, E.J. (1974) Children at Risk from Divorce: A review. In E.J. Anthony and C. Koupernik (eds) *The Child in His Family*. New York: Wiley.

Arnold, Sir John (1985) Open letter to Mr A. Wells.

Askham, J. (1984) *Identity and Stability in Marriage*. Cambridge: Cambridge University Press.

Bentovim, A. and Gilmour, L. (1981) A Family Therapy Interactional Approach to Decision Making in Child Care, Access and Custody Cases. *Journal of Family Therapy* 3: 65–77.

Berger, P.L. and Kellner, H. (1977) Marriage and the Construction of Reality. In P.L. Berger (ed.) *Facing up to Modernity*. Harmondsworth: Penguin.

Bernard, J. (1982) *The Future of Marriage*. Harmondsworth: Penguin.

Blampied, A. and Timms, N. (1985) *Intervention in Marriage: The experience of counsellors and their clients*. University of Sheffield Social Services Monograph.

Blom-Cooper, L. (1985) *A Child in Trust. Report of the Panel of Inquiry into the circumstances surrounding the death of Jasmine Beckford*. London: Borough of Brent.

Booth, the Hon. Mrs Justice (1985) *Report of the Matrimonial Causes Procedure Committee*. London: HMSO.

Bowlby, J. (1969) *Attachment (Attachment and Loss* Vol. 1) London: Hogarth Press/Institute of Psycho-Analysis.

——(1975) *Separation, Anxiety and Anger (Attachment and Loss* Vol. 2). Hogarth Press/Institute of Psycho-Analysis.

——(1980) *Loss: Sadness and Depression (Attachment and Loss*, Vol. 3). Hogarth Press/Institute of Psycho-Analysis.

Brannen, J. and Collard, J. (1982) *Marriages in Trouble: the process of seeking help*. London: Tavistock.

Brown, G.W. and Harris, T. (1978) *The Social Origins of Depression*. London: Tavistock.

Burgoyne, J. and Clark, D. (1984) *Making A Go Of It: A Study Of Stepfamilies In Sheffield*. London: Routledge & Kegan Paul.

Campbell, L. and Johnston, J. (1985) The Use of Groups in the Mediation of Child Custody Disputes. Paper presented to the 62nd Annual Meeting of the American Orthopsychiatry Association. New York.

Caplan, G. (1981) Mastery of Stress: Psychosocial Aspects. *American Journal of Psychiatry* 138 (4): 413–20.

Central Statistical Office (1985) *Social Trends* 15. London: HMSO.

Chester, R. (1971) Health and Marriage Breakdown: experience of a sample of divorced women. *British Journal of Preventative and Social Medicine* 25: 231–35.

——(1984) Mass Divorce and its Implications. In C. Guy (ed.) *Relating to Marriage*. Rugby: National Marriage Guidance Council.

Chiriboga, D., Coho, A., Stein, J. and Roberts, J. (1979) Divorce, Stress and Social Supports: a study in help-seeking behaviour. *Journal of Divorce* 3 (2): 121–35.

Clulow, C., Dearnley, B. and Balfour, F. (1986) Shared Phantasy and Therapeutic Structure in a Brief Marital Psychotherapy. *British Journal of Psychotherapy* 3 (2): 124–32.

Daniell, D. (1985) Love and Work: Complementary Aspects of Personal Identity. *International Journal of Social Economics* 12 (2): 48–55.

Davis, G. (1982) Conciliation: A Dilemma for the Divorce Court Welfare Service. *Probation Journal* 29 (4): 123–28.

——(1985) The Theft of Conciliation. *Probation Journal* 32 (1): 7–10.

Davis, G., MacLeod, A. and Murch, M. (1983) Undefended Divorce: Should Section 41 of the Matrimonial Causes Act 1973 be Repealed? *Modern Law Review* 46 (22): 121–46.

Denning Committee (1947) *Final Report Of The Committee On Procedure In Matrimonial Causes* (Cmnd 7024). London: HMSO.

Dicks, H.V. (1967) *Marital Tensions*. London: Routledge & Kegan Paul.

Dillon, Lord Justice (1986) Function of the Court Welfare Departments. In *The Times*, 2 April 1986.

Dingwall, R., Eekelaar, J., Murray, T. (1983) *The Protection of Children*. Oxford: Blackwell.

Dominian, J. (1983) An estimate given verbally at a symposium on marriage related problems organised by the Marriage Research Centre.

——(1984) Marital Breakdown and Health: An overview. Paper presented at a conference on Marital Breakdown and Health organized by the Marriage Research Centre.

Donzelot, J. (1980) *The Policing of Families*. London: Hutchinson.

Eekelaar, J. (1982) Children in Divorce: Some Further Data. Oxford. *Journal of Legal Studies* 2 (1): 63–85

Eekelaar, J. and Clive, E. with Clarke, K. and Raikes, S. (1977) *Custody after Divorce*. Oxford: Centre for Socio-Legal Studies.

Ewbank, Mr Justice (1985) *Judgment* on Metropolitan Borough of Bury v Heart. 19.12.85. Manchester High Court.

Finer, M. (Chmn) (1974) *The Report of the Committee on One-Parent Families* Cmnd 5629. London: HMSO.

Francis, P., Heygate, S., King, S. and Jones, M. (1983) Mightier than the Sword. *Social Work Today 14* (17): 8–10.

Fraser, D. (1982) *What Happens to the Children?* A study into the custody and access patterns adopted by a group of families experiencing divorce. Avon Probation Service.

Furlong, M. (1981) *Divorce: one woman's view*. Mothers Union.

Garber, B. (1984) Parenting Responses in Divorce and Bereavement of a Spouse. In R. Cohen, B. Cohler and S. Weissman (eds) *Parenthood: A Psychodynamic Perspective*. New York: Guildford Press.

Gingerbread and Families Need Fathers (1982) *Divided Children: A survey of access to children after divorce*. (pamphlet) London.

Goldstein, J., Freud, A. and Solnit, A.J. (1973) *Beyond the Best Interests of the Child*. New York: The Free Press.

——(1980) *Before the Best Interests of the Child*. London: Burnett Books.

Gordon, R. (1986) No Longer Just Passive Bystanders. *Community Care*, 26 June: 30–32.

Hagestad, G. and Smyer, M. (1982). Dissolving Long-Term Relationships: patterns of divorcing in middle age. In S. Duck (ed.) *Dissolving Personal Relationships*. London: Academic Press.

Halsey, A.H. (1985) Family and State. *Noel Buxted Lecture* given at the Family Policy Studies Centre, 11 June.

Hart, N. (1976) *When Marriage Ends: A study in status passage*. London: Tavistock.

Haskey, J. (1982) The Proportion of Marriages Ending in Divorce. *Population Trends* 27. London: HMSO.

——(1983) Children of Divorcing Couples. *Population Trends* 31. London: HMSO.

——(1984) Social Class and Socio-Economic Differentials in Divorce in England and Wales. *Population Studies* 38: 419–38.

Haynes, J.M. (1981) *Divorce Mediation*. New York: Springer.

Haynes, J.M. (1984) Problem Solving in Mediation. Paper given at the International Conference on Conciliation in Divorce, 25–27 October, London.

Hetherington, E.M., Cox, M. and Cox, R. (1982) The Effects of Divorce on Parents and Children. In M.E. Lamb (ed.) *Non-Traditional Families: Parenting and child development*. New Jersey: Erlbaum.

Hetherington, E.M. and Camara, K.A. (1984) Families in Transition: The processes of dissolution and reconstitution. In R.D. Parke (ed.) *Review of Child Development Research in the Family*. University of Chicago Press.

Hills, A. (1983) Divorce Conciliation: A step beyond the traditional *Community Care*, September 22: 16–18.

Himmel, S. (Chmn) (1985) *Policy, Management and Structure for Civil Work in the Probation Service*. Civil Work Committee of the Association of Chief Officers of Probation, March 6.

Hipgrave, A. (1986) New Zealand: A Team Approach. *Community Care*, 26 June: 18–19.

Hunt, P. (1985) *Clients' Responses to Marriage Counselling*. Research Report No. 3. National Marriage Guidance Council.

Home Office Statistical Department (1983) *Probation Statistics, England and Wales*. London: HMSO.

Jackson, B. (1984) *Fatherhood*. London: Allen & Unwin.

James, A.L. and Wilson, K. (1983) Divorce Court Welfare – Present and Future. *Probation Journal* **30** (2): 50–55.

——(1984a) Reports for the Court: The Work of the Divorce Court Welfare Office. *Journal of Social Welfare Law* March: 89–103.

——(1984b) The Trouble with Access: a study of divorcing families. *British Journal of Social Work* **14**: 487–506.

Johnston, J.R., Gonzalez, R. and Campbell, L.E.G. (1985) Ongoing Post-Divorce Conflict as a Predictor of Child Disturbance. Paper presented at the Annual Meeting of the American Psychological Association.

Kressel, K., Jaffee, N., Tuchman, B., Watson, C. and Deutsch, M. (1980) A Typology of Divorcing Couples: Implications for mediation and the divorce process. *Family Process* **19** (2): 101–16.

Law Commission (1986) *Family Law Review of Child Law: Custody*. Working paper No. 96. London: HMSO.

Leete, R. (1979) Changing Patterns of Family Formation and Dissolution. *Studies on Medical and Population Subjects* No.37. London: HMSO.

Levy, A. (1983) *Custody and Access*. London: Longman.

Little, M. (1982) *Family-Breakup: Understanding marital problems and the mediating of child custody disputes*. San Francisco: Jossey-Bass.

Lord Chancellor's Department (1984) Private correspondence. 7 December 1984.

Lund, M. (1984) Research on Divorce and Children. *Family Law* **14** (7): 198–201.

Lyons, A. (1981) *'Justice in Family Relationships: The relationship between the law and the family.'* Unpublished paper.

McGredie, G. and Horrox, A. (1985) *Voices in the Dark: Children and Divorce*. London: Allen & Unwin.

MacGillavry, D. and Bijkerk, H. (1986) An Experimental Approach to Divorce Aid. Paper presented at an international conference organised by IUFO Commission on marriage guidance. Lisbon 13 – 16th June 1986, on Help in Decision Making during Separation and Divorce.

Maclean, M. and Eekelar, J. (1984) The Economic Consequences of Divorce for Families with Children. In J.M. Eekelar and S.N. Katz (eds) *The Resolution of Family Conflict*. Toronto: Butterworths.

McLoughlin, D. and Whitfield, R. (1985) Adolescents and Divorce. *Marriage Guidance*, Spring: 2–8.

Maddox, B. (1982) Who Pays for No Fault Divorce? *Economist*, April 24: 51–6.

Maidment, S. (1976) A Study in Child Custody. *Family Law* 6: 195–200.

——(1981) *Child Custody: What chance for fathers?* National Council for One Parent Families.

——(1983) *Social Work and Divorce*. Audio teaching tape, Lancaster Information Systems.

——(1984) *Child Custody and Divorce. The Law in Social Context*. London: Croom Helm.

Marris, P. (1974) *Loss and Change*. London: Routledge & Kegan Paul.

Mansfield, P. (1985) *Young People and Marriage*. Scottish Marriage Guidance Council Occasional Paper No. 1.

Mattinson, J. (1975) *The Reflection Process in Casework Supervision*. London: Institute of Marital Studies.

Mattinson, J. and Sinclair, I. (1979) *Mate and Stalemate: Working with marital problems in a social services department*. Oxford: Blackwell.

Mitchell, A. (1981) *Someone to Turn to. Experiences of help before divorce*. Aberdeen University Press.

——(1985) *Children in the Middle*. London: Tavistock.

Mnookin, R.H. (1979) *Bargaining in the shadow of the Law: The case of divorce*. Oxford: Centre for Socio-Legal Studies.

——(1984) Divorce Bargaining: The Limits on Private Ordering. In J.M. Eekelaar and S.N. Katz (eds) *The Resolution of Family Conflict*. Toronto: Butterworths.

Morgan, D.H.J. (1985) *The Family, Politics and Social Theory*. London: Routledge & Kegan Paul.

Mortlock, W. (1972) *The Inside of Divorce: A critical examination of the system*. London: Constable.

Murch, M. (1980) *Justice and Welfare in Divorce*. London: Sweet & Maxwell.

Oberg, B. and Oberg, G. (1978) *I'm Leaving*. Stockholm: Wahlstrom & Widstrand.

OPCS (1983) *County Report of Greater London Part 2*, CEN 81, CR 17. London: HMSO.

——(1985) *Marriage and Divorce Statistics 1982*, SM2 no. 9. London: HMSO.

Parkes, C.M. (1972) *Bereavement: Studies of Grief in Adult Life*. London: Tavistock.

Parkinson, L. (1982) Conciliating Matrimonial Disputes – An International Perspective. *Law Society Gazette*, October 20: 1307–308.

——(1983) Conciliation: a new approach to family conflict resolution. *British Journal of Social Work* 13: 19–37.

——(1985a) Conciliation in Separation and Divorce. In W. Dryden (ed.) *Marital Therapy in Britain*, Vol. 2. London: Harper & Row.

——(1985b) Divorce Counselling. In W. Dryden (ed.) *Marital Therapy in Britain*, Vol. 2. London: Harper & Row.

——(1986) *Conciliation in Separation and Divorce: Finding common ground.* London: Croom Helm.

Pilling, D. and Kellmer Pringle, M. (1978) *Controversial Issues in Child Development.* London: Elek.

Pincus, L. (ed.) (1960) *Marriage: Studies in Emotional Conflict and Growth.* London: Methuen. Reprinted 1973 by IMS.

Popay, J., Rimmer, L. and Rossiter, C. (1982) *One Parent Families: parents, children and public policy.* Study Commission on the Family.

Pugh, G. and De'Ath, E. (1984) *The Needs of Parents. Practice and policy in parent education.* London: Macmillan.

Pugsley, J. and Wilkinson, M. (1984) The Court Welfare Officer's Role: Taking it Seriously? *Probation Journal* 31 (3): 89–92.

Rahe, R.H., McKean, J.D. and Arthur, R.J. (1967) A Longitudinal Study of Life Change and Illness Patterns. *Journal of Psychosomatic Research* 10: 355–66.

Richards, M. (1981) Children and the Divorce Courts. *One Parent Families* 7: 2–5.

——(1982) Post Divorce Arrangements for Children: A Psychological Perspective. *Journal of Social Welfare Law* 4: 133–51.

——(1984) Separation, Divorce and Remarriage: the experiences of children. In C. Guy (ed.) *Relating to marriage.* Rugby: National Marriage Guidance Council.

Richards, M. and Dyson, S. (1982) *Separation, Divorce and the Development of Children: A Review.* Child Care and Development Group. University of Cambridge.

Richards, M.P.M. (1986) Behind the Best Interests of the Child. An examination of the arguments of Goldstein, Freud, and Solnit concerning custody and access at divorce. *Journal of Social Welfare Law* 8: 77–95.

Rimmer, L. and Popay, J. (1982) *Employment Trends in the Family.* Occasional Paper No.10. Study Commission on the Family.

Roberts, S. (1983) Mediation in Family Disputes. *Modern Law Review* 46 (5): 537–57.

Robinson, P.D. (Chmn) (1983) *Report of the Interdepartmental Committee in Conciliation.* London: HMSO.

Rutter, M. (1971) Parent Child Separation: Psychological Effects on Children. *Journal of Child Psychology and Psychiatry* 12: 233–60.

——(1975) *Helping Troubled Children.* Harmondsworth: Penguin.

——(1981) *Maternal Deprivation Reassessed.* Harmondsworth: Penguin.

Samuels, A. (1982) Custody and Access. *Justice of the Peace* **146**: 233–35.

Saposnek, D.T. (1983) *Mediating Child Custody Disputes: A systematic guide for family therapists, court counsellors, attorneys and judges.* San Francisco: Jossey-Bass.

Shepherd, G., Howard, J. and Tomkinson, J. (1984) Conciliation: Taking it Seriously? *Probation Journal* **31** (1): 21–4.

Sluckin, W., Herbert, M. and Sluckin, A. (1983) *Maternal Bonding.* Oxford: Blackwell.

Smail, D.T. (1985) Spouse as Therapist. Paper given at the Rugby Research Seminar on Marriage, Health and Handicap. 19 April.

Spanier, G.B. and Thompson, L. (1984) *Parting: the aftermath of separation and divorce.* Beverly Hills and London: Sage.

Stone, L. (1977) *The Family, Sex and Marriage in England 1500–1800.* Harmondsworth: Penguin.

Sutherland, J. (1979) *The Psychodynamic Image of Man.* Malcolm Miller lecture. Aberdeen University Press.

Sutton, A. (1981) Science in Court. In M. King (ed.) *Childhood, Welfare and Justice.* London: Batsford.

Walczak, Y. and Burns, S. (1984) *Divorce: The Child's Point of View.* London: Harper & Row.

Wallerstein, J.S. (1984) Children of Divorce: Preliminary report of a ten year follow-up of young children. *American Journal of Orthopsychiatry* **54** (3): 444–58.

——(1985) The Overburdened Child: Some long-term consequences of divorce. *American Journal of Work*, March/April: 116–23.

Wallerstein, J.S. and Kelly, J.B. (1980) *Surviving the Breakup. How children and parents cope with divorce.* London: Grant McIntyre.

Weiss, R. (1975) *Marital Separation.* New York: Basic Books.

Wilkinson, M. (1981) *Children and Divorce.* Oxford: Blackwell.

Name Index

Subject Index